▼▼▼▼▼▼▼▼▼▼▼▼▼▼▼▼▼▼▼▼▼▼ Native Liberty

NATIVE

UNIVERSITY OF NEBRASKA PRESS ▼ LINCOLN AND LONDON

LIBERTY

NATURAL REASON AND CULTURAL SURVIVANCE

GERALD VIZENOR

Library of Congress Cataloging-in-Publication Data
Vizenor, Gerald Robert, 1934–
Native liberty : natural reason and cultural survivance / Gerald Vizenor.
    p. cm.
Includes bibliographical references and index.
ISBN 978-0-8032-1892-5 (pbk. : alk. paper)
1. American literature — Indian authors — History and criticism.
2. Indians in literature. 3. Indians of North America — Ethnic identity.
4. Indians of North America — Intellectual life. I. Title.
PS153.I52V6 2009
810.9'897 — dc22
2009020134

Set in Quadraat by Kim Essman.
Designed by Ray Boeche.

Contents

Acknowledgments

The thirteen essays in this edition are selected from original work, lectures, and publications in the past two decades. Four of the essays are original, "Native Liberty," "Mercenary Sovereignty," "Genocide Tribunals," and "Ontic Images," and are published here for the first time. The remaining nine selected essays, first published in books or journals, have been expanded and rewritten for this edition.

"Native Liberty" is an original essay, a comprehensive and personal discussion of The Progress, the first newspaper published on the White Earth Reservation in Minnesota.

"Mercenary Sovereignty" was first prepared as a plenary lecture, "Mercenary Sovereignty: Casinos, Truth Games, and Native American Liberty," at an international symposium, Hybrid Americas: Contacts, Contrasts, and Confluences in New World Literatures and Cultures, Center for Interdisciplinary Study, University of Bielefeld, Germany, October 25, 2002.

"Genocide Tribunals" was prepared for a campus lecture at the Institute for Advanced Study, Nolte Center, University of Minnesota, October 2006. The lecture was broadcast on Public Television. "Genocide Tribunals" was also presented as a keynote lecture at the Swiss Association for North American Studies, University of Geneva, Switzerland, November 2006.

"Ontic Images" was presented as a keynote lecture, "Imagic Moments: Native American Identities and Literary Modernity," at an international conference, Imaginary (Re-)Locations: Traditions, Modernity, and the Market in Recent Native American Literature, University of Erlangen, Friedrich-Alexander-Universitat, Erlangen-Nurnberg, Germany, July 6, 2000. The essay was published with conference lectures, a limited edition, in *Imaginary (Re-)Locations: Tradition, Modernity, and the Market in Contemporary Native American Literature and Culture*, ed. Helmbrecht Breinig (Stauffenburg Verlag: Tubingen, 2003).

The nine other essays selected in this edition have been previously published. One section of the introduction was first published as an introduction to a book catalog (Ken Lopez, bookseller, in 2006).

Several sections in the essay "Unnamable Chance" were first published as an autobiographical essay in *Contemporary Authors*, vols. 22 (1996) and 205 (2003).

"Survivance Narratives" was first published as "Native American Narratives: Theories of Resistance and Survivance," in *A Companion to American Fiction 1865–1914*, ed. Robert Lamb and G. R. Thompson (Oxford, UK: Blackwell Publishing, 2005). The original essay was a keynote lecture at the Red River Conference on World Literature, North Dakota State University, Fargo, April 22, 2005.

"Aesthetics of Survivance" is a concise version of the essay "The Aesthetics of Survivance: Literary Theory and Practice,"

in *Survivance: Narratives of Native Presence*, ed. Gerald Vizenor
(Lincoln: University of Nebraska Press, 2008).

"Anishinaabe Pictomyths," an expanded essay in this edition, was first published in a different form as the foreword to Bruce White, *We Are at Home: Pictures of the Ojibwe People* (St. Paul: Minnesota Historical Society Press, 2006).

"Edward Curtis" was presented as a keynote lecture, "Edward S. Curtis: Pictorialist and Ethnographic Adventurist," at a conference, Visual Representations and Cultural History: The Edward S. Curtis Photographs of North American Indians, Claremont Graduate University, October 7, 2000. The essay was first published in *True West*, ed. Bill Handley (Lincoln: University of Nebraska Press, 2004).

"George Morrison" was a lecture in the series Voices and Visions, School of American Research, Santa Fe, New Mexico, January 2004. The essay was first published in the *Inaugural Exhibition Catalogue* (Washington DC: National Museum of American Indian Art, Smithsonian Institution, 2004).

"Bradlarian Baroque" was first published in *David Bradley: American Indian Gothic*, exhibition catalog (Casper WY: Nicolayson Art Museum, 2009).

"Mister Ishi of California" was first published as "Mister Ishi: Analogies of Exile, Deliverance, and Liberty," in *Ishi in Three Centuries*, ed. Karl Kroeber and Clifton Kroeber (Lincoln: University of Nebraska Press, 2003).

"Haiku Traces" was a keynote lecture, "Haiku Culturalism," at an international conference, Haiku North America, Northwestern University, July 10, 1999. The essay was first published as "Fusions of Survivance: Haiku Scenes and Native Dream Songs," *Modern Haiku* 31, no. 1 (2000). "The Envoy to Haiku," an early variation of the essay, was published in the *Chicago Review* 39, nos. 3, 4 (1993).

▼▼▼▼▼▼▼▼▼▼▼▼▼▼▼▼▼▼▼▼▼▼▼▼ Native Liberty

Introduction
Literary Aesthetics and Survivance

Native storiers create, at their best, a singular sense of presence by natural reason, customary words, perceptive tropes, observant irony, and imagic scenes. That aural sense of presence is the premise of a distinctive aesthetics of survivance.

Theories of survivance are elusive and imprecise by definition and in translation. The practices of survivance, however, are obvious and unmistakable in native stories. The nature of survivance creates a sense of narrative resistance to absence, literary tragedy, nihility, and victimry. Native survivance is an active sense of presence over historical absence, the dominance of cultural simulations, and manifest manners. Native survivance is a continuance of stories.

The strain of early oral storiers to create a sense of presence in the face of disease, deracination, and genocide was obviously much greater than the burdens of modern literary artists who provoke governments and controvert simulations of native cultures. The continental liberty once

2   perceived by indigenous native storiers has become the literature of survivance and sovereignty.

These selected essays and original narratives are fusions of survivance. That native oral storiers once encountered the heinous consequences of military and mercenary dominance with liberal irony and stories of survivance necessitates that modern storiers create narratives of resistance and denounce manifest manners, recast literary tragedy, and revoke victimry.

Native storiers teased the obvious, created a sense of presence by natural reason, tease, totemic associations, transmutations, and, by tricky tropes, once balanced the mighty moods and spirits of the world. These are lofty poetic maneuvers, to be sure, and yet these comparable sentiments have inspired and motivated many scholars and modern literary artists.

Native storiers have secured a singular humane practice of the cultural tease, that potential parody and tricky *tease* of situational commerce, communal ceremonies, the concerted caricature of strangers, mockery of dogged academics, and the transformation of animals in stories.

Only a shaman, and the most elusive native storiers, would dare rouse a bear in hibernation by curiosity or risky parodies of ursine masturbation, but a hearty tease of rodents, federal factors, Boy Scouts, and earnest ethnologists can be practiced without fear of rhetorical retribution.

Thick description, for instance, has always been an invitation to the pitch and turn of native mockery and irony. The pretentious, prosaic analogies of thick and thin descriptions of native cultures are unreliable translations that both provoke and induce tricky conversions and liberal irony.

Gilbert Ryle, the philosopher, created the notion of thick
and thin descriptions based on the elaborate interpretations of gestures, such as the twitch and wink of an eye.
The context of a wink, then, would determine what the gesture means, but that, too, could be reductive, thick or thin,
an unreliable semiotic representation.

The "object of ethnology," declared Clifford Geertz in *The
Interpretation of Cultures*, is a "stratified hierarchy of meaning-
ful structures in terms of which twitches, winks, fake-winks,
parodies, rehearsals of parodies are produced, perceived
and interpreted." Moreover, culture, "this acted document,
thus is public, like a burlesqued wink or a mock sheep raid.
Though ideational, it does not exist in someone's head;
though unphysical it is not an occult entity."

Geertz noted that the "ethnographer 'inscribes' social
discourse; *he writes it down*. In so doing, he turns it from a
passing event, which exists only in its own moment of occurrence, into an account, which exists in its inscriptions
and can be reconsulted." Actually, natives by communal
stories, memory, and potentiality create a sense of presence not an inscribed absence.

"In Bali, to be teased is be accepted," declared Geertz in
"Deep Play: Notes on a Balinese Cockfight." That perceived
acceptance was a "turning point so far as our relationship
to the community was concerned, and we were quite liter-
ally 'in.' The whole village opened up to us, probably more
than it ever would have otherwise."[1] That "perceived acceptance" was created by a cultural tease, the aesthetics of survivance. Geertz perceived the tease and parody as political
gestures, and by his own methods of interpretation, a thin
semiotic representation of culture.

4   Giorgio Agamben argued in *Means without End: Notes on Politics*, "What characterizes gesture is that in it nothing is being produced or acted, but rather something is being endured and supported. The gesture, in other words, opens the sphere of *ethos* as the more proper sphere of that which is human. But in what way is an action endured and supported? In what way does a *res* become a *res gestae*, this is, in what way does a simple fact become an event?"[2] The *res*, a thing, a matter, the crux, and *res gestae*, circumstances and events of the past, are never final gestures. The tease is a gesture of native ethos, a continuation of stories.

Geertz might have considered the practice of the cultural tease, a political gesture, as potentiality, a great idea, marvelous enough to change his associations with and interpretations of cultures.

Geertz espoused that the "concept of culture" is "essentially a semiotic one."[3] Consequently, the interpretations, or simulations by translation, are reductive systems of linguistic signs, symbols, and representations. The closure of meaning by cultural representation, however thick, provides the situational potentiality of native tease, parody, mockery, and irony.

These selected essays and narratives strive to discover the intricate, worthy associations of nature, natural reason, human rights and liberty, and the customary tease of personal experience, by chance, myth, theory, archive resistance, and history. My narratives create a sense of survivance over manifest manners, and resistance to cultural separatism, and the commercial, passive notions of tragic victimry.

I write to create a memory and to change the cockeyed views and simulations of the *anishinaabe*, Ojibwe or Chippewa, and Native American Indians. Cultural simulations of natives abound in museums, monuments, commerce, art, cinema, literature, and history. These detractions are the derisive signifiers of manifest manners. Yet, that sense of native presence, survivance, and continental liberty is dynamic, and elusive, as it always has been in native oral stories and literature.

I create imagic scenes, means, and trickster characters and tease traditions and memories in narratives and stories. My own surname is a tease, an oral conversion by early federal agents on the White Earth Reservation in Minnesota. "Vezina," selected as a pay name by a native ancestor in the fur trade, was transcribed in the first reservation census as "Vizenor." My surname is original to the White Earth Reservation. Family histories last in active stories, and inscrutably, sometimes arise in the memories and critical turns of serious readers. Native names create a sense of presence, a tease that undermines the simulations of absence and cultural dominance.

The tricky flight of ravens, the rush of a kingfisher, moccasin flowers in a storm, geese on an ice float, moths at the window are instances of presence and sentiments of natural reason in the narratives and literature of native storiers. Consider the concise images in these three original haiku poems in my book *Cranes Arise: Haiku Scenes*.[4]

> redwing blackbird
> rides the cattails at the slough
> curtain calls

mounds of foam
downriver from the waterfall
float silently

fat green flies
square dance across the grapefruit
honor your partner

My poetic images create a sense of survivance not victimry, a signature of natural reason. I write to creation not
closure, to the treat of trickster stories over monotheism,
linear causality, and victimry. I write to the imagic scenes
of nature not the simulations of dominance, and to the eternal tease of totemic consciousness, gender, mortality, and
other contradictions in the natural world.

These literary practices are the traces of a native aesthetics, the natural reason of native stories. There are many
cultural distinctions, ambiguities, exceptions, and incon-
sistencies, but the native pleasures and worries of essays,
narratives, and creative stories are more than mere commerce and simulations of romance and nostalgia.

I write to create a distinctive literary aesthetics of natural reason and survivance inspired by native stories, oral,
in translation, and original. Ancestral natives created a
sense of aesthetics, a natural presence by sound, motion,
the traces of seasons, a summer in the spring; by imagic,
totemic associations with birds and animals; by customary
transmutations, and evasive, unrehearsed trickster stories.
These perceptions of natural reason, stories of inspired, visionary transmotion,[5] and tricky conversions are the traces
of a distinctive native aesthetics.

My presence is a native trace.

My names are forever in the book.

My tease is natural reason.

My memory endures in stories.

My vision is survivance.

Ancestral storiers hunted their words by sound, shadow, ecstatic conversions and by the uncertainties of creation and the seasons. The native literary artist creates the metaphors of sound in silence, the imagic scenes of totemic transmutation and natural reason. These aesthetic practices arise in contemporary native literature. Many native novelists are hunters by shamanic conversions and figurative roves in time and place.

I wrote in *Manifest Manners: Narratives on Postindian Survivance* that shadows, or the traces of native names in stories, are the ventures of a continent, a habitat and landscape, even in the distance of translation. Native imagination, experience, and remembrance are the real landscapes of liberty in the literature of this continent; discoveries and dominance are silence, absence, want, and cultural nostalgia.[6]

Wallace Stegner wistfully situates the western landscape in the literature of dominance, a postwestern literary salvation. "No place is a place until things that have happened in it are remembered in history, ballads, yarns, legends, or monuments," he declared in *Where the Bluebird Sings to the Lemonade Springs.* "No place, not even a wild place, is a place until it has had that human attention that in its highest reach we call poetry." His apparent reluctance to honor native names and stories of continental liberty is the regrettable cause of manifest manners.[7] Stegner was lost without the christened names of colonial discovery.

8 Native American Indian literature is not a newcomer in the course of literary resistance to dominance. Natives have resisted discovery and dominance for centuries, from the first stories of touch and breach of trust. The stories were wise and tricky. Keeshkemun, for instance, the nineteenth-century *anishinaabe* aural artist and diplomat teased a British military officer with stories of natural reason and survivance. Keeshkemun, in that memorable encounter, created an avian presence. "I am a bird who rises from the earth, and flies far up, into the skies, out of human sight; but though not visible to the eye, my voice is heard from afar, and resounds over the earth."[8]

Tragically, many readers consider native literature as an absence not a presence, a romantic levy of the enlightenment, a heroic separatism and disappearance, and others review native stories as cryptic representations of cultural promises obscured by victimry.

Michael Dorris, the late novelist, argued against the aesthetic distinctions of native literature. Other authors and interpreters of native literature have resisted the concept and notion of a singular literary aesthetics. Duane Niatum, for instance, proclaimed that there is no distinctive native aesthetics. Yet, in his preface to *Harper's Anthology of 20th Century Native American Poetry* he wrote, "Native American poets carry with them the spirit of a common cultural heritage, expressed in divergent and often stunning ways, in their individual poetry. That spirit has not died. On the contrary, it has grown and is growing." The simulation of a "common cultural heritage" suggests a literary nuance but apparently not a discrete native aesthetics.[9]

David Treuer asserted in *Native American Fiction: A User's*
Manual that the "vast majority of thought that has been
poured onto Native American literature has puddled, for
the most part, on how the texts are positioned in relation
to history or culture." Treuer provided the reader with only
three summations, or puddle-jumper notions: Native American literature reflects experience, is linked to storytelling,
and "acts out, by virtue of its cultural material, a tribally
inflected ancient form of 'postmodern' discourse." Moreover, he declared that what "makes the intelligent interro-
gation of Native American literature difficult is the degree
to which the literature has become a central part of an argument about authenticity." His "final thoughts" about literature are incurable notions that do not clearly portray the
literary discourse, visionary power, or traces of native survivance. Treuer feigns an argument about "authenticity,"
that awful diatribe on the bona fides of native literary art
and the most obscure, remote, and improbable review of
creative literature. "We can evoke a connection to the past
in our writing, but novels are wishes, fantasies, fairy tales.
Writing doesn't represent reality; it creates new realities.
Literature has reality, but not life, to offer," he construed
broadly.[10] The crude reduction of literature to "wishes, fantasies, and fairy tales" is nostalgia for dominance. Treuer,
a novelist, critiques the practice, stature, and representations of native literature, but he rarely observes in his com-
mentaries the marvelous traces of native aesthetics.

I practice in my narratives the sentiments, figuration,
patterns of motion, and syntax of a native literary aesthetics. I strongly disagree, in other words, with the spurious
notion that there is no singular native aesthetics. Consider,

for instance, the ancestral storiers who created animal characters with a tricky sense of consciousness, the natural reason of a native aesthetics of survivance. Many contemporary native novelists present the imagic consciousness of animals in dialogue and descriptive narratives, and overturn the monotheistic separation of humans and animals. N. Scott Momaday, Leslie Silko, Gordon Henry, Louis Owens, and other native authors have created memorable animals and reveal a native aesthetics in their stories and novels. Momaday created lusty bears, Silko native witchery, Henry and Owens spirited mongrels, as distinctive characters in their novels. These practices and sentiments are a native literary aesthetics of survivance.

"Stories with animals are older than history and better than philosophy," wrote Paul Shepard in *The Others*. "History tries to describe the world as if it began with writing and only humans mattered."[11]

Native novelists are figurative hunters, literary shamans, and ghost dancers. Commonly, natives have been represented and associated with nature and totemic animals. That attribution, however, is more nostalgia for animism in the commercial world than an imagic sense of nature as a sense of native presence, and animals as a narrative voice in literature. Many culturists fashion natives and nature as an absence, as a tragic, nostalgic closure of the enlightenment, and straitened by victimry.

Momaday, Silko, Henry, and Owens use simile as motion, and comparisons to be sure, but not as mere description or attributions of animal and human characteristics. Janet Martin Soskice noted in *Metaphor and Religious Language* that simile is more than "like" or "as" or mere "same

saying" in literature. Metaphor, on the other hand, is a "figure of speech whereby we speak about one thing in terms
which are seen to be suggestive of another." She argues
that there is only a slight difference between metaphor and
simile.[12] That difference, however, is more significant in
native stories. Animals and humans are either compared,
a mundane similitude, or, as in native aesthetics, animals
are literary figures with voice and consciousness; in other
words, animals are characters.

John Searle argued in his essay "Metaphors" that the
"knowledge that enables people to use and understand metaphorical utterances goes beyond their knowledge of the
literal meaning of words and sentences." He wrote that a
"literal simile" is a "literal statement of similarity" and that
a "literal simile requires no extralinguistic knowledge for
its comprehension." The "literal simile" is the most limited trope or figuration.[13]

Louise Erdrich used a style of trope in her novel Tracks
that is closer to the literal or prosaic simile than the metaphors of a native animal presence. For instance, "she shivered all over like a dog," and "hiding from you like a dog,"
and "head shaggy and low as a bison bull."[14] Dogs are the
most common authored animals in Tracks, and yet the literal similes are mere comparisons of generic animals and
humans, not a wise or tricky perception of native transmutation or aesthetic tropes. The generic authored animal in
literature is a generic and literal simile. Momaday, Silko,
Henry, and Owens seldom create generic animals or use
literal similes.

Grey, the main character in The Ancient Child by Momaday,
"dreamed of sleeping with a bear. The bear drew her into his

massive arms and licked her body and her hair. It hunched over her, curving its spine like a cat, until its huge body seemed to have absorbed her own. Its breath which bore a deep, guttural rhythm like language, touched her skin with low, persistent heat."[15]

Momaday told Charles Woodward in *Ancestral Voices* that he was "serious about the bear" and "identified with the bear" because he is "intimately connected with that story. And so I have this bear power. I turn into a bear every so often. I feel myself becoming a bear, and that's a struggle I have to face now and then."[16] Momaday became a bear in his own stories.

Leslie Silko encircles the reader with mythic witches, an ironic metaphor of creation stories in *Ceremony*. The hard-hearted witches invented white people in a competition, a distinctive figuration that overcame the mere comparison of natives with the racial extremes of dominance.

Betonie, the old man, "shook his head. 'That is the trickery of the witchcraft,' he said. 'They want us to believe all evil resides with white people. Then we will look no further to see what is really happening. They want us to separate ourselves from white people, to be ignorant and helpless as we watch our own destruction. But white people are only tools that the witchery manipulates; and I tell you, we can deal with white people, with their machines and their beliefs. We can because we invented white people; it was Indian witchery that made white people in the first place.'"[17]

Louis Owens pointed out in *Other Destinies* that "Betonie's words and the story of witchery underscore an element central to Native American oral tradition and worldview: responsibility." This sentiment of personal responsibility

is survivance, a native aesthetics, and a metaphor that denies closure. "To shirk responsibility and blame whites, or
any external phenomenon, is to buy into the role of helpless victim."[18]

Gordon Henry created a wild, tricky scene of two dogs
stuck together in a natural, sexual, totemic dance, a white
dog, a brown dog, and in the end, one dead dog, in his
novel *The Light People*. Boozhoo tried to separate the figurative white and brown dogs, and then he turned to his own
magic, "my sideline vocation, my years of training. First I
tried mental magic: I attempted to project the image of a
piece of meat into the mind of the dancing white dog. For
a minute I thought it worked, since I heard the white dog
give off a low growl and I thought I saw his mouth water.
But the dogs remained stuck together."[19]

Custer, the authored mongrel in *Bone Game* by Louis Owens, is a memorable character in the tensive metaphor of
his name. The names of some animals are ironic, and other
authored animals have a sense of presence and character
without a name. In one scene a character in the novel rec-
ommends a guard dog: "I mean it. You should get a dog.
... A big, mean one. And remember, dogs don't like ghosts
or witches. We keep them around the hogans at home just
for that."[20]

Ravens and crows are native tricksters, a union of pushy,
avian mongrels, trust breakers, thieves, and astute healers.
Consider the ravens who stole my lunch in Hibiya Park near
the Imperial Palace in Tokyo. "The palace ravens search the
restaurant trash at first light, and then, in smart teams, they
raid the parks. By dusk they return to their roosts in the imperial sanctuary. My bento sushi became one of their stories of the day," I wrote in *Hiroshima Bugi: Atomu 57*. "Tokyo

was firebombed at the end of the war and the ravens quickly moved to the secure trees of the Imperial Palace. The more guttural ravens of the industrial areas, nearby docks, and remote sections of the city, resent the imperial strain, their haughty relatives, the palace ravens who survived the war as aesthetic victims." The imperial ravens "descend at great speed from nearby buildings, a trace of silent black motion, a perfect flight, and snatch a cracker from a child, a rice cake from a schoolgirl, a sandwich from a tourist." The crown ravens are my relatives, "a tribute to a criminal empire, the great, tricky warriors of Hibiya Park."[21]

I wrote in *Fugitive Poses: Native American Indian Scenes of Absence and Presence* that "monotheistic creation is a separation of animals, birds, and humans in nature and literature; the common unions since then have been both domestic and aesthetic." My idea of a native literary aesthetics is a tricky, totemic union of animals, birds, humans and others. "The more obscure tropes in literature must be closer to nature and animal consciousness than a literal simile."[22] The authors are animals. The readers are animals. The animals are humans, native relatives, and that promotes a native literary aesthetics. The hunters, authors, and readers are tropes, the animals of their own narratives.

The native literary aesthetics of survivance transmutes by imagination the obvious simulations of dominance and closure, and that mighty turn must be shamanic, godly, and pretentious. The creation of native scenes by oral stories and written words forever changes by sound, silence, and scripture. The actual moment of an aesthetic conversion in stories is figurative, an imagic tease of literary mortality.

1. Unnamable Chance

The certificate of my birth was duly recorded on October 22, 1934, in Minneapolis, Minnesota. There were accurate, manifest entries for my father, Clement William Vizenor, a house painter born on the White Earth Reservation, and for my mother, LaVerne Lydia Peterson, a seventeen-year old white housewife.

I was a hybrid document, unnamable on delivery. My names were chance, a nominal absence, a mere voucher of presence. My mother might have considered adoption at the time, but finally she recorded my names by affidavit some eighteen years later.

I was a child of native chance, the unnamable son of an *anishinaabe* newcomer from the reservation and a romantic, lonesome adolescent mother who loved the movies. The *anishinaabe* were forsaken at the time by the federal government, and my mother was surely influenced by the popular simulations of savagism and civilization, but such notions of racial separatism did not restrain her sentimental passions.

16   George Raft, the movie actor, was an inspiration to my mother, and in that sense, he was responsible for my chance conception that winter at the end of the Great Depression. President Franklin Delano Roosevelt had been inaugurated the year before, and he told the nation, "The only thing we have to fear is fear itself." Lovey, my adolescent mother, and millions of other lonesome women stranded in cold rooms, heard that presidential assurance on radio. My mother, however, was roused more by romantic movie actors than by executive promises.

"The first time I saw your father he looked like George Raft, not the gangster but the dancer," my mother told me a few years before her death. "He was handsome and he had nerve." Lovey saw the actor in my father and married an exotic *anishinaabe* expatriate from the White Earth Reservation.

George Raft appeared in four movies that year of my birth. He danced with Carole Lombard in *Bolero*. He was a paroled convict in *All of Me*, a mixedblood Chinese racketeer in *Limehouse Blues*, and a Mexican bullfighter in *The Trumpet Blows*. And he played a romantic detective in *The Midnight Club* a year before my father moved to the city. Raft was a taxicab driver who gave a paroled woman shelter in bad weather in *Pick-Up*, and he was a dark neighborhood gang leader in *The Bowery*.

Clement William Vizenor, or Idee, a native nickname that praised his eyes, lived with his mother, Alice Beaulieu Vizenor, his two sisters, and four brothers in a crowded tenement in downtown Minneapolis. My father and uncles worked as house painters for the same contractor.

Raft, an Italian actor, and my father were swarthy, and they both wore fedoras. Idee must have smiled and waved to my mother, a memorable, theatrical moment. He might have flipped a coin, a signature gesture in the movies, and overturned the Great Depression in that winter tenement of my conception. Lovey, that marvelous night, might have been Carole Lombard in the arms of my virtual father George Raft.[1]

The chance of my conception and the absence of my names on a birth certificate have become the stories of an uncommon literary presence. My stories honor chance, create a sense of presence, and celebrate survivance. Chance cannot easily be reduced by causal reason or cultural contrasts. Chance is my actual sense of the real, a coincidence, an existential venture of uncertainty, and unnamable contradictions. Chancy, natural reason is a communal adjective of survivance over dominance and the causes of victimry.

Clement, my father, was a teaser, a man of uncommon native stories in a constitutional democracy. He encountered the mundane ironies of politics, exclusions, and the violence of the thirties. Idee was newcomer to the city, but not to the contingencies of poverty. He was never a native poser in the name of victimry.

My father and uncles were not hired as *indians*, but they were counted as *indians* on the census. Clement was never asked to name his *tribe* or his proportion of "*indian* blood" in the United States Census of 1930 on the White Earth Reservation. However, his parents, and other natives, were asked questions on the reservation about identity and native affinity in an earlier national census. My father and his generation were enumerated as *indians*, the first national census simulation; the votive politics of archive assimilation, and transethnic triage.

Transethnic in the sense that the simulation of the *indian* is the absence of the native, and the *indian* is the other in the archive of *institutive* simulations. Triage, the decisive sacrifice of the *real*, the unnamable, and the antecedence of natives. The simulation of the *indian* is the "archive fever" of preservation, simplification, and the cause of narrative dominance. Natives are evermore the other, actually twice the other in the transethnic sentiments of *indian* victimry.

The *indian* is an archive: the simulations, discoveries, treaties, documents of ancestry, comparative traditions in translation, museum remains, and the aesthetics of victimry. Cultural studies are common cues to the *indian* archive, but not to an actual native presence, or native stories, that unnamable sense of cultural distinctions. The *indian* archive is *institutive* and, at the same time, the conservation and deconstruction of an elusive native presence in literature and history.

Minnesota, at the time my father moved to the city, counted only about eleven thousand *indians*, about 3 percent of the state population; some 10 percent of the total *indian* population in the nation lived in urban areas, 3 percent more than were counted a decade earlier in the census. The national enumeration of the *anishinaabe* was 21,549 in 1930, compared to more than 100,000 today.

My father was native, an *anishinaabe* by reservation ancestors, and an *indian* by simulation. The census counted him an *indian*, the absence of a native presence, and twice an absence in the city. He was the *other* in the archive, and the double other in the enumeration of *indians* on the census. These representation of the *anishinaabe* in national documents are exclusions of a native sense of presence.

Clement, his brothers, and other natives in urban areas, were *indians* by simulation, transethnic by separation, but native in their stories of survivance. One contractor refused to hire my father and uncles as house painters because they were *indians*. The contractor reasoned that *indians* never lived in houses, and therefore would not know how to paint one. Consequently, my father, uncles, and other natives had to present themselves to subsequent contractors as some other emigrant; at last my father and uncles were hired to paint houses as Greeks and Italians.

The *Minneapolis Tribune* reported that the arrest of a "Negro in Chicago promised to give Minneapolis police a valuable clue to the murder of Clement Vizenor, 26-year-old half-breed Indian, who was stabbed to death in an alley near Washington avenue and Fourth street early June 27 [1936]. Vizenor's slaying was unsolved." Racial violence was indicated in many newspaper stories of homicide, but there was no evidence in the investigations that race was a factor in the murder of my father.

The *Minneapolis Tribune* reported, "Captain Paradeau said he was convinced Clement had been murdered but that robbery was not the motive. The slain youth was reported to have been mild tempered and not in the habit of picking fights. Police learned he had no debts, and, as far as they could ascertain, no enemies." The same newspaper that reported the death of my father by homicide hired me thirty-two years later as a journalist.[2]

Alice Mary Beaulieu, my grandmother, was born January

3, 1886, and nineteen years later she married Henry Vizenor. They were both born on the White Earth Reservation. Sixteen years later, abandoned by her husband, she moved away from the reservation with her children, first to nearby rural towns, and then to the city. The family lived for several years in a coldwater flat in downtown Minneapolis.

My grandmother was *anishinaabe* by ancestors, a native presence, by reservation experience, and she was an *indian* by absence, an emigrant in the city. She endured many seasons of extreme poverty, winters over tricky stories, but she never lost her soul to victimry. She teased lonesome memories and, in her late sixties, married a generous, sightless, younger man.

Alice told newsy stories of survivance in the city. She must have been wary of reservation men and their promises of traditions. Yet, she teased chance and created a new native "giveaway" of survivance in the city. She never used the word *potlatch*, in the sense of native economies, but surely understood the ceremonial give and game of wealth and power.

Alice lived on Social Security, a minimal income, and she told ironic stories about the reservation culture of lace, music, medicine, motorcars, and more, not as envies, and not as rue, but as a trace of the *potlatch* in the creative, narrative giveaway of her uncommon experiences. She had always been a mighty healer, and then, on the move with her blind husband, she became an unnamable reassurance to lonesome women lost in the new suburbs of Minneapolis. She listened to their grants and told curative stories in an ironic native giveaway.

Earl Restdorf and his wife set out, once a week at times,

on a metropolitan bus, and rode to the end of the line. There, they went door-to-door and sold brushes and brooms to housewives. The native emigrant and her blind husband were strangers in the suburban community; however, they were always invited into fine new houses by lonely women. They were served lunch, and then shown pictures of children and families. Alice was a newcomer to the envies and loneliness of suburbia.

Alice could heal a worried heart by humor and a natural tease, the most common unities in trickster stories. She was a healer by just the right touch of survivance. Together, my grandmother, the native emigrant, and her sightless husband, conceived of a new giveaway ceremony. There, at the end of the bus line, they had so much to give as storiers in the suburban estates of cultural absence and victimry.

There are two crucial dimensions of the native *potlatch* ceremony. The first is the distribution of wealth, and the destruction of personal property. The distribution of resources is a common convention in native communities, otherwise named a giveaway; philanthropy, charitable donations, and even certain measures of taxation could be considered in a wider sense of the custom. The destruction of resources, however, and the curse of wealth is a tricky convention to understand as a differentiation of power and prestige.

"Once the resources are dissipated, there remains the prestige acquired by the one who wastes," observed Georges Bataille in *The Accursed Share*. "The waste is an ostentatious squandering to this end, with a view to a superiority over others that he attributes to himself by this means. But he misuses the negation he makes of the utility of the resources he wastes, bringing into contradiction not only himself but man's entire existence." He pointed out that the *potlatch* is "like commerce, a means of circulating wealth, but it excludes bargaining. More often than not it is the solemn giving of considerable riches, offered by a chief to his rival for the purpose of humiliating, challenging and obligating him. The recipient has to erase the humiliation and take up the challenge; he must satisfy the *obligation* that was contracted by accepting. He can only reply, a short time later, by means of a new potlatch, more generous than the first: He must pay back with interest."[3]

Alice, and many other natives, seemed to actuate a postmodern *potlatch* in the city. My grandmother teased the sacred, that moral mime of *indian* traditions, and told new trickster stories in the suburbs where the wealth was only simulated by the lonely. The outcome was a new giveaway. Alice favored the chance of humor over sacrifice, and native survivance over victimry.

The White Earth Reservation was established by concessions, federal coercion, and a treaty, a caricature of native sovereignty. The treaty was an invitation to a perverse giveaway, and a century later, the outcome of that ironic covenant would be the rise of casinos, that crafty union of avarice and mercenary sovereignty.

My grandmother conceived of the reservation in stories, not in the metes and bounds of land allotments, or wily timber concessions. She created a homeland in the memories of native humor, a cultural tease of survivance, not in a nation of traitorous *indians* and federal agents, and never in the rites of tragic victimry. These ironies, teased at the heart of scorn, deceit, and false pity, were the very counter sources of her humor, natural reason, mediative ethos and ethics, and new giveaway stories in the city.

Alice teased the sunrise at the windows, and reassured the lonesome heirs in the suburbs that the old traces of dominion were erased in a native giveaway.

Native giveaways, the wink of trickster stories, and memories of a comic nation, and reservation, are creases outside the institutive surveillance and sway of the government. Always, the double agents of the social sciences were abused by their own measures and could not bear the tease and humor of trickster stories.

My grandmother, a mighty storier, was deft and worthy of laughter and the tease of native reason. Native stories are a natural giveaway, and only laughter is the appropriate response. The obvious obligation of my generation is liberal irony and literature.

Many native authors have actuated a literary giveaway in their stories, a narrative deconstruction of cultural dominance. William Apess, Luther Standing Bear, N. Scott Momaday, Leslie Silko, James Welch, Louise Erdrich, Louis Owens, Thomas King, Kimberly Blaeser, Gordon Henry, Diane Glancy, and many other natives, have created a literature of humor, tragic wisdom, and survivance.

This native literature of survivance is a new aesthetic giveaway.

Survivance is an unnamable narrative chance that creates and teases a sense of presence. The word *Indian*, for instance, is a colonial invention, an absence in literature because it is a simulation without a real reference. The *anishinaabe* and other natives are an unnamable presence; their stories create a sense of presence, and that presence is survivance, my signature and epitome of literature. The stories that grieve over absence are the burdens of victimry.

I wrote in my first autobiographical essay for *Contemporary Authors* that my "visions, scares, and stories are traces of the unnamable," that very countenance of oral stories and narratives. The native author must bear the eternal nature of the unnamable, the chance of names, the ironies of simulations and contested cultural histories, and create a sense of presence in stories, a sense of survivance over dominance and victimry. That "unnamable presence in stories is not the mere antithesis of absence or silence." Survivance is an active, creative force that braves manifest manners, the wicked mien of manifest destiny, and tragic victimry.[4]

I commented later in *Postindian Conversations*, a collection of interviews with A. Robert Lee, that most of the characters in my novels and stories "outwit, reverse, and overturn the wiles of dominance, and they contradict the simulations of natives," that is, the ironic simulations of victimry. Survivance, the union of active survival and resistance to cultural dominance, is an obvious spirit of native sovereignty in my novels. Maybe "upsetting binaries and resistance are the same as survivance, but a tricky, visionary resistance is more than a structural reversion."[5]

My novel *Chancers*, for instance, is about the volatile issue of the repatriation of native skeletal remains. The Solar Dancers, a group of native college students, resurrect the native remains that are housed in the Phoebe Hearst Museum of Anthropology at the University of California, Berkeley. Those faculty and administrators associated with the possession of native remains were sacrificed in gruesome

ceremonies. The Solar Dancers replaced the native remains   25
with those of the academics, and by this ghastly substitu-
tion, the ancient natives were resurrected and became the
Chancers. The comic conclusion of the novel is a spectacular graduation ceremony that includes Ishi, Pocahontas,
Phoebe Hearst, Alfred Kroeber the anthropologist, and
many native Chancers.[6]

Ishi had endured the hate crimes of miners, racial terrorists, bounty hunters, and government scalpers in northern California. Many of his family and friends were murdered in the course of manifest destiny. California natives
barely survived the gold rush and colonial missions. Only
about fifty thousand natives, or one in five of the original
estimated population a century earlier, were alive in the
state at the turn of the twentieth century.

Ishi was one of those survivors. "He was the last of his
tribe," wrote Ashe Miller in the San Francisco Call, September 6, 1911. "Probably no more interesting individual could
be found today than this nameless Indian." Sheriff Weber
secured a "pathetic figure crouched upon the floor" of a
slaughterhouse, the Oroville Register reported on August 29,
1911. Ishi was not a criminal, but he was detained because
no one could understand his native language.

Alfred Kroeber, the first director of the Museum of Anthropology, then located in San Francisco, read the newspaper reports, contacted the sheriff, and federal agents
granted custody of Ishi to Kroeber. Ishi was moved to the
museum and lived in rooms furnished by Phoebe Apperson Hearst.

Ishi was christened the last of the stone agers, and overnight he became the curious savage of a vanishing race

26   overcome by modernity. I read about his capture, imagined his desperation and sense of separation, and was easily persuaded by his many museum friends that he was never contemptuous or servile. His stories were never given to victimry. Ishi was a native humanist in exile, and a storier of survivance.

Ishi, a generous storier, was there at the graduation ceremony in my novel with his admirers to receive an honorary degree, *honoris causa*, a doctor of humane letters from the University of California. Alfred Kroeber presented the academic hood and solemnly honored Ishi as a natural philosopher.

I formally proposed in October 1985 that a section of Dwinelle Hall be named Ishi Hall. My initiative won wide support from students and faculty and was unanimously endorsed by the student union at the University of California, Berkeley.

I argued that Ishi had made significant contributions in the early nineteen hundreds to the University of California. Professor Alfred Kroeber, the first anthropologist and director of the museum, noted that Ishi "had mastered the philosophy of patience." Saxton Pope, a medical doctor who admired the native hunter, pointed out that Ishi "knew nature, which is always true," and that he had the mind of a philosopher.

Ishi was not his native name; he was rescued by cultural anthropologists and named by chance, not by vision. The spirit of this native hunter, captured almost a century ago, has been sustained as cultural property. Ishi was humanely secured in a museum at a time when other natives were denied human and civil rights on reservations. A few years later my *anishinaabe* great uncle, John Clement Beaulieu, and other reservation natives were offered citizenship if they served in the United States Army in the First World War.

Ishi served with distinction the curatorial associations of the new Museum of Anthropology at the University of California. He was generous with his stories, endured without rancor a museum nickname and was, after all, vested as the first native employee of the University of California.

Ishi died of tuberculosis on March 25, 1916. His brain was removed during an autopsy, and the rest of his cremated remains were stored in a cinerary urn at the Mount Olivet Cemetery in Colma, California. Recently his brain was repatriated and buried with his ashes in a secret place near Mount Lassen.

None of this information, however, impressed the faculty committee that first considered my proposal. Ishi, in name and service, was denied a byword presence on the campus by the Dwinelle Hall Space Subcommittee. After a hearty discussion of toilets and closet space the subcommittee denied my initiative and the decision could not be overturned by any other campus committee.

Ishi was connected to the museum by chance, and he was twice denied a presence by name; however, seven years later my direct petition to the chancellor resulted in an acceptable compromise. The actual decision had more to do with the politics of federal funds and compliance with the law to repatriate native skeletal remains. There was an urgent interest to avert criticism by supporting native issues and academic programs.

Ishi Court was dedicated on May 7, 1993. Gary Strankman, justice of the First District California Court of Appeals, said the ceremony concerns names, and he pointed out an irony of memorial names on campus buildings, that for "every student or visitor who can give you some personal history of Wheeler, Boalt, Sproul, or Dwinelle, [he could] find a hundred, no a thousand, who can tell you the story of Ishi. Without a name he has achieved a fame and a respect that they can only envy."[7]

I first read Ishi in Two Worlds and Alfred Kroeber: A Personal Configuration by Theodora Kroeber some thirty years ago. Ishi, more than any other native outside of my family, is a presence in my creative memory. I admire his courage, humor, patience, the irony of his service in a museum, and his sense of survivance. He is my virtual, visionary relation, an honorable elder of native memory.

Ishi never revealed his sacred name, but at the museum he created an eternal sense of presence. He endured by chance, unnamable, and yet he is remembered by millions of people around the world. Ishi was a man of survivance not victimry.

Albert Camus, the novelist and philosopher, and Ishi, the native humanist and storier, both lived in exile. Camus created a literature of separation and exile. Ishi created songs and stories of natural reason, survivance, and liberty. These two storiers were more at ease in nature, and the memory of seasons, than they were in the causes of culture and measures of history.

Ishi was a fugitive of nature and an outsider in a museum, an ethnographic archive. Camus was at home in his memories of nature, and in memories and stories of his beloved Algeria. Ishi was at home by natural reason and in his oral stories of survivance.

Camus never mentioned native oral stories in his essays, 29
but he shared an obvious vision of nature with Ishi. They
were betrayed by nations, by cultures, but not by nature.
These two storiers of exile were not weakened by the absence of ancestral scenes; rather, they created by nature a
visionary scene of liberty.

Ishi and Camus were exiled from distinctive landscapes,
and yet their stories consecrate a primordial sense of nature. "History explains neither the natural universe which
came before it, nor beauty which stands above it," wrote
Camus in "Helen's Exile," an essay in *Lyric and Critical Essays*. "Consequently it has chosen to ignore them." Nature,
however, is always there. "Her calm skies and her reason
oppose the folly of men."[8]

Camus observed that the artist and the historical mind
"seek to remake the world. But the artist, through an obligation of his very nature, recognizes limits the historical
mind ignores. This is why the latter aims at tyranny while the
passion of the artist is liberty. All those who struggle today
for liberty are in the final analysis fighting for beauty."

Ishi, Albert Camus, and Eric Hoffer, influenced the early
development of my thoughts as a writer. Hoffer, the long-
shoreman and philosopher, published *The True Believer* in
the early fifties. I was a sophomore college student, and
he introduced me to the idea of mass movements, ecstatic
dominance, and the fanatical causes of those who believe
in the absolute. The "true believer" has no sense of chance.
These ideas became part of my early interpretation of simulations. I augmented his idea of the true believer as "terminal creeds" in my critique of native racialists, essential
separatists, and those who stand by the simulation of the

"Indian" as the real. Terminal, rather than true, because
of federal termination policies and the absence of natives
in history; creed, rather than believer, because of the romantic pursuit of native cultures, shamans, and curious
spiritual connections. Hoffer introduced me to the true believer, and his ideas influenced my thoughts and theories
of native literature, the contradictions of those who must
possess the other by ideology and simulations.

Macalester College honored me with a degree of Doctor
of Humane Letters, *honoris causa*, at the commencement on
May 23, 1999, in Saint Paul, Minnesota. "Gerald Vizenor
has written more books and has gone farther with them
than any other native writer," said Diane Glancy, who presented the honorary citation. "I have permission to create
new thought, new words, because of him. I am not stuck
without a voice. I can think in ways I had not thought before.
In a time when a people were looking for *wordage*, for place,
for re-creation of tribal meaning, for facing the unknown,
which you will face as graduates this very afternoon, Vizenor
found the imaginative tools with which to speak. May you
have the same courage to continue to say new things and
keep presenting us with ideas, blessed ideas."

President Michael McPherson, the trustees, faculty, graduates, and guests, heard me honor, in turn, the memory of my
parents at the commencement. My lecture started with my
father and ended with a story about Hubert Humphrey.

Clement Vizenor moved to Minneapolis from the White
Earth Reservation with his family during the Great Depression. Clement and his brothers found work as house painters, but not at first. Some contractors, at the time, thought
that Indians were not the best painters because they did

not live in houses. My father and uncles told similar stories of their experiences, but not always in the context of the White Earth Reservation. They were storiers of survivance, and, because their experiences were similar to those of emigrants, they were hired as painters, Italian, Greek. I am the son of a painter, and my father was an ironic emigrant in the city.

My father never read N. Scott Momaday, Isaiah Berlin, Albert Camus, Hannah Arendt, Edmond Jabès, Primo Levi, Samuel Beckett, Louis Owens, or Diane Glancy, to name a few authors that come to mind, but surely he would have compared his own stories to their narratives of survivance.

"We are what we imagine," wrote N. Scott Momaday, the author of *House Made of Dawn*. "Our very existence consists in our imagination of ourselves. . . . The greatest tragedy that can befall us is to go unimagined."[9] Clement, my father, imagined his advantage as a native newcomer to the city. I create stories of survivance in his name.

Isaiah Berlin wrote in *The Roots of Romanticism*, "We owe to romanticism the notion of the freedom of the artist, and the fact that neither he nor human beings in general can be explained by oversimplified views. . . . We also owe to romanticism the notion that a unified answer in human affairs is likely to be ruinous. . . . The result of romanticism, then, is liberalism, toleration, decency and the appreciation of the imperfections of life."[10] My father was a storier of liberal irony, decency, and the imperfections of native survivance.

"We enter New York harbor. A terrific sight despite or because of the mist," wrote Albert Camus in *American Journals*. "The order, the strength, the economic power are there. The heart trembles in front of so much admirable inhumanity."[11] My father might have written as much in the journal of a house painter, and he might have noted the tease of winters, the humor, chance, and the "admirable inhumanity" of Minneapolis in 1934.

"Just as our hunger is not that feeling of a missing meal, so our way of being cold has need of a new word," wrote Primo Levi in *If This Is a Man*. "We say 'hunger,' we say 'tiredness,' 'fear,' 'pain,' we say 'winter' and they are different things. They are free words, created and used by free men who lived in comfort and suffering in their homes."[12]

Native Americans were cursed by racialism and separatism on federal reservations in a constitutional democracy, and the stories of that time necessitate new words. My ancestors resisted the arbitrary authority of federal agents and published *The Progress*, the first newspaper on the White Earth Reservation. Their testimony is not the same as the survivors of concentration camps. My father suffered, but he was free. *The Progress* honored the stories of survivance and liberty.

"The act of writing defies all distance," wrote Edmond Jabès in *The Little Book of Unsuspected Subversions*. "Is it not every writer's ambition to raise the fleeting—the profane—to the level of the lasting, the sacred?"[13] Clement, my father, surely would agree, and with a native sense of humor. I was a child when he was murdered, the victim of an unsolved homicide in Minneapolis. My stories of survivance dare and defy that distance.

Samuel Beckett wrote in the *Unnamable*, "Perhaps they have carried me to the threshold of my story, before the door that opens on my story, that would surprise me, if it opens, it will be I, it will be the silence, where I am, I don't know, I'll never know, in the silence you don't know, you must go on, I can't go on, I'll go on."[14] That threshold is my story of survivance, "you must go on."

Louis Owens observed in *Other Destinies*, "Traditionally, a storyteller's audience consisted of tribe or clan members, who could be counted on to contribute a wealth of intimate knowledge to the telling of any story, to thus actively participate in the dynamics of the story's creation."[15] My father, grandmother, uncles, and other native ancestors were storiers, and my first literary audience is their presence in memory.

Diane Glancy wrote in *Claiming Breath*, "I think poetry evolves out of ordinary circumstances—the ideas I write about often come from the hardness of prairie life. Poetry is road maintenance for a fragmented world which seeks to be kept together."[16]

My road was chance, the unnamable, and a dare, first held together by the images of haiku poetry, and then the book. Jabès wrote in *The Book of Questions*, "I am in the book. The book is my world, my country, my roof, and my riddle. The book is my breath and my rest."[17] My father writes by my hand in memory, his native blood and breath, my book, and my rest.

LaVerne, my mother, was a high school dropout and worked all her life as a union waitress in restaurants. Lovey was shy and wrote more poetry than she ever read. She honored one politician more than any other. His name was Hubert H. Humphrey, and she praised me for writing about him more than anyone in my career as a journalist.

Vice President Humphrey accepted an invitation to join the faculties at Macalester College and the University of Minnesota a month after he lost the presidential election

34   to Richard Nixon. I was a staff writer for the *Minneapolis Tribune* at the time.

Humphrey told the audience at the Janet Wallace Fine Art Center in 1968, "I was on this campus twenty-five years ago and I've had, you might say, a rather extended sabbatical, and I want to thank you for your patience."

Arthur Fleming, then the president of Macalester College, pointed out that when Humphrey lost his first bid for mayor of Minneapolis, he came to teach at Macalester, and the next time he ran for mayor he was elected. Humphrey returned to the Senate two years later, but he was never again a presidential candidate.

Humphrey was my assignment the day after the presidential election. He arrived at his daughter's house in Burnsville, near Minneapolis. I followed him with permission down the basement stairs. A card table was set with miniature teacups. Jill Solomonson, who was six years old at the time, took her grandfather by the hand and led him to a blackboard in the basement room. Vicky stood at his side. Humphrey read out loud this printed message:

> A vote for Humphrey
> Is a vote for me.
> Love
> Jill, Amy and Vicky.
> Do not vote for Nixon.
> Boo!

I reported on the front page of the *Minneapolis Tribune*, November 8, 1968, that the weary grandfather who almost became the thirty-seventh president of the United States turned to Vicky, who was celebrated at an early birthday party, and said, "I tell you, don't we have fun."

2. Native Liberty

Daily newspapers observe the moment and then vanish the morning after, as the commerce of news awaits an invitation to history. I was a journalist for about five years and never gave much time to consider my stories in the last edition of the newspaper. Every morning was the start of new stories on the elusive road to history.

Newspapers delivered on federal reservations may linger a few more days, but the fade is even more pronounced by content, a distinct treaty boundary of news and information *outside* the politics of cultural dominance.

The *Cherokee Phoenix*, one of the first native newspapers, was established in 1828. Native newspapers "grew slowly" and were "considered an oddity until the last two decades of the nineteenth century," noted Daniel Littlefield in the *Encyclopedia of North American Indians*. These early native "newspapers were aimed primarily at the American public as well as the local population and promoted an image of 'civilization' to the outside world."[1]

I discovered that civilization in *The Progress*, a weekly newspaper published by my native ancestors more than a

century ago on the White Earth Reservation in Minnesota.
I was inspired by the dedication of the editor, and the news
stories created a singular sense of native presence, the culture and politics of the inside, and provided a privy trace of
assurance to consider a career as a writer, although the actual associations and connections were more involved and
political. The Progress has forever been in my imagination
and sense of native liberty.

I was a graduate student at the time, more than forty
years ago, at the University of Minnesota. During my early
research on native writers, tribal leaders, and treaties at
the Minnesota Historical Society, a generous reference li-
brarian directed me to the original bound volumes of The
Progress, the first newspaper published on the White Earth
Reservation. The Progress was published about twenty years
after the federal reservation was established by removal
treaty in 1886.

I was transformed, inspired, and excited by a great and
lasting source of a native literary presence and survivance.
The newspaper countered the notion of a native absence,
and sustained instead a personal source of solace, enlightenment, and a unique historical identity. I slowly, almost
reverently, turned the fragile pages of the newspaper and
read news stories, editorials, and notes by and about my
distant relatives.

The Progress was founded by Augustus Hudon Beaulieu,
the publisher, and Theodore Hudon Beaulieu, the editor.
They were directly related to my paternal grandmother Alice Beaulieu Vizenor. John Clement Beaulieu, my great uncle, and my grandmother never mentioned the family newspaper to me. At the time their need to remember was not as

great as mine by discovery. *The Progress*, two years later, became *The Tomahawk*. The number of pages increased slowly, and national news reports, or syndicated patent insides, were published in each issue of *The Tomahawk*.

Reading the newspaper that afternoon at the Minnesota Historical Society was truly transformational, a moment that lasts in my stories and memory, in spite of the unreasonable, dismissive response by the faculty graduate advisor. He refused to accept my research paper, a historical, descriptive content analysis of the reservation newspaper, because, he said, it was not an acceptable subject of graduate study. The primary reason for his rejection, however, was mundane, the exploitation of graduate students. He demanded that students study national newspaper advertising space to serve his own funded research project. His manifest manner was grievous and unacceptable to me. I never returned to graduate school. Obviously it was time for me to become a journalist. *The Progress* provided a sense of higher civilization.

Bower Hawthorne, the executive editor of the *Minneapolis Tribune*, at the time, offered me a position as a journalist after he heard my critical lecture at a conference of newspaper editors and read my publication on Thomas James White Hawk. The Dakota college student had been convicted of murder and sentenced to death in South Dakota. I had published, with foundation support, five thousand copies of a free pamphlet on the facts of the case.

My presentation to the editors at the conference was a fierce indictment, the historical inventions and political invalidations of tribal cultures right down to the advertisements and editorial columns of the best newspapers in the country. I cited specific violations of human rights by the incitement of racialism in stories and advertisements published in recent issues of the *Minneapolis Tribune*.

Frank Premack, the city editor, provided me with a desk and typewriter on Monday, June 3, 1968. Later that week, Thursday, June 6, 1968, Senator Robert Kennedy died of gunshot wounds in Los Angeles. Sirhan Sirhan was indicted the next day for murder. Premack assigned me to write a feature news story that the nation was *not*, in essence, violent. Three days as a journalist and my first assignment, a feature story that would controvert the public notions on violence. I interviewed a wide range of experts in two days. My story was published on the front page, an extreme initiation as a journalist.

Alice Beaulieu Vizenor, my grandmother, was generous by tease, stories, sentiment, and money. I remember mostly her everlasting liberal humor, love, and the grandeur of her stories. I could not have found a better source to tease her memory than the hearsay column in *The Progress*. Actually, my first historical use of news from the reservation some seventy years earlier was to tease my grandmother. I would casually mention her relatives, noted visitors, one or two great storms, and activities of the priests at the Benedictine Mission. "How did you know that," she would say. She laughed and reasoned the tease of time was a native practice.

The Progress announced one spring morning in the first issue, March 25, 1886, that the "novelty of a newspaper published upon this reservation may cause many to be wary in their support, and this from a fear that it may be revolutionary in character."

The front page of the weekly newspaper carried side column advertisements by local merchants on the reservation: Hotel Hindquarters; R. Fairbanks, Dealer in Groceries Provision; Frank Hume, Clocks, Watches and Jewelry;
G. A. Fairbanks & Bro, Dry Goods, Groceries, Hardware;
and Leecy and McArthur, General Merchandise. Natives
owned every reservation business and service advertised
in the newspaper.

The Progress published a notice in the top right-hand corner of the front page, "Look Out! For Wainnahboozho,"
or naanabozho, the trickster figure in native stories. The
anishinaabe, or Chippewa, create marvelous stories about
the adventures and priapic exploits of naanabozho, a transformational trickster. Priests and federal agents were forever teased, mocked, and outwitted in trickster survivance
stories.

"We shall aim to advocate constantly and withhold reserve, what in our view, and in the view of the leading minds
upon this reservation, is the best for the interests of its residents. And not only for their interests, but those of the tribe
wherever they now are residing."

I was provoked and influenced by the advocacy of the editor, the gestures to the "leading minds" on the reservation,
and imagined my presences as a writer for the newspaper.
I worried, at the same time, about the fragile condition of
the newsprint.

"The main consideration of this advocacy will be the political interests, that is, in matters relative to us and to the
Government of the United States. We shall not antagonize
the Government, not act, in the presentation of our views,
in any way outside of written or moral law."

We intend that this journal shall be the mouth-piece of the community in making known abroad and at home what is for the best interests of the tribe. It is not always possible to reach the fountain head through subordinates, it is not always possible to appeal to the moral sentiment of the country through these sources, or by communication through general press.

We may be called upon at times to criticize individuals and laws, but we shall aim to do so in the spirit of kindness and justice. Believing that the "freedom of the press" will be guarded as sacredly by the Government on this reservation as elsewhere, we launch forth our little craft, appealing to the authorities that be, at home, at the seat of government, to the community, to give us moral support, for in this way only can we reach the standard set forth at our mast-head.

The Progress was dedicated to "A Higher Civilization: The Maintenance of Law and Order."

I was amused by the words "fountain head," the source, or originator, but the sense was ironic, an "appeal to the moral sentiment of the country." I was impressed by the dedication of the editor to "moral law" and, in my view, moral agency. Rightly, the editor argued, it is not possible to communicate to the government "through subordinates." I was already involved in the discourse of early reservation politics and "civilization" by the first few issues of the newspaper.

The Minnesota Historical Society reference room was almost silent, only the faint sound of automobile traffic around the capitol building. I must have been alone in that baronial room for hours, enchanted, leaning over seventy some year old copies of The Progress spread out on the oak

table. I easily return by imagination to that singular time
and place on the reservation. My relatives were there, writers too, and we shared the same general issues of resistance
and survivance, and the ironies of federal dominance in a
constitutional democracy.

The Progress was confiscated by federal agents shortly after the first copies of the newspaper were distributed on the
White Earth Reservation. Theodore Beaulieu, the editor,
and Augustus Beaulieu, the publisher, both tribal members, were ordered by federal agents to leave the reservation.
They avoided the agents and found sanctuary in the mission
church. The Benedictine priests, at the time, were active in
the politics of the reservation, and obviously endorsed the
publication of a newspaper for the community.

The Progress was first published on March 25, 1886, and
the second issue was published on October 8, 1887, more
than a year after federal agents seized the press and property of the newspaper, and after a subcommittee testimony
and favorable hearing in federal court.

T. J. Sheehan, the United States Indian Agent, a malevolent federal appointee, was a nasty, obsessive denier of
native liberty, and he would not tolerate "freedom of the
press" on the reservation without his approval. Sheehan
wrote to the editor and publisher that they had "circulated
a newspaper without first obtaining authority or license so
to do from the honorable Secretary of the Interior, honorable Commissioner of Indian Affairs, or myself as United
States Indian Agent."

Practically every means of communication by federal
agencies about natives was ironic, and in this instance
the mere use of the word "honorable" was an invitation to

42 mockery. The honorific names of secretaries, commissioners, and federal agents are an eternal summons to ridicule
and tricky invectives. The honorable political appointees
were pronounced contradictions, and those who carried
out the policies of dominance were the agents of manifest
ironies, the measures of state dishonor and venality.

The mockery of federal agents has always been a native
theme in stories. These practices of mockery are not the
same as the cultural tease of acceptance. I read about the
corruption of the federal agent on the reservation, and my
mockery increased by the page. The Progress endured, truly
an honorable declaration of native liberty and survivance
on the White Earth Reservation.

Sheehan asserted in his formal letter that the publisher,
Augustus Beaulieu, "did scheme and intrigue with certain
chiefs on White Earth Reservation without the knowledge
of myself and the Indians of this agency, for the said chiefs
to proceed to Saint Paul, Minnesota, for the purpose of sign-
ing a power of attorney for the Mississippi Indians, depu-
tizing a person to act as an attorney for the Indians in certain business interests affecting the welfare of the Indians
on White Earth Agency, all of which I considered revolutionary to the United States Government and a detriment
to the welfare of these Indians."

The editor was an advocate, to be sure, and the syco-
phants of the federal agents no doubt anticipated wary parties, fearful that the newspaper was "revolutionary in character." I looked around the reference room that afternoon
for someone to convince that The Progress was absolutely
revolutionary.

Sheehan continued, "Whereas you have at different times
advised the full and mixedblood Indians to organize and
'kick' against the rule established by myself as United States
Indian Agent, for the suppression of card playing, or other
games which may be detrimental for the Indians on this
agency, in either the hotels or store-buildings of White Earth
Reservation.

"Whereas, Theodore H. Beaulieu has written and caused
to be printed in a newspaper adjacent to White Earth Reservation, false and malicious statements concerning the affairs of the White Earth Reservation, done evidently for the
purpose of breaking down the influence of the Unites States
Indian agent with the Indians of White Earth Agency."

I have no doubts that the editor intended, by ironic courtesy, to discredit and weaken the arbitrary power of federal
agents. Sheehan clearly pitched too hard against the good
nature of natives, and his preachy, defensive manner was
enough evidence to reveal his incompetence and insecurity.
The agent unwisely continued to devalue the ideas and interests of the "leading minds" of the reservation until the
number of complaints about his capricious manner resulted
in an official investigation by a subcommittee of the Committee on Indian Affairs of the United States Senate. The
subcommittee convened a hearing about a year after The
Progress had been confiscated by federal agents.

Clement Hudon Beaulieu was the first witness to testify
on Tuesday, March 8, 1887, before the subcommittee of the
Committee on Indian Affairs. Clement was the father of
Augustus Beaulieu, publisher of The Progress, and uncle of
the editor, Theodore Hudon Beaulieu. There has been some
confusion about names. Clement, who died at White Earth

44   in 1892, had seven sons with his wife Elizabeth Farling. One
son was named Theodore Basile Beaulieu.

Senator John Tyler Morgan, Democrat from Alabama,
studied several documents and then asked the first questions that morning:

> What is your age?
> I was seventy-five years old last September.
> What family have you living with you?
> I have my wife living with me. . . .
> Is your wife Indian or white? Asked Senator
> Morgan.
> She is half Chippewa and half Scotch.
> Are you Chippewa?
> Yes, sir, responded Clement Beaulieu.
> Full blood?
> No, sir; half French and half Chippewa.
> What other members of your family have you living in the house?
> My children are all grown up; there is only one
> living with me. My oldest son, Charles Beaulieu, has
> been in the Army.
> Which Army?
> The Union Army. In 1862 I raised up a company for
> him of mixedblood, Indians and French. I got him a
> hundred men.
> And he took them into the Army?
> Yes, sir.
> He was a captain of the company?
> Yes, sir, he was captain of the company.

Senator Morgan had been a brigadier general, some
twenty years earlier, in the Confederate Army during the
Civil War. He was first elected to the Senate in 1876 and
served as chairman of the Committee on Foreign Relations.

Morgan, a "southern nationalists" was active in the racial
politics of the time. He was a prominent racist and advocated that constitutional liberty was exclusive. "Morgan's
views on limiting suffrage rights through literacy tests
soon gained wide acceptance," observed Thomas Adams
Upchurch in "Senator John Tyler Morgan and the Genesis
of Jim Crow Ideology 1889–1891." His "racist oratory and
publications garnered a national and even international
audience at the time."

Senator Morgan seemed to examine natives in anticipa-
tion of his later racist motions, a direct query of racial blood-
lines, education, intermarriage, and voting rights.

> What children have you living in the house with
> you?
>> Theodore, one of my youngest sons. . . .
>> Where do you reside?
>> I reside at the White Earth Agency.
>> How long have you been there?
>> For fifteen years. . . .
>> What other sons have you?
>> I have another, a minister. . . .
>> Where does this minister reside?
>> He is now in Mason City, Iowa.
>> What church is he minister of? asked Senator
> Morgan.
>> The Episcopal Church, said Clement Beaulieu.
>> How long has he been in that calling?
>> He was confirmed about four or five years ago.
>> What is your religion?
>> Catholic; we are all Catholics except that one.
>> Your wife is Catholic?
>> Yes, sir. . . .
>> Have you any daughters?

One.

Is she married?

Yes, sir.

What is her name?

Julia Beaulieu. She is married to one of our relatives of some distance, said Clement Beaulieu.

A cousin, I suppose?

Yes, sir, a second cousin.

What is her husband's name?

Theodore H. Beaulieu.

So that he has the same name as your son?

No, sir, the other one is Theodore B. Beaulieu. . . . How much of a family has Julia?

She has had three children.

Where do they live?

They live about a mile from me. . . .

On the reservation?

Yes, sir, on the reservation. . . .

What order has been made by the Secretary of the Interior in regard to the removal of your family or your daughter's family? asked Senator Morgan.

The only way we can tell there is to be a removal is by the letters of the Secretary of the Interior to the agent, said Clement Beaulieu.

Does that include your wives and children?

No, sir, only ourselves alone.

So that you are to be banished from that country and separated from your families.

Yes, sir, both, as long as this order continues. The agent asks for us to be permanently removed forever. I have not seen it myself.

Other persons have seen the order of removal, but you have never seen it?

No, sir, I have not seen it.

Have you or your son-in-law, Theodore H. Beaulieu,

the means to break up at the reservation and go elsewhere with your families and make a support?

I do not know whether it will come to that. . . .

But have you the means to leave?

No, sir; we have not means at all. He has less than
I have, because he has nothing but his farm.

So that if you are compelled to remove your families from the reservation it will amount to the destruction of all you have earned in your life?

Yes, sir, the whole of it. . . .

Are you a citizen of the United States?

I was born in what is now the State of Wisconsin,
said Clement Beaulieu. My mother was a member of
the Chippewa tribe, and my father was a Frenchman.
I was born before any treaty was made between the
Chippewas and the Unites States. The first treaty was
made in 1837. No removal of the Indians was made to
any tract, but they ceded our land to us. No reservation was made, but we had a right to occupy the land
and to hunt as usual. . . .

When did you move to Minnesota?

I was two years in Canada and in 1838 I came to Wisconsin and have remained there just on the edge of
Minnesota ever since until 1846, and then I removed
as an agent for the American Fur Company to Minnesota. . . .

When did you first join the body of Indians of which
you are now a member, the White Earth Indians?

I joined them under the treaty of 1854, when there
was a separation between the Lake Superior Indians
and the Mississippi Chippewas. I joined that band because I could not go so far back as Lake Flambeau. Under the provisions of that treaty we were allowed to go
either with the Mississippi Chippewa or with the Lake
Flambeau Indians, and they would be considered as

the Lake Superior Chippewa, and from that time I have always been with the Chippewas of Mississippi.

Have you ever been a voter?

I have, responded Clement Beaulieu. I voted in Crow Wing County, Minnesota, near Brainerd. . . .

Was this voting done under the laws of the State of Minnesota?

I don't know whether it was or not, but I was allowed to vote.

You thought it was under the laws of Minnesota?

We thought it was, because it was outside the reservation. We did not see anything to prevent us. I don't know whether it was done to get the votes of the half-breeds.

But all the half-breeds outside the reservation voted?

Yes, sir. . . .

Did you muster with the militia?

No, sir, but when Mr. Sibley was governor he appointed me lieutenant-colonel in the State militia, and that is the reason they call me colonel now.

Have you held office and paid taxes?

Yes, sir. I held office only once; that was in 1842, I think, at Duluth. Before we had any laws we elected our own people as officers, and I was elected a justice of the peace; and I was at the same time sheriff, lawyer, and judge. When a man had committed any wrong I drew the writ myself, brought the man before me, pleaded his case, condemned him, and put him in lock-up. In one case I prosecuted a man for stealing and locked him up and afterwards found out I had made a mistake, and we relieved him from arrest and I paid him for the time he was there, and settled for everything. The poor fellow had no chance to gain his case when I did it all myself.

Where was that?

That was in Duluth.

In what county?

We had no county established at that time. . . .

Under what law did you do all these things?

I thought I had the law of Minnesota, or Wisconsin as it was then, to go by.

The Territory or the State law?

The law of the Territory, said Clement Beaulieu. I had a few pieces of the printed laws; I do not know where I picked them up or whether they were the laws of Michigan or Wisconsin, and I used them to dictate to me what to do. But it was all a mistake, I suppose.

You were elected to the office of justice of the peace, were you? asked Senator Morgan.

Yes, I was elected by the people to the office of justice of the peace.

Were you also elected to the office of sheriff?

No, sir, but I thought as justice of the peace, having no constable, lawyer, or judge, I had the right to elect myself to those offices.

And the judgments you rendered as justice of the peace had to be carried into execution?

Yes, sir, and so I appointed myself judge, sheriff, and lawyer.

Did you get along pretty well under that arrangement?

Yes sir, I had no trouble.

What was your reason for wanting all this power?

To keep the peace; that was the only motive.

Was there much trouble with the Indians up there?

There was a good deal of stealing.

And you wanted to prevent that?

Yes, sir.

That is your answer then as to the question I put to you, whether you were a citizen of the United States?

Yes, sir.

I suppose you leave that for other persons to determine whether you are a citizen or not?

Yes, sir, I do.

Did you take an oath when you were appointed justice of the peace, before any person?

No, sir.

Have you ever taken an oath to support the Constitution of the United States?

Not that I know of.

Did you take an oath of office when you were made lieutenant-colonel? asked Senator Morgan.

No, sir.

Have you ever held an office of any kind since you have been on the White Earth Reservation?

None that I know of.

Is Theodore H. Beaulieu a farmer?

Yes, sir, he is a farmer; he does nothing but farm.

Is he a thrifty, good farmer?

He is a good farmer, a good worker. . . .

Are your children educated people?

My children pass to be educated. They are the best educated boys; I think, there on the reservation, my boys are.

Where did you educate them?

When I was at Brainerd there, I had a teacher that came from below. I sent for a teacher and kept him there as long as I could, and then sent them down to Saint Paul, and then, after they were there, I thought they hadn't enough, hadn't but a small education and I sent them down to New Jersey and kept them there as long as I could.

All of your children?

No, sir, four of them. The other one didn't want to be educated, he wanted to be a farmer, and I could not get him to go away from home.

Which one is that?

That is the one now living with me, Theodore B. Beaulieu.

Is your daughter educated?

Yes, sir, I sent her to a convent, and I gave her all the education in music and everything.

Where was the convent?

At Saint Paul, responded Clement Beaulieu.

Under what treaty did you receive these certificates for lands?

Under the treaty of 1867. Formerly it was all in a body, all together in a reservation. . . .

How many Indians now, about, belong to the White Earth Reservation? asked Senator Morgan.

Altogether I think there are between 1,700 and 1,800 of the Mississippi, Otter Tail, and Pembina bands.

And those 1,800 Indians comprise the body which are included in the White Earth Reservation?

Yes, sir.

Amongst those White Earth Indians I suppose you include all the half-breeds and quarter-breeds?

Yes, sir, all the half and quarter breeds.

All that belong to the Chippewa tribe of Indians are included?

Yes, sir.

Have you any stranger Indians amongst you at all?

No, sir. We had two Sioux, but one took his wife away, and the other one died last fall, so that we have no strangers now.

Senator Morgan continued to question Clement Beaulieu about the mixedblood population, education, alcohol

52   consumption on the reservation, food supplies, game and
       fish, maple sugar and wild rice, and the attitudes and be-
       havior of federal agents and missionaries, and, the pri-
       mary reason for the examination of witnesses, the publi-
       cation of The Progress.

       The secretary of the interior received a letter signed by
       more than two dozen tribal leaders that denounced the re-
       moval order issued by T. J. Sheehan, the United States Indian
       Agent. White Cloud; Ignatius Hole-in-the-Day; Wahjimah
       Wahmegons; Mahjikeshig; Nahtanub; Charles Wright, a
       missionary; Albert Fairbanks, a practical farmer; and many
       others resolved to denounce the charges against Clement
       Hudon Beaulieu, and Theodore Hudon Beaulieu, the editor
       of The Progress, "as false and malicious." "[They are] mem-
       bers, residents, and neighbors of our reservation, and we
       cheerfully bear testimony to their ability and unblemished
       character." And the signatories further resolved that "no
       action should be taken tending to their removal until a fair
       and just hearing is granted to them, and a public and im-
       partial investigation of all the facts in the matter be also
       granted, to the end that justice may be done in the prem-
       ises." The letter was published with the official subcommit-
       tee transcript of the Committee on Indian Affairs.

       John Johnson Enmegahbowh, the tribal missionary who
       established the Episcopal Saint Columba Church on the
       White Earth Reservation, wrote to the committee that he
       knew Clement Hudon Beaulieu to be "always upright and
       honorable and zealous in the civilization and advancement
       of his tribe." Enmegahbowh, the son of a trapper, had been
       ordained as a priest by Bishop Henry Whipple. His letter
       was particularly important because of the mettlesome

competition between the Episcopal and Catholic missions
on the White Earth Reservation. Clement Beaulieu and his
family, with the exception of one son, were members of the
Catholic Church.

Senator Morgan considered a letter, included in the report of the subcommittee, from T. J. Sheehan. The agent accused Theodore Hudon Beaulieu, and his family, of printing
in The Progress "false and malicious statements concerning
the affairs of White Earth Reservation, done evidently for
the purpose of breaking down the influence" of the federal agent.

> This paper appears to contain the reasons why Mr.
> Sheehan, the agent at that place, White Earth, thought
> fit to prohibit the publication of a newspaper, the same
> paper which had already been offered in evidence?
> Yes, sir.
> Had any copy of that newspaper appeared before
> that was written? asked Senator Morgan.
> No, sir, said Clement Beaulieu.
> If this paper had been printed in Saint Paul or at
> Detroit, Minnesota, do you know of any authority or
> power on the part of this agent to prevent its being
> carried into the reservation and circulated through
> the mails?
> No, sir, he cannot suppress any paper that comes
> in there, and I do not think he would be able to sup-
> press this one.[2]

The Progress published the second issue of the newspaper on October 8, 1887, more than a year after the editor
and publisher were ordered removed from the reservation
by federal agents, and six months after an investigation

54   by the subcommittee of the Senate Committee on Indian
Affairs.

Theodore Hudon Beaulieu, the editor, wrote the following on the front page of the second issue:

> [In the] month of March last year, we began setting
> the type for the first number of The Progress and were
> almost ready to got to press, when our sanctum was
> invaded by T. J. Sheehan, the United States Indian
> Agent, accompanied by a posse of the Indian police.
> The composing stick was removed from our hands,
> our property seized, and ourselves forbidden to pro-
> ceed with the publication of the journal. We had, prior
> to this time, been personally served with a written no-
> tice from Mr. Sheehan detailing at length, surmises
> beyond number as to the character of The Progress, to-
> gether with gratuitous assumptions as to our moral
> unfitness to be upon the reservation, charging the
> publisher with the voicing of incendiary and revolu-
> tionary sentiments at various times.
>
> We do not believe that any earthly power had the
> right to interfere with us as members of the Chippewa
> tribe, and at the White Earth Reservation, while peace-
> fully pursuing the occupation we had chosen. We did
> not believe there existed a law which should prescribe
> for us the occupation we should follow. We knew of
> no law which could compel us to become agricultur-
> alists, professionals, "hewers of wood and drawers
> of water," or per contra, could restrain us from en-
> gaging in these occupations. Therefore we respect-
> fully declined obeying the mandate, at the same time
> reaching the conclusion that should we be restrained
> we should appeal to the courts for protection.
>
> We were restrained and a guard set over our
> property. We sought the protection of the courts,

notwithstanding the assertion of the agent that there
would be no jurisdiction in the matter.

The United States district court, Judge Nelson in session, decided that we were entitled to the jurisdiction we sought. The case came before him, on jury trial. The court asserted and defended the right of any member of a tribe to print and publish a newspaper upon his reservation just as he might engage in any other lawful occupation, and without surveillance and restrictions. The jury before whom the amount of damage came, while not adjudging the amount asked for, did assess and decree a damage with a verdict restoring to us our plant. . . .

Now that we are once more at sea, fumigated and out of quarantine, and we issue from dry dock with prow and hull steel-clad tempered with truth and justice, and with our clearance registered, we once more box our compass, invite you all aboard, and we will clear port, set sails to favorable breezes, with the assurance that we will spare no pains in guiding you to a "higher" civilization.

The Progress was not the first newspaper to be published on a federal reservation, but it was the first tribal newspaper to be seized capriciously by federal agents. The Progress continued weekly publication for about two years and then changed its name to The Tomahawk. The editor and publisher remained the same. The newspapers published reservation, state, and national news stories, and controversial editorials.

Theodore Hudon Beaulieu, the feisty editor, strongly opposed the federal allotment of reservation land, the provisions of the Dawes General Allotment Act of 1887. One front-page report, for instance, was introduced by this verbose

56   feature headline: "Is it an Indian Bureau? About some of
the freaks in the employ of the Indian Service whose actions are a disgrace to the nation and a curse to the cause
of justice. Putrescent through the spoils system."

The Progress created a sense of presence, survivance, and
native liberty by situational stories, editorial comments,
reservation reportage, and by the resistance of the editors.
The native editors and readers were denied the ordinary
rights of citizens in a constitutional democracy by arbitrary federal dominance, historical absence, and by the
sentiments of victimry.

3. Survivance Narratives

"What boy would not be an Indian for a while when he thinks of the freest life in the world? This life was mine," wrote Charles Alexander Eastman in *From the Deep Woods to Civilization*. "Every day there was a real hunt. There was real game. Occasionally there was a medicine dance away off in the woods where no one could disturb us, in which the boys impersonated their elders."[1]

Natives of Appomattox

The Civil War ended with the surrender of General Robert E. Lee at Appomattox Court House in Virginia on April 9, 1865. The carnage had been horrific, but the republic survived with a wounded spirit. Then, Abraham Lincoln, the sixteenth president, was assassinated four days later.

Native American Indians have been rived, deracinated, and removed by constant colonial, cultural, and territorial conflicts, but the total, bloody war between the Union and the Confederacy forever abated an original native sense of presence, cultural sovereignty, and continental liberty.

Francis Paul Prucha pointed out in *American Indian Treaties* that at the end of the Civil War the federal government
was "intent on dealing strongly" with those natives who
had "disowned their treaty obligations" and "formed alli-
ances" with the Confederacy.[2] An estimated twenty thousand natives fought in the Civil War, slightly more for the
Confederacy than for the Union.

Prucha argued in *The Indians in American Society* that by the
time natives were "crushed militarily, they had already lost
status as independent political entities" to negotiate treaties with the United States. Ely S. Parker, the first native to
serve as commissioner of Indian Affairs, insisted that the
"treaty system be scrapped, since it falsely impressed upon
the tribes a notion of national independence. 'It is time,'
Parker said, 'that this idea should be dispelled, and the government cease the cruel farce of thus dealing with its helpless and ignorant wards.'" Native "dependency increased,"
observed Prucha, "as the traditional means of survival were
weakened and destroyed in the passage of time."[3]

The military, however diminished, moved against natives
on the western frontier at the end of the Civil War. Railroads
were soon built across the continent, natives were deceived
by treaties and removed to reservations, and bison, the primary source of food and income for natives, were slaughtered by the millions in the hide trade.

The Civil War was not the first act of savagery to rouse a
native sense of survivance—the sensibilities of diplomatic,
strategic resistance, and the aesthetics of literary irony. The
new warriors of survivance had a vision of futurity. Natives
created many spirited narratives in the very ruins of racism

and chauvinistic crusades on the elusive frontier of a constitutional democracy.

Colonel Ely S. Parker, for instance, a Seneca sachem of the Iroquois Confederacy, was military secretary to General Ulysses S. Grant and transcribed the actual surrender terms that ended four years of war. Parker was born in 1828 at Indian Falls on the Tonawanda Reservation in New York. Thirty-seven years later he was present for the surrender of Robert E. Lee at Appomattox Court House.

Robert Utley wrote in *The Indian Frontier of the American West* that Parker "loyally served his chief as adjutant, military secretary, and aide-de-camp," and two years later he directed a "comprehensive plan of Indian management, including transfer of the Indian Bureau to the War Department." The plan "won strong support in the Congress."[4]

Jay Winik noted in April 1865 that after the two generals had "signed the preliminary papers, Grant proceeded to introduce Lee to his staff. As he shook hands [with Parker], Lee stared for a moment and finally said, 'I am glad to see one real American here.' If this account is true, Parker responded to the general, 'We are all Americans.'" There is, of course, "some debate as to whether this exchange ever actually happened," observed Winik. "It has also been speculated that Lee at first may have thought Parker was a black man."[5] The irony is doubled either way.

Grant was elected president four years later and appointed Parker the commissioner of Indian Affairs. Parker wrote that General Grant "showed his love for his military family by doing kindness for them whenever he could." As president "he sought them out, and without solicitation on their part, provided for many of them." Grant "never forgot a favor rendered him when he was poor and he was kind to such people when he had the power."⁶

Appomattox, the actual place of the surrender, is derived from a native word. The name was first recorded about four centuries ago and has now become a part of a national narrative history. John Smith observed in "The Description of Virginia," his seventeenth-century adventure stories, the "pleasant river of *Apamatuck*" and some thirty "fighting men" of that name.

Brigadier General Stand Watie is another significant name in the history of the Civil War. Cherokee by birth and politics, he was the only native general in the Confederacy. Praised and promoted for his raids on federal supply lines, he was the last officer to surrender his forces in June 1865. Educated at the Moravian Mission School in Georgia, he supported the removal of the Cherokee to Indian Territory in what is now Oklahoma.

Utley pointed out that Stand Watie "set up a rival Cherokee government with himself as chief."⁷ Several tribes were divided by their loyalties to the Union and the secession of the Confederacy. Watie supported slavery and was a member of the Knights of the Golden Circle, an association that countered the abolition movement. Many southern natives were slavers and enlisted in the cause of the Confederacy.

Native American Indians served as scouts for colonial regimes, and much later for the army on the frontier and in other countries. Their military service was obviously an escape from reservations. Thomas Britten argued in *American Indians in World War I* that native veterans were more experienced, and "more effectively" resisted the "encroachments on their lands, cultures, and liberties." Natives served in the military to ensure their survivance, however ironic, and as warriors to "obtain security, honor, prestige, and wealth, and to enact revenge on enemies."[8] Most natives served in integrated military units.

Britten pointed out that the War Department "continued its policy of conscious assimilation of Indians into white units." Natives fought in integrated units in the Spanish American War, the Filipino Revolution, and the Boxer Rebellion in China.[9] The narratives of their service as common soldiers were seldom included in war histories.

Ten thousand natives served in the American Expeditionary Force during the First World War. Britten wrote that many native soldiers returned with "emotional scars" and memories of horror, but "others gained a sense of purpose, discipline, and pride." The Society of American Indians and many native progressives of the time supported the war and encouraged natives to serve their country to "win respect and high valuation in the estimation of the world." Meanwhile, natives were forever burdened by the corruption and bureaucratic abuses of federal agents at home on reservations. A Lakota elder told an ironic story about the war and torment of reservation policy. The German Kaiser, said the elder, should be confined on a reservation, and the federal agent should say to him, "Now you lazy bad man, you farm and make your living by farming, rain or no rain; and if you do not make your own living don't come to the Agency when you have no food in your stomach and no money, but stay here on your farm and grow fat till you starve."[10]

Newspaper Indians

"The Civil War changed American journalism," declared John Coward in *The Newspaper Indian*. The number of readers increased, there was more "competition between urban newspapers," and there were new economic incentives to report and publish the news promptly. Coward pointed out that the "telegraph helped put speed ahead of accuracy."[11]

Indian news reports were "distributed more efficiently and consistently," and as a consequence of speed and consolidation, the news was standardized.[12] Native cultures, resistance, wars, and removal were reported in simplistic, descriptive, and romantic narratives. Many news stories contributed to the simulation of native images in the dominant culture.

The Civil War "set a pattern for news coverage of the Indian wars," noted Coward. "In both cases, reporters sometimes resorted to inventing sensational or dramatic details in order to improve the copy."[13]

Charles Sanford Diehl, for instance, reported on the surrender of the Nez Perce for the *Chicago Times*. Many newspapers at the time reported daily on the military pursuit of the Nez Perce by General Nelson Miles, and covered the surrender of Chief Joseph on October 5, 1877, at the Bear Paw Mountains in Montana.

Chief Joseph, the Nez Perce diplomat and political leader, was reported to have said at surrender, "Hear me, my chiefs. I am tired. My heart is sick and sad. From where the sun now stands, I will fight no more forever."[14] That eloquent statement was reported widely, and has become a romantic signifier of a native vanishing point in art, literature, and history.

Lieutenant Charles Erskine Scott Wood may have construed the speech, but there is no secure record or document to explain how or when the actual surrender sentiment was transcribed and translated from an emotive oral expression to a written language. Wood, an acting aide-de-camp at the time of the surrender, was named the transcriber, but the handwritten evidence does not support his story.

Mark Brown noted in *The Flight of the Nez Perce* that the "story that Joseph surrendered his rifle with this touching little speech, while Wood stood by 'with a pencil and a paper pad' to record it does not have a word of truth in it." Brown observed that the "formal surrender took place near evening" and only a "small group were present to receive the surrender."[15]

Thomas Sutherland, a correspondent for several newspapers, including the *San Francisco Chronicle* and the *New York Herald*, described the scene of surrender in somber, tragic metaphors. "As the sun was dropping to the level of the prairie and tinging the tawny and white land with waves of ruddy lights, Joseph came slowly riding up the hill," wrote Sutherland. Joseph raised his head and "with an impulsive gesture, straightened his arm toward General Howard, offering his rifle, as if with it he cast away all ambition, hope and manly endeavors leaving his heart and his future down with his people in the dark valley where the shadows were knitting about them a dusky shroud."[16]

Bruce Hampton argued in *Children of Grace* that Lieutenant Wood later disavowed an earlier account and claimed that Chief Joseph had delivered the surrender notes. "Still, there is a resonance to the speech that closely resembles other declarations attributed to Joseph. If not his explicit words, Wood—probably with some literary polish—seems to have captured their gist."[17]

"Diehl was not with General Miles and was not a witness to the surrender of the Nez Perce," wrote Coward.

"I wrote my story, by candlelight, in a cold army tent," explained Diehl, "and dispatched it by courier to Helena, Montana." Diehl was a respected war reporter because he created a sense of "action and excitement." Coward pointed out that the "job of the Indian reporter was to find excitement, even when it was inspired by fiction."[18]

Chief Joseph, the august native diplomat, Yellow Bull, and Ad Chapman, an interpreter, visited Washington DC in January 1879, two years after their surrender, to argue for tribal recognition and the return of the exiled Nez Perce to their homeland in the Pacific Northwest. Members of Congress, the cabinet, diplomats, and commercial leaders listened to a memorable, heartfelt entreaty for liberty.

Chief Joseph heard a standing ovation at the end of his speech. Bruce Hampton pointed out that "Washington newspapers praised the speech and several philanthropic organizations, including the Indian Rights Association and, strangely enough, the Presbyterian Church, began to show an interest in the exiles."[19] Chief Joseph's purported speech, and there are several versions, was published as an article a few months later in the *North American Review*.[20]

> If the white man wants to live in peace with the Indian he can live in peace. There need be no trouble. Treat all men alike. Give them all the same law. Give them all an even chance to live and grow. All men were made by the same Great Spirit Chief. They are all brothers. The earth is the mother of all people, and all people

should have equal rights upon it. You might as well expect the rivers to run backward as that any man who was born a free man should be contented not penned up and denied liberty to go where he pleases. When I think of our condition my heart is heavy. I see men of my race treated as outlaws and driven from country to country, or shot down like animals. I know that my race must change. We cannot hold our own with the white men as we are. We only ask an even chance to live as other men live. We ask to be recognized as men. We ask that the same law shall work on all men.

Whenever the white man treats the Indian as they treat each other, then we shall have no more wars. We shall be all alike—brothers of one father and one mother, with one sky above us and one country around us, and one government for all. Then the Great Spirit Chief who rules above will smile upon the land, and send rain to wash out the bloody spots made by brothers' hands upon the face of the earth. For this time the Indian race are waiting and praying. I hope that no more groans of wounded men and women will ever go to the ear of the Great Spirit Chief above, and that all people may be one people.[21]

Congress received fourteen petitions of support for the cause of Chief Joseph. Otis Halfmoon noted in the *Encyclopedia of North American Indians* that on "May 22, 1885, the Nez Perce boarded railroad cars in Arkansas City to return home to the reservation. The charisma and diplomacy of Chief Joseph had prevailed." Sadly, the Nez Perce were not allowed to return to the Wallowa Valley in Oregon. They were removed to the Colville Reservation in Washington where Chief Joseph died on September 21, 1904.[22]

66   Robert Utley pointed out in *Frontier Regulars* that Chief Joseph "refused to give up hope of returning to his beloved
Wallowa Valley in Oregon." Once more, in 1897, "he jour-
neyed to Washington and urged his cause on President
McKinley." General Nelson Miles and other military leaders supported his initiative, but the "whites of the Wallowa
refused to part with any land for Indian occupancy."

The Nez Perce created a great narrative of resistance,
tragic retreat, surrender, and survivance. Utley wrote, "Their
just cause, their unity of purpose and action, their seemingly
bottomless reservoirs of courage, endurance, and tenac-
ity, their sheer achievement and final heartbreaking failure
when on the very threshold of success, have evoked sympathy and admiration for almost a century."[23] The Nez Perce
are truly the patriots of a continental native liberty.

Higher Civilization

"The novelty of a newspaper published upon this reservation may cause many to be wary in their support, and this
from a fear that it may be revolutionary in character," announced Theodore Beaulieu, the native editor of *The Progress*, the first newspaper published on the White Earth Reservation in northern Minnesota, March 25, 1886. "We shall
aim to advocate constantly and withhold reserve, what in
our view, and in the view of the leading minds upon this
reservation, is the best for the interests of its residents. And
not only for their interests, but those of the tribe wherever
they now are residing.

"We may be called upon at times to criticize individuals
and laws, but we shall aim to do so in a spirit of kindness
and justice. Believing that the 'freedom of the press' will

be guarded as sacredly by the Government on this reservation as elsewhere, we launch forth our little craft, appealing to the authorities that be, at home, at the seat of government, to the community, to give us moral support, for
in this way only can we reach the standard set forth at our
mast-head." *The Progress* was dedicated to "A Higher Civilization: The Maintenance of Law and Order."[24]

The United States Indian Agent confiscated the press
and ordered the editor and Augustus Beaulieu, the publisher, both of whom were tribal members, removed from
the White Earth Reservation. The Indian Agent alleged that
The Progress printed "false and malicious statements concerning the affairs of the White Earth Reservation, done
evidently for the purpose of breaking down the influence
of the United States Indian Agent with the Indians."[25]

The second issue of *The Progress* was published more than
a year later on October 8, 1887, after a hearing in federal
court and a government investigation. Theodore Beaulieu
observed, "We began setting type for the first number of
The Progress and were almost ready to go to press, when our
sanctum was invaded by T. J. Sheehan, the United States
Indian Agent, accompanied by a posse of the Indian police. The composing stick was removed from our hands,
our property seized, and ourselves forbidden to proceed
with the publication of the journal." Beaulieu continued,
"We did not believe that any earthly power had the right to
interfere with us as members of the Chippewa tribe, and
at the White Earth Reservation, while peacefully pursuing
the occupation we had chosen. We did not believe there existed a law which should prescribe for us the occupation we
should follow. We knew of no law which could compel us

to become agriculturists, professionals, 'hewers of wood and drawers of water,' or per contra, could restrain us from engaging in these occupations. Therefore we respectfully declined obeying the mandate, at the same time reaching the conclusion that should we be restrained we should appeal to the courts for protection.

"We were restrained and a guard set over our property. We sought the protection of the courts, notwithstanding the assertion of the agent, that there could be no jurisdiction in the matter. The United States district court, Judge Nelson in session, decided that we were entitled to the jurisdiction we sought. The case came before him, on jury trial. The court asserted and defended the right of any member of the tribe to print and publish a newspaper upon his reservation just as he might engage in any other lawful occupation, and without surveillance and restrictions. The jury before whom the amount of damage came, while not adjudging the amount asked for, did assess and decree a damage with a verdict restoring to us our plant."[26]

The Progress was the first newspaper published on the White Earth Reservation, and it was the first native newspaper seized by federal agents in violation of the Constitution of the United States. *The Progress* was published weekly for two years; the newspaper was enlarged and the name was changed to *The Tomahawk*. The native editor and publisher remained the same; both newspapers published reservation, state, and national news stories, and critical, controversial editorials. The newspapers opposed the federal act that allotted collective native land to individuals. One article, for instance, carried this headline on the front page: "Is it an Indian Bureau? About some of the freaks in the

employ of the Indian Service whose actions are a disgrace
to the nation and a curse to the cause of justice. Putrescent
through the spoils system."[27]

Messiah of Survivance

Wovoka was a shaman, an envoy of the sacred world. His
concise narrative envisioned the resurrection of native reason and a sense of presence. He revealed new, crucial ceremonies that would exalt the ancestors to return, revive
the bison to the prairie, and restore a native continental
liberty.

Wovoka, or Jack Wilson, a Northern Paiute who was born
near Smith Valley, Nevada, inspired thousands of natives
by his direct, temperate, and humane instructions to wear
sacramental paint, dance in a circle for five days, bathe in
the river, feast, and "not refuse to work for the whites and
do not make any trouble with them until you leave them.
When the earth shakes do not be afraid."

The native dead would be resurrected by the dance, and
the "great change will be ushered in by a trembling of the
earth, at which the faithful are exhorted to feel no alarm,"
observed James Mooney in The Ghost-Dance Religion and the
Sioux Outbreak of 1890. "The moral code inculcated is as pure
and comprehensive in its simplicity as anything found in
religious systems from the days of Gautama Buddha to the
time of Jesus Christ."[28]

Wovoka asked Mooney to present a copy of his narrative
to government officials in Washington. The purpose was
"to convince the white people that there was nothing bad
or hostile in the new religion."[29]

The Arapaho version, the first transcription of the narrative, begins with the direct advice of the messiah of survivance: "What you get home you make dance, and will give the same. When you dance four days and one day, dance day time five days and then fift, will wash for every body."

Wovoka told the concise stories of his vision to several native translators. Casper Edson, an Arapaho who had studied at the federal Carlisle Industrial Indian School, translated and transcribed the first narrative into English, and that became the ironic lingua franca of the Ghost Dance Religion. That original narrative was later translated into other native oral languages on reservations, but the initial doctrine and other renditions were communicated in English. More than twenty thousand natives in some thirty western tribes actively participated in the Ghost Dance.

"No white man had any part, directly or indirectly," in the first translation and production of the narrative. Nor was the doctrine of the messiah "originally intended to be seen by white men," wrote Mooney. "In fact, in one part the messiah himself expressly warns the delegates to tell no white men."

Mooney, who had several conversations with Wovoka, years after his shamanic vision, pointed out in a rather reductive manner that while the messiah was "sick there occurred an eclipse of the sun, a phenomenon which always excites great alarm among primitive peoples. In their system the sun is a living being, of great power and beneficence, and the temporary darkness is caused by an attack on him by some supernatural monster which endeavors to devour him, and will succeed, and thus plunge the world into eternal night unless driven by incantations and loud noises."[30]

Wovoka stated that he was "stricken down by a severe fever" and experienced an ecstatic, shamanic vision. "When the sun died"—a reference to a solar eclipse—he was entranced and taken to heaven. Later he returned from the spirit world with a revelation. Wovoka was probably in his early thirties at the time of his vision, a cosmic ideation, and a total eclipse on January 1, 1889.

Mooney pointed out that there were three early versions of the translated narrative in English: Arapaho, Cheyenne, and the third, a free rendering, the most familiar version of the transcribed narrative. Here is the free rendered version of the entire narrative. The "good cloud" probably refers to rain, and "each tribe there" suggests reservations and native country. The reference to a "young man" is probably the first translator of the narrative, Casper Edson.

When you get home you must make a dance to continue five days. Dance four successive nights, and the last night keep up the dance until the morning of the fifth day, when all must bathe in the river and then disperse to their homes. You must all do in the same way.

I, Jack Wilson, love you all, and my heart is full of gladness for the gifts you have brought me. When you get home I shall give you a good cloud which will make you feel good. I give you a good spirit and give you all good paint. I want you to come again in three months, some from each tribe there.

There will be a good deal of snow this year and some rain. In the fall there will be such a rain as I have never given you before.

Grandfather says, when your friends died you must not cry. You must not hurt anybody or do harm to anyone. You must not fight. Do right always. It will give you satisfaction in life. This young man has a good father and mother.

Do not tell the white people about this. Jesus is now upon the earth. He appears like a cloud. The dead are all alive again. I do not know when they will be here; maybe this fall or in the spring. When the time comes there will be no more sickness and everyone will be young again.

Do not refuse to work for the whites and do not make any trouble with them until you leave them. When the earth shakes do not be afraid. It will not hurt you.

I want you to dance every six weeks. Make a feast at the dance and have food that everybody may eat. Then bathe in the water. That is all. You will receive good words again from me some time. Do not tell lies.[31]

Many natives wrote letters to the messiah of survivance. The letters were translated from dictation by the first generation of natives who had attended federal and mission schools. Several letters were published in I Wear the Morning Star, an exhibition catalog on the Ghost Dance, published by the Minneapolis Institute of Arts. Cloud Horse, for instance, sent his letter to the messiah on April 11, 1911, from Pine Ridge, South Dakota:

Jack Wilson,

Dear Father: Why do you not write to me. I sit with you and I write to you this letter. I hope I will come to see you. I send you a dollar bill. Why dont you answer me?

When you get this letter answer soon, Father. This man writing a letter for me but he lives far and this man write for me this letter.

This man a good man write for me this letter. I sit with Cloud horse and we write this letter.

Your loving son, I shake hands with you, Answer quick when you get this letter.

Cloud Horse

Address answer to Red Star

Pine Ridge, So. Dak.

The English language and the postal service became the
primary means of communicating the Ghost Dance Religion. Cloud Man Horse wrote this letter to Jack Wilson from
the Kyle Post Office, South Dakota, on December 13, 1911:

Dear Father:

Your letter has been received and I was very glad indeed to hear
from you dear father

Now I am going to send you a pair of mocissions but if they are
not long enough for you when you write again please send me you
foot measure from this day on—I will try to get the money to send
to you. I wish I had it just at present I would send it wright away.

I think I might get the money soon enough to send it so that is
why I say that so. I will get it just as soon as possible and be sure to
send it so if you get a letter from me I may have the money in that
letter so dear Father this will be all. I can answer you so for your sake
all the Indians out here make fun of me but I allways think dear Father that around me you would give me strength. so if you get the
money I want that medican and some good feathers & that paint
so that is what I want you to send me.

So this is all for this time. I give a good & hard shaking of the
hands to you I hope you have pity on me

I remain your son

Cloud Man Horse[32]

Wovoka was a storier of transcendence and survivance,
a clairvoyant of the weather and, in at least one instance,
an apparent seer of familial futurity. Harlyn Vidovich, his
grandson, became a pilot and fulfilled a prophecy.

Michael Hittman wrote in *Wovoka and the Ghost Dance* that
the messiah said his grandson would attend school, become a "credit to his people" and fly. Harlyn, born in 1919,
was the son of Andrew Vidovich, a Death Valley Shoshone,

74 and Alice Wilson, the illegitimate daughter of Jack Wilson. Wovoka said at the baptism, according to Andrew, that Harlyn would be "flying in the skies." Andrew pointed out that there were few airplanes at the time of his prophecy. Wovoka continued, "And then he's going to join the United States Flying" and "lead the white men in the skies. He will become a great captain."

Hittman reported that Harlyn Vidovich was "posthumously awarded" the Distinguished Flying Cross as a fighter pilot in the Flying Tigers.[33] Captain Vidovich, however, was listed in official Air Force records as a pilot in the 74th Fighter Squadron, Flying Tigers, in China, but not the earlier American Volunteer Group, Flying Tigers, under the celebrated commanded of General Claire Lee Chennault.

Wounded Knee

Wovoka, Charles Alexander Eastman, Luther Standing Bear, and Sophia Alice Callahan were born in the era of migrations, treaty reservations, and moral duplicities of the Civil War. They matured at a time of monstrous cultural burdens, military vengeance, and state violence; a native generation forsaken at the end of a great continental liberty, and yet they created narratives of chance and survivance.

Lakota Ghost Dancers were on the move that winter with visions of native survivance. Big Foot and his escorts had resisted removal to reservations and were pursued with a vengeance by the military. Fourteen years after the defeat of General George Custer at the Little Bighorn River the Seventh Cavalry massacred destitute men, women, and children at Wounded Knee Creek, South Dakota, on December 29, 1890.

"No one on either side that morning had any thought of a fight. Certainly not the Indians, as the army later charged; they were outnumbered, surrounded, poorly armed, and had their women and children present," argued Robert Utley in *The Indian Frontier of the American West*. "Wounded Knee assumes a larger significance, for it marks the passing of the Indian frontier."[34]

The bodies of the dreamers were frozen in the snow; some three hundred natives were slaughtered, and more than a hundred of the dead were buried in a mass grave. Big Foot, the traditional elder, weakened by pneumonia, was wounded and did not survive the massacre. His frozen head, shoulders, and arms were raised and braced in the snow, an enervated simulation by a mercenary photographer.

William Coleman wrote in *Voices of Wounded Knee* that Dewey Beard saw the soldiers murder the Ghost Dancers. Beard was wounded and "surrounded by soldiers." He "fought his way toward the ravine." Beard said, "I saw my mother standing and singing. She was waving a pistol. She told me to take it, she was dying. I cried and helped her sit down. I felt like I couldn't get up, I looked down and saw I had been shot again, in the lap.

"I was badly wounded and pretty weak too. While I was lying on my back, I looked down the ravine and saw a lot of women coming up and crying. When I saw these women, little girls, and boys coming up, I saw soldiers on both sides of the ravine shoot at them until they had killed every one of them."[35]

Turning Hawk said, "Those who escaped that first fire got into the ravine, and as they went along up the ravine for a long distance they were pursued on both sides by the soldiers and shot down, as the dead bodies showed afterwards."[36]

Celene Not Help Him survived the massacre. She said, "My grandfather was shot in the back; it went through his lung in the first volley of gunfire. He was again shot in the right calf and in the hip. He was coughing blood. He had lost a lot of blood. He could hear someone singing a death song. Whenever someone moved, the soldiers shot them."[37]

The Seventh Cavalry returned to the Pine Ridge Agency with their dead and wounded soldiers. Most of them had been shot "by their own comrades, who had encircled the Indians." Very few of the natives had guns, wrote Charles Alexander Eastman in *From the Deep Woods to Civilization*. "A majority of the thirty or more Indians wounded were women and children, including babies in their arms." There were not enough tents so the mission chapel, "in which the Christmas tree still stood," was offered as a "temporary hospital": "We tore out the pews and covered the floor with hay and quilts. There we laid the poor creatures side by side in rows, and the night was devoted to caring for them as best we could. Many were frightfully torn by pieces of shells, and the suffering was terrible." Eastman, a medical doctor, was placed in charge. The army surgeons were ready to assist, but the "tortured Indians would scarcely allow a man in uniform to touch them."[38]

Eastman, Santee Dakota, was born in 1858 near Redwood Falls, Minnesota. Many Lightnings, his father, was imprisoned for his active resistance in the Dakota Uprising of 1862. Seth Eastman, his maternal grandfather, was a graduate of West Point. Later he was the commander of Fort Snelling in Minnesota.

Charles attended the Santee Normal Training School, Beloit College, Knox College, Dartmouth, and graduated from the Boston Medical College, one of the first native medical doctors. Susan LaFlesche Picotte and Carlos Montezuma were two other native medical doctors at the time. Eastman had been in practice for about a month when he treated the survivors of the Wounded Knee Massacre. His Dakota nicknames were Hakadah, The Pitiful Last, and Ohiyesa, The Winner.

Wounded Knee was buried in snow. Eastman, who searched for survivors after the storm, wrote,

> Fully three miles from the scene of the massacre we found the body of a woman completely covered with a blanket of snow, and from this point on we found them scattered along as they had been relentlessly hunted down and slaughtered while fleeing for their lives. Some of our people discovered relatives or friends among the dead, and there was much wailing and mourning. When we reached the spot where the Indian camp had stood, among the fragments of burned tents and other belongings we saw the frozen bodies lying close together or piled upon one another. I counted eighty bodies of men who had been in the council and who were almost as helpless as the women and babes when the firing began, for nearly all their guns had been taken from them. A reckless and desperate young Indian had fired the first shot when the search for weapons was well under way. Immediately the troops opened fire from all sides, killing not only unarmed men, women, and children but their own comrades who stood opposite them, for the camp was entirely surrounded.
>
> It took all of my nerve to keep my composure in the

face of this spectacle and of the excitement and grief of my Indian companions, nearly every one of whom was crying aloud or singing his death song. The white men became very nervous, but I set them to examining and uncovering every body to see if any were living. Although they had been lying untended in the snow and cold for two days and nights, a number had survived. Among them I found a baby of about a year old warmly wrapped and entirely unhurt. I brought her in, and she was afterward adopted and educated by an army officer. One man who was severely wounded begged me to fill his pipe. When we brought him into the chapel, he was welcomed by his wife and daughters with cries of joy, but he died a day or two later.[39]

Luther Standing Bear, or Plenty Kill, was in the first class of native students to attend the Carlisle Indian School, a former military barracks, in 1879. He survived the extreme experience with distinction and was hired to teach in the government school on the Rosebud Reservation. Later, he moved to the Pine Ridge Agency.

Standing Bear noted in *My People the Sioux* that the soldiers were sent to escort and protect Big Foot and the Ghost Dancers. "The following morning the news arrived of the terrible slaughter of Big Foot's whole band. Men, women, and children—even babies were killed in their mothers' arms!" he wrote many years later. "When I heard this, it made my blood boil. I was ready myself to go and fight then. There I was, doing my best to teach my people to follow in the white man's road—even trying to get them to believe in their religion—and this was my reward for it all! The very people I was following—and getting my people to follow—had no respect for motherhood, old age, or babyhood. Where was all their civilized training?"[40] Days later he visited the site of the massacre. The bodies had been buried. "The place of death was forsaken and forbidding. I stood there in silence for several minutes, in reverence for the dead, and then turned and rode toward the agency."[41]

Indian Agents were determined to turn natives into "citizen farmers" observed L. G. Moses in *The Indian Man: A Biography of James Mooney*. The "Ghost Dance religion would not be permitted to challenge the tidiness of the process." Natives watched the military parades in silence. Grievously, "faith in the prophet was no longer enough to inspire armed resistance to the combined forces of civilization."[42]

Fictional Shoulders

Sophia Alice Callahan had almost completed her novel *Wynema* at the time of the war crimes at Wounded Knee Creek. She included a descriptive, omniscient scene about the "day of the skirmish," one of the first fictional comments of the massacre.

Wounded Knee is introduced at the very end of the novel by two characters in a passive, romantic conversation about a singular newspaper editorial: "The great Indian war is over—nothing was done except what was intended to be done." "[Defenseless] Indians were murdered; the Indian agents and contractors reaped a rich harvest; that's all."

"I think the editor is rather bitter," said Genevieve.

"Yes dear," answered Robin, "but if you had seen the Indians slain on the battle-field as we did, and could have heard the groans of the wounded you would not think so."

Robin placed his hands over his eyes and said, "I shall never forget that battle-field all strewn with dead and dying men and women and children, and the three little babies resting sweetly and unconsciously in their dead mothers' bosoms."[43]

Callahan created Wildfire, a noble warrior of omniscience, who maintained that he would never surrender his arms, and "my followers shall not. They are ours to use for our pleasure, or defense if need be."

Carl Peterson, a missionary, counsels Wildfire to surrender on a reservation, assume a "submissive attitude" and the government "will protect you; you will not be starved again, for those criminal agents have been discharged and better ones employed."[44]

"May the Great Father hear me say, let this arm wither, let these eyes grow dim, let this savage heart still its beating, when I stand and make peace with a Government whose only policy is to exterminate my race," said Wildfire.

This is "not a policy to live by," said Peterson.

"Then let it be a policy to *die* by," declared Wildfire. "If we cannot be free, let us die. What is life to a caged bird, threatened with death on all sides?"[45]

Big Foot and the Ghost Dance are not directly named in the novel. The omission creates an absence of actual natives, and the fictional natives, revised in sentimental conversations, are a double absence, not a presence in the novel or history.

Callahan died at age twenty-six in 1894. *Wynema* is one of the first novels written by a native, and the first published by a native woman. Apparently the novel was not widely read in the first edition. A. LaVonne Brown Ruoff pointed out in the historical introduction to *Wynema* that the only notice of the original publication was in *Our Brother in Red*:

Callahan "is an intelligent Christian lady and we look forward with pleasure to a time when our other duties will permit us to read the book."[46]

"Callahan combines the themes of domestic romance and protest novel" and "uses multiple voices and perspectives, Indian and non-Indian, female and male, to educate her readers," observed Ruoff. Of the last section of the novel Ruoff observed, "Sioux hostilities, the murder of Sitting Bull, and the massacre at Wounded Knee, is such an abrupt departure from the earlier romance plot that it was probably added to an almost completed novel."[47]

Pagan Sentiments

Gertrude Bonnin was eight years old when she left the Yankton Reservation for the first time to attend White's Indiana Manual Labor Institute in Wabash, Indiana. The institute was sponsored by the Society of Friends.

"The first turning away from the easy, natural flow of my life occurred in an early spring," she wrote in Atlantic Monthly. "At this age I knew but one language, and that was my mother's native tongue." Gertrude spied the missionaries that morning and heard the promises of "red, red apples." Her mother resisted but then agreed that her daughter would "need an education when she is grown, for then there will be fewer real Dakotas, and many more palefaces. This tearing her away, so young, from her mother is necessary, if I would have her an educated woman."[48]

Bonnin was indeed an educated woman. She assumed a native literary name, Zitkala Sa, and wrote traditional and autobiographical stories for several magazines at the time. She taught at the Carlisle Indian School, played the violin with the band, and performed as a soloist at the Paris Exposition in 1900. Suddenly, she returned to the Yankton Reservation, ended her engagement to Carlos Montezuma, the medical doctor, and married Raymond Bonnin, a native who worked for the Indian Service. Later she transcribed native melodies and collaborated on the production of *The Sun Dance Opera* that was performed in Salt Lake City, Utah, in 1913. She became a native activist and was elected secretary of the Society of American Indians, and, with her husband, founded the National Congress of American Indians in 1926.

"Controversial to the end, Gertrude Bonnin remained an enigma," observed Dexter Fisher in "Zitkala Sa: The Evolution of a Writer." She was "a curious blend of civilized romanticism and aggressive individualism. Her own image of herself eventually evolved into an admixture of myth and fact, so that by the time of her death in 1938, she believed, and it was erroneously stated in three obituaries, that she was the granddaughter of Sitting Bull, though the Yankton tribal rolls indicated that her own mother was older than Sitting Bull."[49]

Ruth Heflin wrote in "I Remain Alive": The Sioux Literary Renaissance that Gertrude Bonnin, like Charles Alexander Eastman, "at first wrote both autobiographical essays and short stories, later merging her literary talents with political rhetoric." She wrote blatant political "essays and appeals, seeking equity and suffrage for Indians."[50]

Zitkala Sa published "Why I Am a Pagan" in the *Atlantic Monthly*. She returned to the reservation and in this essay responded to the criticism of missionaries. "I prefer to their dogma my excursions into the natural gardens

where the voice of the Great Sprit is heard in the twitter-
ing of birds, the rippling of mighty waters, and the sweet
breathing of flowers. If this is Paganism, then at present,
I am a Pagan."[51]

Ely Samuel Parker, Chief Joseph, Theodore Beaulieu, Wovoka, Charles Alexander Eastman, Luther Standing Bear,
Sophia Alice Callahan, and Gertrude Bonnin, and many
other natives, were neither pagans nor evangelists of dominance; they were by visions, words, and actions, the new
warriors of survivance between the Civil War and the First
World War. Their narratives of survivance have inspired
many generations of natives.

4. Aesthetics of Survivance

Theories of survivance are elusive, obscure, and imprecise by definition, translation, comparison, and by catchword histories, but survivance is invariably true and just in native practice and cultural company. The nature of survivance is unmistakable in native songs, stories, natural reason, remembrance, traditions, customs, and clearly observable in narrative sentiments of resistance, and in personal attributes such as the native humanistic tease, vital irony, spirit, cast of mind, and moral courage. The character of survivance creates a sense of native presence and actuality over absence, nihility, and victimry.

Native survivance is an active sense of presence over absence, deracination, and oblivion; survivance is the continuance of stories, not a mere reaction, however pertinent. Survivance is greater than the right of a survivable name.

Survivance stories are renunciations of dominance, detractions, obtrusions, the unbearable sentiments of tragedy, and the legacy of victimry. Survivance is the heritable right of succession or reversion of an estate, and, in the course

86   of international declarations of human rights, a narrative
estate of native survivance.

Fourth Person

Charles Aubid, for instance, declared by stories his native
presence, human rights, and sovereignty. He created a crucial course and sense of survivance in federal court and defied the hearsay of historical precedent, cultural ethnologies, absence, and victimry.

The inspired storier was a sworn witness in federal court
that autumn more than thirty years ago in Minneapolis,
Minnesota. He raised his hand, listened to the oath for the
first time in the language of the *anishinaabe*, Chippewa or
Ojibwe, and then waved, an ironic gesture of the oath, at
United States district judge Miles Lord.

Aubid testified by visual memory, an inseparable sensibility of natural reason, and with a singular conception of
continental native liberty. His stories intimated a third person other than the apparent reference, the figurative presence of a fourth person, a sui generis native discourse in
the oral language of the *anishinaabe*.

That native practice of survivance, the storied presence
of a fourth person, a visual reminiscence, was repudiated
as hearsay, not a source of evidence in common law or federal court precedent.

Aubid was a witness in a dispute with the federal government over the right to regulate the *manoomin*, wild rice,
harvest on the Rice Lake National Wildlife Refuge in Minnesota. Federal agents had assumed the authority to determine the wild rice season and regulate the harvest, a bureaucratic action that decried a native sense of survivance
and sovereignty.

Aubid, who was eighty-six years old at the time, testified through translators that he was present as a young man when the federal agents told Old John Squirrel that the *anishinaabe* would always have control of the *manoomin* harvest. Aubid told the judge that the *anishinaabe* always understood their rights by stories. John Squirrel was there in memories, a storied presence of native survivance. The court could have heard the testimony as a visual trace of a parol agreement, a function of discourse, both relevant and necessary.

Justice Lord agreed with the objection of the federal attorney, that the testimony was hearsay and not admissible, and explained to the witness that the court could not hear as evidence what a dead man said, only the actual experiences of the witness. "John Squirrel is dead," said the judge. "And you can't say what a dead man said."

Aubid turned brusquely in the witness chair, bothered by what the judge had said about John Squirrel. Aubid pointed at the legal books on the bench, and then, in English, his second language, he shouted that those books contained the stories of dead white men. "Why should I believe what a white man says, when you don't believe John Squirrel?"

Judge Lord was deferential, amused by the analogy of native stories to court testimony, judicial decisions, precedent, and hearsay. "You've got me there," he said, and then considered the testimony of other *anishinaabe* witnesses.[1]

Monotheism is hearsay, the literary concern and ethereal care of apostles, and the curse of deceivers and debauchery. The rules of evidence and precedent are selective by culture and tradition, and sanction judicial practices over native presence and survivance.

88   Charles Aubid created indirect linguistic evidence of a fourth person by visual reminiscence. His stories were intuitive, visual memories, a native sense of presence, and sources of evidence and survivance.

Natural Estates

The native stories of survivance are successive and natural estates. Survivance is an active resistance and repudiation of dominance, obtrusive themes of tragedy, nihilism, and victimry.

The practices of survivance create an active presence, more than the instincts of survival, function, or subsistence. Native stories are the sources of survivance, the comprehension and empathies of natural reason, tragic wisdom, and the provenance of new literary studies.

Native storiers of survivance are prompted by natural reason, by a consciousness and sense of incontestable presence that arises from experiences in the natural world, the turn of seasons, sudden storms, migration of cranes, the ventures of tender lady's slippers, chance of moths overnight, unruly mosquitoes, and the favor of spirits in the water, rimy sumac, wild rice, thunder in the ice, bear, beaver, and faces in the stone.

Survivance is not a mere romance of nature, not the overnight pleasures of pristine simulations, or the obscure notions of transcendence and signatures of nature in museums. Survivance is character by natural reason, not by monotheistic creation stories and dominance of nature.

Survivance stories create a sense of presence and situational sentiments of chance. Monotheism takes the risk out of nature and natural reason and promotes absence, dominance, sacrifice, and victimry.

Survivance is a practice, not an ideology, dissimulation, or a theory. The theory is earned by interpretations, the critical construal of survivance in creative literature, and by narratives of cause and natural reason. The discourse on literary and historical studies of survivance is a theory of irony. The incongruity of survivance as a practice of natural reason, and as a discourse on literary studies, anticipates a rhetorical or wry contrast of meaning.

Antoine Compagnon observes in *Literature, Theory, and Common Sense* that theory "contradicts and challenges the practice of others," and that ideology "takes place between theory and practice. A theory would tell the truth of a practice, articulate its conditions of possibility, while an ideology would merely legitimate this practice by a lie, would dissimulate its conditions of possibility."

Theory, then, "stands in contrast to the practice of literary studies, that is, literary criticism and history, and it analyzes this practice," and "describes them, exposes their assumptions—in brief, criticizes them (to criticize is to separate, discriminate)," wrote Compagnon. "My intention, then, is not in the least to facilitate things, but to be vigilant, suspicious, skeptical, in a word: critical or ironic. Theory is a school of irony."[2]

Bear Traces

The presence of animals, birds, and other creatures in native literature is a trace of natural reason, by right, irony, precise syntax, by literary figuration, and by the heartfelt practice of survivance.

Consider a theory of irony in the literary studies of absence and presence of animals in selected novels by Native

90   American Indians. The creation of animals and birds in literature reveals a practice of survivance, and the critical interpretation of that literary practice is theory, a theory of irony and native survivance. Verbal irony is in the syntax and ambiguous situations of meaning, absence, and presence, as one concept turns to another.

The *anishinaabeg*, for instance, are named in "several grand families or clans, each of which is known and perpetuated by a symbol of some bird, animal, fish, or reptile," observed William Warren in *History of the Ojibway Nation*. The *ajijaak*, or crane totem, is the word for the sandhill crane, a dancer with a red forehead, and a distinctive wingbeat. "This bird loves to soar among the clouds, and its cry can be heard when flying above, beyond the orbit of human vision." Warren, an *anishinaabe* historian, declared more than a century ago that native crane leaders in "former times, when different tribes met in council, acted as interpreters of the wishes of their tribe."[3]

Keeshkemun, an orator of the crane totem at the turn of the nineteenth century on Lake Superior, encountered a British military officer eager to enlist native support for the war. Michel Cadotte translated the stories of the orator. Keeshkemun created an avian presence by his totemic vision and natural reason.

"I am a bird who rises from the earth, and flies far up, into the skies, out of human sight; but though not visible to the eye, my voice is heard from afar, and resounds over the earth," said Keshkemun.

Englishman, "You have put out the fire of my French father. I became cold and needy, and you sought me not. Others have sought me. Yes, the Long Knives found me. He has

placed his heart on my breast. It has entered there, and
there it shall remain."[4]

Metaphors are persuasive in language, thought, and action. "Our ordinary conceptual system, in terms of which
we both think and act, is fundamentally metaphorical in
nature" and "not merely a matter of language," observed
George Lakoff and Mark Johnson in *Metaphors We Live By*.
"Metaphor is one of our most important tools for trying to
comprehend partially what cannot be comprehended totally: our feelings, aesthetic experiences, moral practices,
and spiritual awareness. These endeavors of the imagination are not devoid of rationality; since they use metaphor,
they employ an imaginative rationality."[5]

Metaphors create a sense of presence by imagination and
natural reason, the very character and practice of survivance. The critical interpretation of native figurations is a
theory of irony and survivance. The studies of oratory and
translation, figuration, and native diplomatic strategies are
clearly literary and historical, text and context, and subject
to theoretical interpretations.

N. Scott Momaday, for instance, created a literary landscape of bears and eagles in his memoirs and novels. "The
names at first are those of animals and of birds, of objects
that have one definition in the eye, another in the hand, of
forms and features on the rim of the world, or of sounds
that carry on the bright wind and in the void," declared Momaday in *The Names*. "They are old and original in the mind,
like the beat of rain on the river, and intrinsic in the native
tongue, failing even as those who bear them turn once in
the memory, go on, and are gone forever."[6]

Clearly, metaphors provide a more expansive sense of

signification and literary survivance than simile. John
Searle argued in "Metaphor" that the "knowledge that enables people to use and understand metaphorical utterances goes beyond their knowledge of the literal meaning of words and sentences." Searle declared that a "literal
simile" is a "literal statement of similarity" and that "literal simile requires no special extralinguistic knowledge
for its comprehension."[7]

Metaphor is that "figure of speech whereby we speak
about one thing in terms which are seen to be suggestive
of another," observed Janet Martin Soskice in *Metaphor and
Religious Language*. The "greatest rival of metaphor, simile,
in its most powerful instances does compel possibilities.
Simile is usually regarded as the trope of comparison and
identifiable within speech by the presence of 'like' or an 'as,'
or the occasional 'not unlike.'" Simile, she argued, "may be
the means of making comparisons to two kinds, the comparison of similars and dissimilars, and in the latter case,
simile shares much of the imaginative life and cognitive
function of its metaphorical counterparts." However, simile cannot "be used in catachresis," the excessive or misuse
of words. Simile cannot create the lexicon, as does "dead
end" or the "leaf of a book."[8]

James Welch, for instance, created a precise sense of presence, a landscape by simile. "Tumble weeds, stark as bone,
rocked in a hot wind against the west wall," and, "I was as
distant from myself as a hawk from the moon," he wrote
in *Winter in the Blood*.[9]

I "have this bear power. I turn into a bear every so often.
I feel myself becoming a bear, and that's a struggle I have

to face now and then," Momaday told Charles Woodward in *Ancestral Voices*.[10]

Momaday became a bear by visionary transformation, an unrevealed presence in his novel *House Made of Dawn*. Angela, the literary voyeur, watched Abel cut wood, "full of wonder, taking his motion apart. . . . She would have liked to touch the soft muzzle of a bear, the thin black lips, the great flat head. She would have liked to cup her hand to the wet black snout, to hold for a moment the hot blowing of the bear's life." Later, they came together, in the bear heat of the narrative. "He was dark and massive above her, poised and tinged with pale blue light."[11]

Leslie Silko encircles the reader with mythic witches, an ironic metaphor of survivance in *Ceremony*. The hardhearted witches invented white people in a competition, a distinctive metaphor that resists the similative temptations of mere comparison of natives with the structural extremes of dominance and victimry.

"The old man shook his head. 'That is the trickery of the witchcraft,' he said. 'They want us to believe all evil resides with white people. Then we will look no further to see what is really happening. They want us to separate ourselves from white people, to be ignorant and helpless as we watch our own destruction. But white people are only tools that the witchery manipulates; and I tell you, we can deal with white people, with their machines and their beliefs. We can because we invented white people; it was Indian witchery that made white people in the first place.'"[12]

Louise Erdrich created tropes in her novel *Tracks* that are closer to the literal or prosaic simile than to the metaphors that inspire a sense of presence and survivance. She names moose, bears, cats, and other animals, but the most common is the dog. For instance, "she shivered all over like a dog," and, she "leaned over the water, sucking it like a heifer," and, his "head shaggy and low as a bison bull."[13]

David Treuer created a few animals and birds in his novel *The Hiawatha*. Deer, mallards, and a goose kill in the city. Conceivably, only the curious, astray, and then dead deer, an erudite sacrifice, was necessary. That scene in the first few pages becomes the singular metaphor of the novel, a sense of absence and melancholy. Any sentiments of native survivance are overturned by woe and mordancy. The omniscient narrator alleged, "So memory always murders the present."[14] Many of the scenes are heavy, overbooked irony. The natives and other characters, however, arise with glory and grandeur as construction workers on a skyscraper, a material metaphor of survivance, but grounded they are separated, dissociated, tragic, and enervated by cultural dominance, nihility, and victimry.

"The earth would treat them with the same indifference as loose steel, a dropped hammer, a windblown lunch," wrote Treuer in *The Hiawatha*. "This was the secret: the building wanted to stay standing, to grow, to sway but hold on, and so did they." The "tower wanted to be noticed and admired, as did the Indian crew. Its bones of steel and skin of glass were treated roughly by the wind, heat, and ice as were their skin and bones."[15]

March, the streets are "dirty with sand," and homeless men reach out to touch a wild deer astray in a "church parking lot." Truly, a tensive scene as the men reach out in silence to warm their hands on the deer, hesitant, and the deer walks untouched through a "channel of men." Then,

heedless, one man placed his hand on the deer, and in an
"instant it was running." The men "hook their fingers" on
the fence "and watch the deer bound down the weedy and
trash-strewn slope to the freeway and into the traffic."[16]

Treuer, who slights the distinct character of native literature, pronounced the deer dead in five pages, and evoked
a weighty metaphor of want and victimry. The scene of the
deer astray in rush hour traffic is obvious, portentous. The
intention of the author is clear, a dead deer. The choice dis-
heartens, and yet appeases by the familiar simulations of
sacrifice. That emotive scene provokes the pity and sympathy of some readers, those who may concede the simulations of victimry. Surely, other readers might imagine
the miraculous liberty of the deer by natural reason and
survivance.

The Hiawatha closes in a second person crescendo of nihility. "You move stones with your feet but there is no impression, no remnant of your life, your action. Whatever
you do is not accommodated, it is simply dropped onto
the hard earth you pass. You will be forgotten. Your feet,
your hands are not words and cannot speak. Everything
we accumulate—our habits, gestures, muscles trained by
the regimen of work, the body remembering instead of the
mind—it is of no use."[17]

House Made of Dawn by N. Scott Momaday, as a comparison, ends with a song, a sense of presence and native survivance. Abel "was alone and running on. All of his being
was concentrated in the sheer motion of running on, and
he was past caring about the pain. Pure exhaustion laid
hold of his mind, and he could see at last without having
to think. He could see the canyon and the mountains and

the sky. He could see the rain and the river and the fields beyond. He could see the dark hills at dawn."

Abel "was running, and under his breath he began to sing. There was no sound, and he had no voice; he had only the words of a song. And he went running on the rise of the song. *House made of pollen, house made of dawn.*"[18]

Treuer declared in *Native American Fiction: A User's Manual* that native fiction, "if there is such a thing," should be studied as literature, and, by "applying ourselves to the word, and, at least at the outset of our endeavors, by ignoring the identity of the author and all the ways the author constructs his or her authority outside the text, we will be better able to ascertain the true value of that text."

The "true value" of any text is elusive, as truth is only the ironic intention of the author, and, forevermore, the consciousness of the reader. Treuer creates a fallacy of the "true value" of literature, and he seems heartened by the implied death of the author, and by the strains of formalism and erstwhile New Criticism. Yet, he does not appear to be haunted by the wake of literary intentionalism, or the implied intentions of the native author. "Over the past thirty years, Native American fiction has been defined as, exclusively, literature written by Indians," he noted. The sentiment, however, that "Native American literature should be defined by the ethnicity of its producers (more so than defined by anything else) says more about politics and identity than it does about literature. This is especially true, and especially clear, when we see that our books are constructed out of the same materials available to anyone else. Ultimately, the study of Native American fiction should be the study of style."[19]

Treuer shows his own intentional fallacy that counters silky ideas about literature, style, and identity. The symbol of a broken feather enhances the cover of his book, a trace of image and identity politics, and the biographical note that he is "Ojibwe from the Leech Lake Reservation in northern Minnesota," implies that he would rather favor being read for his ethnicity.

So, if there is only literature by some dubious discovery of the "true value" of the cold, white pages of style, then there is no sense of native presence and survivance. Treuer teases the absence of native survivance in literature, but apparently he is not an active proponent of the death of the author. Surely, he would not turn native novelists aside that way, by the ambiguities of cold print, only to declare, as a newcomer, his own presence as a native author.

Tragic Wisdom

Native American Indians have resisted empires, negotiated treaties, and, as strategies of survivance, participated by stealth and cultural irony, in the simulations of absence to secure the chance of a decisive presence in national literature, history, and canonry. Native resistance of dominance, however serious, evasive, and ironic, is an undeniable trace of presence over absence, nihility, and victimry.

Many readers consider native literature an absence not a presence, a romantic levy of heroic separatism and disappearance, and others review native stories as cryptic representations of cultural promises obscured by victimry.

The concurrent native literary nationalists construct an apparent rarefied nostalgia for the sentiments and structures of tradition, and the inventions of culture, by a reductive reading of creative literature. The new nationalists would denigrate native individualism, visionary narratives, chance, natural reason, and survivance for the ideologies that deny the distinctions of native aesthetics and literary art. Michael Dorris, the late novelist, argued against the aesthetic distinctions of native literature. Other authors and interpreters of literature have resisted the idea of a singular native literary aesthetic.

Native literary artists, in the furtherance of natural reason, create the promise of aesthetic sentiments, irony, and practices of survivance. The standard dictionary definitions of survivance do not provide the natural reason or sense of the word in literature. Space, time, consciousness, and irony are elusive references, but critical in native history and literary sentiments of the word *survivance*.

The sectarian scrutiny of essential individual responsibilities provokes a discourse of monotheist conscience, remorse, mercy, and a literature of tragedy. The ironic fullness of original sin, shame, and stigmata want salvation, a singular solution to absence and certain victimry. There is a crucial cultural distinction between monotheism, apocalypticism, natural reason, and native survivance.

Dorothy Lee observed in *Freedom and Culture* that the "Dakota were responsible for all things, because they were at one with all things. In one way, this meant that all behavior had to be responsible, since its effect always went beyond the individual. In another way, it meant that an individual had to, was responsible to, increase, intensify, spread, recognize, experience this relationship." Consider, for the "Dakota, to be was to be responsible; because to be was to be related; and to be related meant to be responsible."

Personal, individual responsibility, in this sense, is communal, and creates a sense of presence and survivance. Responsibility, in the course of natural reason is not a cause of
nihility or victimry. "The Dakota were responsible, but they
were accountable to no one for their conduct," wrote Lee.
"Responsibility and accountability had nothing in common
for them. Ideally, everyone was responsible for all members
of the band, and eventually for all people, all things."

Yet, Lee declared, no "Dakota was accountable to any one
or for any one. Was he his brother's keeper? Yes, in so far
as he was responsible for his welfare; no, in so far as being
accountable for him. He would never speak for him, decide
for him, answer prying questions about him. And he was
not accountable for himself, either. No one asked him questions about himself; he gave information or withheld it, as
his own choice. When a man came back from a vision quest,
when warriors returned, they were not questioned. People
waited for them to report or not as they pleased."[20]

Original, communal responsibility, greater than the individual, greater than original sin, but not accountability,
animates the practice and consciousness of survivance, a
sense of presence, a responsible presence of natural reason, and resistance to absence and victimry.

Survivance is related to the word *survival*, obviously, and
the definition varies by language. The *Robert & Collins dic-
tionnaire français–anglais, anglais–français* defines survivance
as a "relic, survival; cette coutume est une survivance de
passé this custom is a survival *ou* relic from the past; survivance de l'âme survival of the soul (after death), afterlife."
The New Shorter Oxford English Dictionary defines survivance
as the "succession to an estate, office, etc., of a survivor

nominated before the death of the previous holder; the right of such succession in case of survival." And -*ance*, the suffix, is a quality of action, as in *survivance, relevance, assistance.* The *American Heritage Dictionary* defines the suffix -*ance* as a "state or condition," or "action," as in *continuance.* Survivance, then, is the action, condition, quality, and sentiments of the verb *survive*, "to remain alive or in existence," to outlive, persevere with a suffix of survivancy.

The word *survivance* has been used more frequently in the past few years, since the publication of *Manifest Manners: Narratives on Postindian Survivance* and *Fugitive Poses: Native American Indian Scenes of Absence and Presence* by the University of Nebraska Press. "Survivance is an active sense of presence, the continuance of native stories, not a mere reaction, or a survivable name," I wrote in *Manifest Manners.* "Native survivance stories are renunciations of dominance, tragedy, and victimry. Survivance means the right of succession or reversion of an estate, and in that sense, the estate of native survivancy."[21]

The word *survivance* has been used in many titles of essays and at least one recent book. Anne Ruggles Gere, for instance, used the word in the title of her essay "An Art of 'Survivance,' Angel DeCora of Carlisle," in *American Indian Quarterly*, 2004. Rauna Koukkanen, "'Survivance,' in Sami and First Nation Boarding School Narratives," *American Indian Quarterly*, 2003.

Survivance, the word, is more commonly used in the political context of francophone nationalism and the Québécois in Canada. Other instances of the word include "Cadjins et creoles en Louisiane. Histoire et survivance d'une francophonie" by Patrick Griolet, reviewed by Albert Valdman in *Modern Language Journal*, 1989.

Ernest Stromberg, in the introduction to his edited collection of essays *American Indian Rhetorics of Survivance*, declared that "'survivance' is the easiest to explain," but he does not consider the compound history of the word. "While 'survival' conjures images of a stark minimalist clinging at the edge of existence, survivance goes beyond mere survival to acknowledge the dynamic and creative nature of Indigenous rhetoric."[22] Stromberg does not cite, consider, or even mention, any other sources, exposition, or narratives on survivance. His rhetoric on survivance is derivative.

Clifford Geertz used the word *survivance* in a structural sense of global differences, the "recurrence of familiar divisions, persisting arguments, standing threats," and notions of identity. Geertz declared in *Available Light* that a "scramble of differences in a field of connections presents . . . a situation in which the frames of pride and those of hatred, culture fairs and ethnic cleansing, *survivance* and killing fields, sit side by side and pass with frightening ease from the one to the other."[23] Survivance, printed in italics in his personal essay, is understood only in the context of an extreme structural binary.

"Each human language maps the world differently," observed George Steiner in *After Babel: Aspects of Language and Translation*. He relates these "geographies of remembrance" to survivance. "Thus there is, at the level of human psychic resources and survivance, an immensely positive, 'Darwinian' logic in the otherwise battling and negative excess of languages spoken on the globe. When a language dies, a possible world dies with it. There is no survival of the fittest. Even where it is spoken by a handful, by the harried remnants of destroyed communities, a language contains within itself the boundless potential of discovery, or re-compositions of reality, of articulate dreams, which are known to us as myths, as poetry, as metaphysical conjecture and the discourse of law."[24]

Steiner considered the aesthetic experience of survivance in the responses of readers, listeners, and viewers to music, painting, and literary art. "Responding to the poem, to the piece of music, to the painting, we re-enact, within the limits of our own lesser creativity, the two defining motions of our existential presence in the world: that of the coming into being where nothing was, where nothing could have continued to be, and that of the enormity of death," he wrote in *Real Presences*. "But, be it solely on a millennial scale, the latter absolute is attenuated by the potential of survivance in art. The lyric, the painting, the sonata endure beyond the life-span of the maker and our own."[25]

Jacques Derrida used the word *survivance* once in a collection of essays and interviews, *Negotiations: Interventions and Interviews*. The interviewers for the monthly review *Passages* continued a point about Karl Marx and Marxism, and asked Derrida if he would be "surprised if there were some kind of return—in a different form and with different applications—of Communism, even if it is called something else? And if what brought it back were a need within society for the return of a little hope?"

Derrida responded, "This is what we were calling justice earlier. I do not believe there will be a return of Communism in the form of the Party (the party form is no doubt disappearing from political life in general, a 'survivance'

that may of course turn out to have a long life) or in the return of everything that deterred us from a certain kind of
Marxism and a certain kind of Communism." Derrida seems
to use the word *survivance* here in the context of a relic from
the past, or in the sense of an afterlife.[26]

Derrida, in *Archive Fever*, comments on a new turn of forms
in the recent interpretations of *Moses and Monotheism* by Sig-
mund Freud, the "phantoms out of the past" compared to
the form of a "triumph of life." Derrida observed that the
"afterlife [survivance] no longer means death and the return of the specter, but the surviving of an excess of life
which resists annihilation."[27]

Derrida would surely have embraced a more expansive
sense of the word *survivance*, as he has done by the word
différance. Peggy Kamuf pointed out in *A Derrida Reader* that
the suffix *-ance* "calls up a middle voice between the active
and passive voices. In this manner it can point to an operation that is not that of a subject or an object," a "certain
nontransitivity."[28] Survivance, in this sense, could be the
fourth person or voice in native stories.

5. Mercenary Sovereignty

The Treaty of Westphalia ended more than thirty years of war against the hegemonic power of the Holy Roman Empire. The treaty of October 24, 1648, provided the political opportunity for peace and dominion, the very foundations of territorial borders, security, and state sovereignty.

Native American Indian communities, at about the same time, were not secure by mere treaties of peace and sovereignty. Natives, already under colonial siege and disease, were decimated by that first fatal contact with the dominions of "globalization." An estimated hundred million natives perished from fatal diseases delivered by the breath and blood of monotheism and civilization.[1] Ancient, native hemispheric trade routes were obstructed by foreign "discovery," invasion, colonial occupation, and state dominance. Natives were denied a sense of presence and continental liberty.

Natives of the Americas have lived in virtual exile for more than five centuries. Thousands of distinct native cultures were decimated by diseases, slavery, colonial border wars, and by devious codes of extermination. Since then many generations of native survivors have endured nominal discoveries, treaty removal to federal exclaves, monotheistic collusions, and unnatural conversions; thousands of ancestral, native communities were denied their sense of presence, cultural hybridity, hemispheric contact and liberty.

"Behind the supposed inviolability of national borders, liberal democratic institutions took hold in some countries, while in others rulers carried out genocide against their own citizens," wrote Peter Singer in One World: The Ethnics of Globalization. The idea of state sovereignty must be reconceived to protect human rights in the world, "or more accurately, an abandonment of the absolute idea of state sovereignty that has prevailed in Europe since the Treaty of Westphalia," argued Singer.[2]

Giorgio Agamben declared in Means without End that sovereignty is an undecidable connection. "The concepts of sovereignty and constituent power, which are at the core of our political tradition, have to be abandoned or, at least, to be thought all over again. They mark, in fact, the point of indifference between right and violence, nature and logos, proper and improper, and as such they do not designate an attribute or an organ of the juridical system or of the state; they designate, rather, their own original structure. Sovereignty is the idea of an undecidable nexus between violence and right, between the living and language."

Agamben argued, "Sovereignty, therefore, is the guardian who prevents the undecidable threshold between violence and right, nature and language, from coming to light."[3]

Stephen Krasner pointed out in Sovereignty: Organized Hypocrisy that the authority of the term has been "commonly

used in at least four different ways." The first is "domestic
sovereignty," or the "organization of public authority within
a state." The second is "interdependence sovereignty, referring to the ability of public authorities to control trans-
border movements." The third use is "international legal
sovereignty, referring to the mutual recognition of states
or other entities." The last is "Westphalian sovereignty, referring to the exclusion of external actors from domestic
authority configurations."[4]

Native American Indians were denied by discovery and
occupation their ordinary human rights and continental
liberty, and early courts controverted native resistance,
transmotion, and sovereignty. Chief Justice John Marshall,
for instance, ruled in *Johnson v. McIntosh*, 1823, that the "title by conquest is acquired and maintained by force. The
conqueror prescribes its limits. Humanity, however, acting on public opinion, has established, as a general rule,
that the conquered shall not be wantonly oppressed, and
that their condition shall remain as eligible as is compatible with the objects of the conquest. . . . The claim of the
government extends to the complete ultimate title, charged
with this right of possession, and to the exclusive power of
acquiring that right."[5]

David Wilkins observed, the "Supreme Court has a power
that is supposed to prevent governmental action which is
prejudicial, arbitrary, or capricious; however the experience of tribal nations too often has been that the Supreme
Court has only sustained and legitimated the political and
policy directives of the federal government."[6]

When federal courts in the past generations have ruled
in favor of native treaty rights, the conditions were more

the sentiments of domestic sovereignty than interdependence or Westphalian Sovereignty. The common authority of continental native liberty, reciprocity, and visionary sovereignty was "diminished" by discovery, occupation, removal to reservations, denial of national citizenship, and by the plenary power of the United States Congress.

"The discovery doctrine was a rule developed and observed by the Christian colonizing powers of Europe to help manage their collective ambitions to empire around the world," declared N. Bruce Duthu. "The doctrine created a right of 'first dibs' in favor of the discovering nation to acquire the soil—through purchase or conquest—from the native inhabitants."[7]

Memorably, native transmotion, that inspired sense of natural motion and singular, visionary sovereignty, abides in stories of survivance; yet, the native as outcast is assured by the manifest manners of institutional dominance, and the romantic, misused historical and literary notions of tragic victimry.

The United States of America has never vouched for a serious, bilateral, or multilateral, humane dialogue or agreement with Native American Indians. Executive ventures over land and culture were deceptions, outright political lies, and legislative expediency; terminal exile was the outcome of that failure of a democratic constitution and government agencies to honor native transmotion and visionary sovereignty. Natives braved state dominance as the fugitives of frontier, imperial, mercenary sovereignty.

Yes, fugitives because natives are forever burdened by the subornation of frontier dominance. Natives have been denied an actual native presence in the hemisphere. The tragic wisdom of nature, creative, visionary resistance, and native political strategies now arise more from reservation experiences as fugitives of dominance than from natural reason, or creative ideas that are presented by nature, *transmotion*, and native liberty.

The missions of frontier monotheism denounced shamanism, that elusive tease of nature, an unrevealed sense of absolute presence, and *transmotion*, the visionary sensibilities of time, space, and native sovereignty.

The United States Constitution has seldom served or protected the rights of natives. Frontier liberty in the new nation was the recision not the protection of native sovereignty. Manifest destiny was a terminal intervention that decimated natives.

The Constitution did not outlaw slavery, for instance, and "failed to guarantee the right of suffrage, leaving the qualifications of suffrage to the states," wrote Robert Dahl in *How Democratic Is the American Constitution?*[8] Implicitly, the Constitution excluded women, African Americans, and Native American Indians.

Fabricated Landscapes

"The North American terrain can be imagined as empty only by willfully ignoring the existence of the Native Americans," wrote Michael Hardt and Antonio Negri in *Empire*. "Just as the land must be cleared of trees and rocks in order to farm it, so too the terrain must be cleared of the native inhabitants. Just as the frontier people must gird themselves against the severe winters, so too they must arm themselves against the indigenous populations. Native Americans were regarded as merely a particularly thorny element of nature, and a continuous war was aimed at their expulsion."[9]

Clearly the United States Constitution did not protect natives on the simulated frontier. Frederick Jackson Turner noted in his essay "The Significance of the Frontier in American History" that natives were a "common danger, demanding united action." His thesis on the exceptional social evolution of the imperial frontier excluded native civilizations from the very history and character of the nation.[10]

Martin Ridge pointed out in Frederick Jackson Turner that the 1890 Census Report revealed "for the first time in one hundred years the nation no longer possessed a distinct boundary or frontier line between settled and unsettled portions of the West."[11] Turner described the frontier as the "meeting point between savagery and civilization," a frontier that created a national character.[12] Turner's celebration of a national character did not include war crimes against natives or the premeditated breach of treaties. The Fort Laramie Treaty, for instance, was understood as a distinct boundary between immigrants, miners, and native communities; however, the federal government did not honor the treaty rights of natives.

"Here we are faced with a contradiction that could not be absorbed within the constitutional machine," observed Hardt and Negri. "Native Americans could not be integrated in the expansive movement of the frontier as part of the constitutional tendency; rather, they had to be excluded from the terrain to open its spaces and make expansion possible. If they had been recognized, there would have been no real frontier on the continent and no open spaces to fill. They existed outside the Constitution as its negative foundation."[13]

Hardt and Negri argue that the exclusion of natives was

an essential condition to the very function of the new Constitution. This contradiction of constitutional rights posed by notions of frontier sovereignty, and exclusion of native rights, are not easily enacted in literature or resolved in history.

"Imperial sovereignty must always overcome barriers and boundaries both within its domain and at the frontiers," wrote Hardt and Negri. "This continuous overcoming is what makes the imperial space open. The enormous internal barriers between black and white, free and slave, blocked the imperial integration machine and deflated the ideological pretense to open spaces." Clearly the new nation demanded a redefinition of space. "At stake was the question whether the free exodus of the multitude, unified in a plural community, could continue to develop, perfect itself, and realize a new configuration of public space."[14] The debased notion of a national frontier excluded native rights to that space.

Hardt and Negri pointed out that the "new democracy had to destroy the transcendental idea of the nation with all its racial divisions and create its own people, defined not by old heritages but by a new ethics of the construction and expansion of the community. The new nation could not but be the product of the political and cultural management of hybrid identities."[15]

Native hybridity, transmotion, and that sense of an ancient presence and continental liberty were sacrificed by colonial, territorial greed, and mercenary sovereignty. Yet, at the same time, the Constitution accommodated an immigrant hybridity on the frontier. Native communities, the beaver, and other animals were sacrificed in the interactive fur trade. Only a change of occidental fashions, fur to silk, alleviated the decimation of the environment. The want of bison hides created another drastic global market on the early frontier.

Tyler Cowen observed in *Creative Destruction* a common pattern of cultural compromise and interactive trade. "The initial meeting of cultures produces a creative boom, as individuals trade materials, technologies, and ideas. Often the materially wealthier culture provides financial support for the creations of the poorer culture, while the native aesthetic and ethos remains largely intact. For a while we have the best of both worlds from a cultural point of view. The core of the poorer or smaller culture remains intact, while it benefits from trade. Over time, however, the larger or wealthier culture upsets the balance of forces that ruled in the smaller or poorer culture. The poorer culture begins to direct its outputs towards the tastes of the richer culture." Cowan pointed out that contact and "communication with the outside world makes the prevailing ethos less distinct." Consequently, the "smaller culture 'forgets' how to make the high-quality goods it once specialized in, and we observe cultural decline."[16]

The United States Constitution sanctioned dominance, warranted frontier exclusions, denied natives a presence in a civil society, and coerced natives to excuse their distinct cultures and hemispheric liberty. Natives endure in virtual and actual exile; incredibly, that separation was endorsed by the Constitution.

"Democracy, in the sense of the rule of the majority, does not provide a guarantee that human rights will be respected," observed Peter Singer. "But a democratic process requires that the policies of the government must be publicly defended and justified. They cannot simply be implemented from above. Although some of us may have the capacity to commit terrible crimes, many of us also have a moral sense, that is, a capacity to reflect on the rights and wrongs of what we are doing, or what our rulers are doing. That capacity emerges in the public arena."[17]

Empire Sovereignty

The autonomous, colonial nations of the past have been transformed by modern, global economies, an original, but controversial, new form of sovereignty. That hemispheric, economic liberty, once denied natives, has now become the very foundation of a new cause of empire. Territorial boundaries have been revised and "decentered" to warrant and accommodate a new empire of global sovereignty.

"For several centuries, sovereignty has been considered an attribute of states," observed John Boli in *Problematic Sovereignty*, edited by Stephen Krasner. "The state is the locus of ultimate authority in society, uniquely qualified to represent society as a whole in its relations with the external world. No body, no organization, no power stands higher than the state; the world is a basically feudal structure composed of lordly states all jealously guarding their respective domains. As a result, conflict is structural and endemic; cooperation is strategic and fragile."[18]

Most native cultures and communities were not comparable to the authority of a sovereign state, according to Boli's general definition; yet, native interdependence was undermined by colonial occupation and, by contradiction, a great revolutionary, democratic constitution that controverted native *transmotion*, visionary rights, and liberty. Natives, in the past century, have articulated, emulated, and litigated the notion of state sovereignty as independence and autonomy; that minimal view of state or territorial sovereignty, however, has lost significance in the economic globalization of the world.

"Globalisation is blurring the borders between nation states. Yet it is neither uniform nor universal," argued Philippe Legrain in *Open World: The Truth About Globalisation.* "Individual choice is fragmenting the imposed uniformity of national cultures. New hybrid cultures are emerging, and regional ones re-emerging. National identity is not disappearing, but the bonds of nationality are loosening."[19]

Nayan Chanda pointed out in *Bound Together* that throughout "history, increasing integration has provoked resistance from those who were subjected to foreign domination or suffered from the arrival of alien goods or unfamiliar ideas. The resistance of those exposed to the key actors of globalization—traders, preachers, adventurers, warriors, and migrants—has come in many forms, ranging from armed opposition to the closure of borders to the imposition of tariffs and trade barriers."[20]

Daniel Cohen argued in *Globalization and Its Enemies* that the portrayal of "globalization as a 'clash of civilizations' or as a 'world class struggle' has the merit of historical simplicity, but it confuses myth and reality. The principal problem with globalization today is not that it sharpens religious conflicts or class struggles; it is that *globalization does not keep its promises.* Globalization creates a strange world that nourishes the feeling of exploitation while in fact exploiting only a bit or not at all. It creates an image of new closeness between nations that is only virtual, not real."[21]

Native American Indians, meanwhile, have once again become the patsies of nations and domestic sovereignty. Most politicians are enthusiastic about native sovereignty because casino money supports their parties and state budgets. Governor Gray Davis of California, for instance, once proposed a new fees assessment on Indian casinos because the casinos "pay virtually no state taxes. The compacts under which tribes operate gambling halls are up for renegotiation," reported John Broder for the *New York Times*.[22] The Indian Gaming Regulatory Act of 1988 recognizes that native governments have the "exclusive right to regulate gaming" if such activities are not prohibited by state or federal laws. The California Constitution was amended to allow casino operations on native trust land in the state. Public officials are considering the "industry as a potential source of significant new revenue." Many states have courted casinos for the money to avoid tax increases. California and many other states are obliged to defend mercenary sovereignty.[23]

The United States Supreme Court ruled, twenty years ago, the "states had no right to restrict gambling on Indian reservations if they allowed it elsewhere." Today, the "states look covetously at Indian casinos, which pay fewer taxes than businesses off the reservation." Iowa and Michigan have recently allowed community casinos. Arizona, California, and other states have "worked out ways of extracting more taxes from the wealthiest tribes." In the past decade there has been a dramatic increase in the number tribal casinos and gambling operations. There were 391

116   casinos and gambling rooms on reservations and Indian land in 2005. The total revenue from these casinos was more than twenty-two billion dollars, compared to 290 casinos and revenues of almost thirteen billion in 2001. The total annual revenue from tribal casinos almost doubled in four years. "Casinos have been good to those tribes that happened to be in the right place. But few believe the good times will last forever."[24]

Sovereignty "remains attractive," argues Stephan Krasner in *Foreign Policy*. "Although sovereignty might provide little more than international recognition, that recognition guarantees access to international organizations and sometimes to international finance." Sovereignty could provide recognition to native governments and communities. Krasner points out, however, that "the most important impact of economic globalization and transnational norms will be to alter the scope of state authority rather than to generate some fundamentally new way to organize" the politics of governments and communities.[25]

"Empire manages hybrid identities, flexible hierarchies, and plural exchanges through modulating networks of command," argue Hardt and Negri. "The Empire we are faced with wields enormous powers of oppression and destruction, but that fact should not make us nostalgic in any way for the old forms of domination. The passage to Empire and its processes of globalization offer new possibilities to the forces of liberation." Empire, in other words, "presents its rule not as a transitory moment in the movement of history, but as a regime with no temporal boundaries and in this sense outside of history or at the end of history."[26]

Meanwhile, native reservations, or colonial, constitutional

exclaves created in the nineteenth century by racial separatists, continue to be much closer to the old boundaries
of history and the models of imperial dominance than to
the new forms of global empire and sovereignty.

The established boundaries of federal exclaves or reservations were secured in treaties between natives and the
Congress of the United States. Natives were considered nations only as a metaphor of domestic dominance, not in the
sense of a foreign, sovereign state. Congress has the plenary power to reverse even the conception of "diminished"
native sovereignty and abrogate treaties at any time.

The Supreme Court would not likely deny congressional
plenary "power to regulate the tribes," argued T. Alexander
Aleinikoff in *Semblances of Sovereignty*. The Court "has apparently forgotten" that tribal communities and reservations "are more than private, voluntary associations. They
are polities that have somehow survived and continue to
flourish against great odds," moreover, that "Indian sovereignty is expressly secured by treaty is no bar to subsequent congressional defeasance, and, most egregiously,
Congress remains free to abrogate treaty rights and structures unilaterally even in violation of a provision requiring
tribal consent for such action."[27]

The dubious legacies of frontier liberty and the exclusion of natives continue on federal reservations. Colonial
ideologies persist in the administration of treaty services
by government agencies.

Casino Remorse

Casinos are no exception to these contradictions of native
rights and "diminished" sovereignty, as federal gaming
laws obligate reservation governments, territorial, domestic

treaty entities, to negotiate with respective states. Native casinos are not "decentered" global economies, but rather a revision of traditional, territorial boundaries based on federal treaties and the elusive notions of state or national sovereignty. The increase in internet gaming could be a global enterprise, but federal policies may restrict the mercenary, empire reach of reservation or territorial casinos.

Casinos have transformed many native communities. Some native governments invested the mercenary "money of the losers" in education, health care, housing, and community infrastructure; others have made per capita payments to eligible members of reservations. The *Santa Fe New Mexican*, for instance, reported that the "median household income" on two native communities, the Yavapai Prescott Tribe, and the Fort McDowell Yavapai Nation, more than doubled in the past decade. These two reservations operate casinos.[28]

Native casinos are not required by law or custom to report their gaming profits or dispensations. Few native casinos provide annual financial statements for government or public review. The idea of native sovereignty has turned the reservation sentiments of political independence inward, a primary defense of cultural autonomy and domestic authority. Casinos, however, have opened wide the reservations boundaries to a new strain of outsiders, the gamblers who are eager and determined to bet against natives and lose their money.

"The amount of money involved is staggering," reported *Time*. The magazine estimated that "casinos kept more than $5 billion as profit" in 2001. "That would place overall Indian gaming among *Fortune* magazine's 20 most profitable

U.S. corporations, with earnings exceeding those of J.P. Morgan Chase & Co., Merrill Lynch, American Express and Lehman Bros. Holdings combined." About 20 percent of that total annual revenue was lost by gamblers at two of the largest casinos in the world: Foxwoods Resort Casino, of the Mashantucket Pequots, and the Mohegan Sun, both located in Connecticut. Few natives, however, benefit from gaming profits. The investors in casinos have prospered, but the "overwhelming majority of Indians get nothing."

Meanwhile, wealthy "Indian gaming tribes suddenly are pouring millions of dollars into political campaigns at both state and federal levels. They are also influencing gaming and other policies affecting Native Americans by handing out large sums to influential lobbying firms. In 2000 alone, tribes spent $9.5 million on Washington lobbying." Indian casinos, altogether, spend more to influence legislation than several major corporations, including Boeing and General Motors.[29]

Ernest Stevens Jr., chairman of the National Indian Gaming Association, objects strongly to the critical story in *Time*. "Indian gaming revenue is used directly for tribal government purposes, serving as tribal tax revenue," he wrote in a letter to the editor. "When tribes suffer high suicide rates among teens, Indian gaming builds schools, funds scholarships and gives children hope. When Indians suffer diabetes and liver disease, gaming builds hospitals and fitness centers," and, of course, the mercenary money has provided "thousands of new jobs in rural and reservation areas."[30]

"The argument of the story is that only a relatively few Indians have gained financially from gaming" while "wealthy investors have lined their pockets far more than the rank and file tribal members," wrote James May in *Indian Country Today*. "The *Time* article links this problem to vague language and loopholes in the Indian Gaming Regulatory Act." Susan Jensen, a spokesperson for the California Nations Indian Gaming Association, was cited in the same story. She said the federal regulations on gaming are "not supposed to be a panacea for the widespread poverty on Indian reservations."[31]

The *Wall Street Journal*, in an editorial about the casino on the land owned by the Augustine Band of Mission Indians near Los Angeles, California, noted critically that there are only *eight* members of the Augustine Band; the casino is "run by a Las Vegas company." The Indian Gaming Regulatory Act of 1988 "made it easier for federal authorities to recognize tribes, which now means any group with the right combination of Indian blood and political connections to convince the federal Bureau of Indian Affairs. Congress is finally figuring out that this process has become a recipe for political abuse." Census figures show that most natives "remain mired in poverty, and other studies suggest little progress in raising education and health standards. The impact of gambling on the social fabric, including the dangers posed by organized crime, is another concern."[32]

Casinos are mercenary ventures of greed and compulsive behavior, a curious postmodern dimension of native sovereignty. Native governments have not, however, used their new economic and territorial sovereignty to sue for a presence in international political and human rights organizations.

David Chen and Charlie LeDuff wrote in the *New York Times* that inside "Indian territories, which are considered sovereign entities, a battle is raging over whether casinos represent genuine salvation or false temptation. It is a clash between those with a reverence for the old ways and those with a thirst for a revenue stream. It is an argument over who will control the receipts and whether exchanging vows with state governments is worth selling a piece of autonomy."[33]

Indian casino regimes could have considered a more impressive demonstration of sovereignty, an investment in a cosmopolitan presence in the world. Some of the uncounted billions of casino dollars could be used to support a native embassy. Natives could wisely secure a moral international presence, a new hybrid polity of empire sovereignty. Casino avarice with no moral sentiment is the likely end of native sovereignty. "The envies of casino riches incite the enemies" of native rights, those opposed to the domestic "sovereignty honored for more than a century in treaties with the federal government."[34]

Truth Games

The United States Constitution is a truth game inspired by a revolution, and yet that exemplary constitution was used to exclude natives who had resisted colonial and frontier dominion. Slavery, the cruelties of colonial empires and imperial frontier justice were the lies of civilization and denied native cultural hybridity and liberty. The notions of global empire sovereignty, however, are the new truth games of native traditions, casinos, constitutions, and economic globalization.

Native Americans have been the subject of empire and

mission lies from the first instance of contact and the conceits of discovery. Europeans, by word and image, created simulations of natives in the cultural binaries of savagism and civilization. The first pervasive lie of discovery was the invention of the *indian*, and that monotheistic lie has been compounded in truth games as a singular name for thousands of distinct native cultures.

These rather obvious points are made to connect the practice of colonial deception and the promise of moral games of truth with the constitutional renunciation of native rights on the hybrid frontier of the United States of America.

The American Indian is a brand culture, a dubious, customary simulation of distinct native cultures, and revision of specific native experiences, such as *indian* language, *indian* religion, and the more mundane *indian* traditions. Regrettably the brand name of native cultures has been instituted by conviction, covenants, government documents, and based on the truth games of the social sciences. Indians are forever constrained to enter the truth games as fugitives with invented names. Many native communities have tried to enter the global economy with a positive brand name and image. Casinos, for instance, promote the ratified simulations of traditions as brand associations in a new commercial truth game, and without a trace of resistance or apparent irony.

Mark Taylor noted in *The Moment of Complexity* that our "extraordinary complexity" in the modern world has exhausted the strategies to interpret experience. There is a "widespread consensus that the most pressing critical challenge is to find ways to resist systems and structures that totalize by repressing otherness and by reducing differences to same."

These "hegemonic structures," he pointed out, "must be subverted or overturned by soliciting the return of repressed otherness and differences in a variety of guises."[35]

Indian casinos are strategies of survivance, an incredible subversion of "hegemonic structures," but avarice is an odious disguise, and with no manner or remorse for the repression of native ethics and liberty. The mercenary sovereignty and politics of casino money is a truth game that might overturn the honor and assurance of native transmotion and visionary sovereignty.

States, cities, companies, and now reservations, are concerned about brand recognition. "The unbranded state has a difficult time attracting economic and political attention. Image and reputation are thus becoming essential parts of the state's strategic equity," wrote Peter van Ham in *Foreign Affairs*. "Although no doubt unsettling to conservative thinkers, this is actually a positive development, since state branding is gradually supplanting nationalism."[36]

Indian casinos dare not invite revisions of brand simulations of natives because the truism of gaming rights on treaty reservations could be abrogated by the plenary power doctrine of the United States Congress. In other words, the money comes by the historical contradictions of brand name simulations and the federal exclaves of nationalism. Casinos have contrived new fugitives of dominance in a truth game of sovereignty.

Convictions, on the other hand, "are more dangerous enemies of truth than lies," asserted Friedrich Nietzsche in *Human, All Too Human*. He pointed out that "lying demands invention, dissimulation, and good memory" and mused that the "beast in us wants to be lied to; morality is an official lie told so that it shall not tear us to pieces."[37]

Natives might have shared the view that moral convictions on the frontier were dangerous, but surely not more treacherous than the denial of human rights on the continent. Natives who lost their transmotion and liberty on the frontier were doubly tormented by monotheistic convictions and the truth games of the United States Constitution.

"Everyday life contains many truth games," wrote John Forrester in Truth Games. "The social processes and institutions that establish power, expertise, and authority also generate truths," and the games of truth. "From the sheer diversity, resilience, and efficiency of the thousands of languages people use, it is clear that language has very little to do with truth."

Moreover, lying "is always distinguished from error or falsity by its deliberateness," noted Forrester. "The search for origins notoriously haunted the encounter of Europeans with their others, the natives of other lands. In European travelers' tales and stories of far-off lands, the mirroring and projection processes are enmeshed with seeking the origins of civilization, morality, and nobility in the split between self and other. Lying, whose inherent structure reveals the duplicity of consciousness, lends itself particularly well to the seesaw dynamics of all such mirroring encounters with the other, the native."[38]

Natives are the subject of incessant, duplicitous truth games, the scientific, linguistic, ethnographic, and institutional objects of knowledge and political power. Natives, once a hybrid presence in the hemisphere, have become the absent object of various truth games, the fugitives of

simulations, and the romantic promise of absence and eternal exile. National covenants and the truth games of institutions proscribed a native presence as brand cultures on
the continent.

The conception of truth games was derived from the
original philosophical ideas of Michel Foucault in The Order of Things. "I have tried to discover how the human subject entered into games of truth, whether they be games
of truth which take on the form of science or which refer
to a scientific model, or games of truth like those that can
be found in institutions or practices of control," said Foucault in an interview published in The Final Foucault, edited
by James Bernauer and David Rasmussen. The problem is
to "know how games of truth can put themselves in place
and be linked to relationships of power."[39]

Foucault raised three "traditional problems" of humanism, ethics, and models of freedom, in Technologies of the
Self. First, what are the "relations we have to truth through
scientific knowledge, to those 'truth games' which are so
important in civilization and in which we are both subject
and object?" Second, what are the "relationships we have
to others through those strange strategies and power relationships?" Third, what are the "relationships between
truth, power, and self?"[40]

Kennewick Man

Kennewick Man, once a continental hybrid, is much better
known today than he was some nine thousand years ago.
His bones are a scientific treasure, the oldest ever found on
the continent. The right to study or bury his remains has
become a truth game between scientists, various federal
agencies, native scholars, and cultural fundamentalists.

126   The Ancient One, a reverential native name, is better known by the postmark place of his discovery. The unusual skull was uncovered in 1996 near the McNary Dam on the Columbia River in Kennewick, Washington. Scientists soon recovered and protected for study the rest of his skeletal remains, according to the provisions of the federal Archaeological Resources Protection Act.

Mister Kennewick has, in a sense, become an affirmative action skeleton, a proprietary, postmodern tease of the rights of ancient bones. Natives in the area resolved that the remains must be returned to the earth by authority of traditions, a truth game of derived and simulated convictions. The scientists, on the other hand, pointed out that the skull and bones were not similar to those of natives, and argued that the remains were not a cultural connection to modern natives, but to a more complex early history of the Americas.

The Umatilla Nation and other natives were convinced that the remains were found within the ancient territory of several ancestral communities. Natives based their convictions on oral traditions, or, on the unchallengeable stories of elders. The scientists studied the bones, reconstructed the skull, and were convinced that the characteristics of the remains were not similar to other natives.

"Kennewick Man was then in my laboratory, where I was studying him at the local coroner's request," wrote James Chatters in the Wall Street Journal. "I had barely begun when local Indian tribes claimed Kennewick Man was an ancestor and demanded to rebury him immediately, without further study. The federal government moved quickly to comply with the Indians' wishes, and even as requests for study poured in. The anthropologists, alarmed by the

potential loss to America's early heritage," filed a lawsuit
in federal court to protect the remains for scientific and
historical study.[41]

Natives cited the Native American Graves Protection and
Repatriation Act and oral traditions as their cause for reburial. The recent federal law was intended to protect ancient native remains from misuse, and to count native remains in institutions for reburial, but in this instance the
skeletal remains were inconsistent with the characteristics of other ancient natives or Europeans. Scientists argued that because the skeleton was not evidently native
the only pertinent law was the Archaeological Resources
Protection Act.

The truth games over the tease of nature, tradition, conviction, research, simulation, legislation, protection, and
the material bent of the ancient skeletal remains cost some
three million dollars to resolve in federal court.

This ancient continental hybrid may have cost science
and the government more time and money than any other
identity truth game in history. Actually, at a dollar a day
over the past nine thousand years since his death, the cost
of a truth game decided in favor of science, some scholars
would argue, was not exorbitant.

Five government scientists, seven active plaintiff scientists and lawyers, seven federal agents, and at least twelve
other natives and scientists were involved in a federal lawsuit that would determine if scientists had a right to study
the remains over the protective convictions and protests of
natives to rebury the bones of the skeleton.

Bruce Babbitt, secretary of the interior, ruled that natives
had the absolute right to rebury the Ancient One. That ad-
ministrative decision, counter to the recommendation and

truth games of a panel of scientists, was overturned this year in federal court.

"The tribes have sought to control the bones under a federal law, the Native American Graves Protection and Repatriation Act, that requires skeletal remains to be turned over to people who can show a geographic or cultural affiliation with them," wrote Timothy Egan in the *New York Times*. "Babbitt appeared to bypass the conclusion of a panel of scientists who were assigned by the court to determine the ethnic origins of Kennewick Man. That panel said the remains resembled those of people from Asia, particularly the Ainu of northern Japan, and Polynesians from southern Asia."

Babbitt was convinced that natives had demonstrated a cultural connection to the bones. "Although ambiguities in the data made this a close call, I was persuaded by the geographic data and oral histories," said Babbitt. That hasty resolution would not stand in federal court.[42]

Magistrate Judge John Jelderks of the United States District Court in Portland, Oregon, decided on August 30, 2002, in favor of the scientists over the resolution of federal agencies to support the native petition of tribal affiliation and reburial under the Native American Graves Protection and Repatriation Act.

Mister Kennewick, the affirmative action skeleton, would not be reburied because he was not native under the law. Judge Jelderks ruled there was no material evidence that the ancient remains were related, "even indirectly," to modern natives.

Judge Jelderks "repeatedly criticized the Army Corps of Engineers and the Interior Department" during the trial "for the way they handled the case. The judge had said he felt the Corps made a 'hasty decision' to recognize a tribal claim to the bones," reported the Associated Press. "He also criticized the government for delaying tests on the age of the bones and delaying its response to questions about determining cultural affiliation with modern tribes."

Scientists won the right to study the skeletal remains of an ancient hybrid of this continent. Future research has the "potential to change conventional understanding of how the Americas were peopled," observed James Chatters. "Kennewick Man will not be reburied. He and his people, whoever they were, may assume their rightful place in the human story." Moreover, the "past is not a possession," he wrote, but rather a "series of events" and traces. "Archaeologists have been trained to read those traces and serve the public by helping them glimpse the lives of our predecessors. Such knowledge shows us how we fit into the great tapestry of cultural and biological evolution."[43]

The truth games of science, courts, government agencies, oral traditions, and native convictions, moral, ethical, or otherwise, never end, but science has been a big winner for more than a century. Surely, the Ancient One would be honored more by the moves of science in this case, than by the elusive associations that would bury his name and stories of his presence on this continent.

Mister Kennewick was unknown, an absence on the continent for some nine thousand years. Today he has a presence, a hybrid skeletal celebrity. Judge Jelderks and the scientists who sued for the right to study the ancient remains have created a new truth game and a hybrid narrative of bygone liberty.

6. Genocide Tribunals

Charles Aubid declared by stories his *anishinaabe* human rights and sovereignty. He created a vital "fourth person," a sense of presence and survivance, and defied the cultural hearsay of ethnologies, absence and victimry.

The inspired storier was a sworn witness in federal court that autumn more some forty years ago in Minneapolis, Minnesota. He raised his hand, listened to the oath for the first time in the language of the *anishinaabe* and then waved at United States District Judge Miles Lord.

Aubid testified by visual memory, an inseparable sensibility of natural reason, and with a memorable conception of continental native liberty. His stories intimated a third person other than the apparent reference, the presence of a fourth person, a native discourse, or the linguistic obviative in *anishinaabemowin*, the oral language of the *anishinaabe*. That native practice, the storied presence of a fourth person, was repudiated as hearsay, not a source of evidence in common law and federal court. Recently, however, international criminal court tribunals have not excluded "hearsay or indirect evidence." William Schabas pointed out in *An*

Introduction to the International Criminal Court that to be "admissible, evidence must be relevant and necessary."[1]

Aubid was a witness in a dispute with the federal government over the right to regulate the *manoomin*, or wild rice harvest on the Rice Lake National Wildlife Refuge in Minnesota. Federal agents had assumed the authority to announce the wild rice season and regulate the harvest, a bureaucratic action that decried a native sense of survivance and sovereignty.

Aubid, and many other *anishinaabe* witnesses, were in federal court to convince the judge to restrain the government from regulating the *manoomin* harvest on the national refuge, a century after the area had been ceded in treaties, and the refuge established by the government. William Falvey, the federal attorney, argued that control of the refuge was legal and that the natives in court were not elected to represent the interests of the reservation. Federal agents, however, had denied natives an innate cultural practice.

Aubid, who was eighty-six years old at the time, testified through translators that he was present as a young man when the federal agents told Old John Squirrel that the *anishinaabe* would always have control of the *manoomin* harvest. Aubid told the judge that there once was a document, but the *anishinaabe* always understood their rights in stories. John Squirrel was there in memories, a storied presence of native survivance. The court could have heard the testimony as a visual trace of a parol agreement, a function of discourse, both relevant and necessary.

Falvey objected to the testimony as hearsay, and not admissible as evidence. The judge agreed with the objection and explained to the witness that the court cannot hear as evidence what a dead man said, only the actual experiences of the witness. "John Squirrel is dead," said Judge Miles Lord. "And you can't say what a dead man said." The judge waited for his words to be translated and then invited the witness to continue his testimony.

Aubid turned in the witness chair, bothered by what the judge had said about John Squirrel. English was his second language, but he told stories in *anishinaabemowin*, the language of his visual memories. Aubid leaned closer to the judge, pointed at the legal books on the bench, and then, in English, shouted that those books contained the stories of dead white men. "Why should I believe what a white man says, when you don't believe John Squirrel?" Judge Lord was deferential, amused by the analogy of native stories to court testimony, judicial decisions, precedent, and hearsay. "You've got me there," he said, and then considered the testimony of other *anishinaabe* witnesses.[2]

The regulation of the wild rice harvest was not decided then and there; later, in other cases, federal courts acknowledged the inherent rights of natives to regulate natural resources on treaty reservations. Francis Paul Prucha observed that the "treaties, which reformers at the end of the nineteenth century considered an obstacle to the progress of the Indians, have turned out, in the late twentieth century, to be one of the principal bastions of protection for the lands, the political autonomy, and the hunting and fishing rights of present-day reservation Indians."[3]

Aubid created a presence of John Squirrel. That sense of native presence in federal court was the obviative, the fourth

134   person in the poses of linguistic evidence. Monotheism is hearsay, the concern and care of apostles, and the curse of deceivers. The rules of evidence are selective by culture and tradition, and sanction federal cozenage over native presence and survivance.

Charles Aubid was a storier who created indirect linguistic evidence and a native sense of presence. Native stories that arise from visual memories and rouse a sense of presence, the animation of a fourth person, are important sources of evidence and survivance. Stories of natural reason could provide linguistic evidence in the genocide tribunals advocated in this essay. Consider, for instance, the evidentiary stories of those who survived the wars against natives at Sugar Point, Sand Creek, and Wounded Knee. Native testimony, cultural games of adversarial evidence, and hearsay would create narratives of native survivance in genocide tribunals. Many public officials and senior military officers exhorted the removal and extermination of Native American Indians. The perpetrators of genocide, and those who incited crimes against natives, would be prosecuted in absentia at genocide tribunals.

"Tolerance and acceptance of pluralism resulted eventually from a *standoff* between bitterly hostile opposing groups," argued Albert Hirschman in *The Rhetoric of Reaction.* "There remains then a long and difficult road to be traveled from the traditional internecine, intransigent discourse to a more 'democracy-friendly' kind of dialogue. For those wishing to undertake this expedition there should be value in knowing about a few danger signals, such as arguments that are in effect contraptions specifically designed to make dialogue and deliberation impossible."[14]

Lemkin Conventions

The Convention on the Prevention and Punishment of the Crime of Genocide provides that genocide is the "intent to destroy, in whole or in part, a national, ethnical, racial or religious group." The "definition indicates a quantitative dimension," observed Schabas. "The quantity contemplated must be significant, and an intent to kill only a few members of a group cannot be genocide. The prevailing view is that where only part of a group is destroyed, it must be a 'substantial' part."[5]

The General Assembly of the United Nations approved the resolution on December 9, 1948. The convention confirmed that "genocide, whether committed in time of peace or in time of war, is a crime under international law which they undertake to prevent and punish." State sovereignty, by legal concepts, would no longer provide immunity.

Raphael Lemkin created the word *genocide*, a specific name that connotes the singular slaughter of humans and the destruction of cultures. Seventeen years later the genocide convention was ratified, but the new international law has not saved many lives in the past fifty years.

The United States was once a mainstay of the proposed convention, and was persuasive at first, but support was weakened by political grievances and confusion over the precise meaning of *genocide*. Some United States "senators feared the expansive language would be used to target Americans," wrote Samantha Power in "A Problem from Hell." The American Bar Association, for instance, challenged the definition of genocide and opposed ratification of the convention and international law. Power observed that in "criminal law an intent to commit a crime is generally hard to prove, and intent to commit genocide even harder."[6]

Some of those who opposed the ratification of the genocide convention focused narrowly on the concern that the United States could be investigated for crimes against Native American Indians. Rightly, a retroactive tribunal would reveal many violations of every provision of the genocide convention. "Reckoning with American brutality against native peoples was long overdue, but the convention, which was not retroactive, could not be used to press the matter," declared Power.[7]

Senator William Proxmire delivered more than three thousand daily speeches on genocide over nineteen years in the senate. The Genocide Convention Implementation Act was passed in October 1988, and the genocide convention was finally ratified. Alas, when President Reagan and the Senate "got their first chance to enforce the law, strategic and domestic political concerns caused them to side with the genocidal regime of Saddam Hussein."[8] The United States seemed more hesitant, once the convention was ratified, to intervene to stop genocide.

"Never in history had states even resolved to prevent atrocities," noted Power. "But enforcement was another matter entirely." The United States policy of "nonintervention in the face of genocide" is heinous politics, inhumane, and impeachable. Power observed that this is not a failure of policy, but one that is "ruthlessly effective. The system, as it stands now, is working." No United States "president has ever made genocide prevention a priority." Likewise, no "president has ever suffered politically for his indifference

to its occurrence. It is thus no coincidence that genocide
rages on."⁹

Heinous Politics

The United States has constructed by situational ethics,
godly sentiments, resistance, idealism, contrary practices, and by force one of the most provocative histories of
civil and human rights. The political turns of observance,
frenzy, wrath, and denial of human rights in a constitutional democracy have rightly worried citizens of the nation and the world.

America has been a recalcitrant nation in the advancement of international human rights. A "nation much given
to spurts of world leadership followed by periods of self-
regarding isolationism," asserted Geoffrey Robertson in
Crimes against Humanity. "Its scholars have made vast contributions to the literature of human rights, reflecting its
history as the land of the free, but its refusal to qualify its
own sovereignty in any way by accepting international jurisdiction reduces its influence and sets bad examples."¹⁰

Native American Indians, for instance, have petitioned
many international agencies to represent their cause, the
denial of human rights in a constitutional democracy. No
other nation has so grandly negotiated hundreds of treaties with indigenous tribes, and, at the same time, rent,
reproved, or abrogated every treaty. Yet, those very treaties are now the foundations of federal court decisions in
favor of Native American Indians. Hearty contradictions
may be the contrived, mediated course of human rights
in America.

The central, vital, political missions and discourse
on human rights, provided by moral certitude, domain

constitutions, and international conventions, arise and are critically sustained at universities. Native American Indians, in the past generation, have created a serious venue in the academic world to review treaties, federal policy, reservation politics, art, language, literature, and sovereignty. These academic associations are natural reasons to consider human rights, survivance, tolerance, and to initiate tribunals on genocide. The critiques of liberalism and humanistic philosophies at universities are clearly compatible with the discourse on various declarations and conventions of human rights and liberty.

William Galston observed that rights are at the "epicenter of key debates in contemporary philosophy and politics." Moreover, the "main point is that in current circumstances, 'taking rights seriously' entails a number of controversial, and in some cases unfashionable commitments."[11] Tribunals on genocide would be a controversial practice and a commitment to adjudicate the serious rights of Native American Indians.

Survivance Narratives

Native survivance is an active sense of presence over absence, deracination, and oblivion in history; survivance is the obvious continuance of stories, not a mere reaction, or a survivable cultural name. Survivance stories are renunciations of state dominance, obtrusions, and the unbearable sentiments of monotheism, tragedy, and victimry. Survivance means the heritable human right of succession or reversion of a cultural estate, and, in the course of tribunals, a narrative estate of native survivance.[12]

The University of South Dakota, for instance, and many other universities, should heighten this discourse on native

survivance and establish formal tribunals on human rights
to consider provincial, domain, and state genocide, and
crimes against humanity. The convention of a tribunal could
arguably resolve by judicial practices, principles, and standards some of the contentious accusations and denials of
genocide and crimes against Native American Indians.

Colonial genocide and ethnic cleansing are "part of our
civilization," argued Michael Mann in *The Dark Side of Democracy.* "Murder is not distinctively modern, but murder
in order to cleanse particular identities is modern," and the
"dark side of democracy is passing through modern societies," he declared. "By now we can recognize the circumstances in which ethnic cleansing threatens danger and
then goes over the brink into mass murder. From recognition comes the ability to formulate solutions."[13]

Genocide tribunals would provide venues of judicial reason and equity that reveal continental ethnic cleansing,
mass murder, torture, and religious persecution, past and
present, and would justly expose, in the context of legal
competition for evidence, the inciters, falsifiers, and deniers of genocide and state crimes against Native American Indians. Genocide tribunals would surely enhance the
moot court programs in law schools and provide more serious consideration of human rights and international criminal cases by substantive testimony, motivated historical
depositions, document evidence, contentious narratives,
and ethical accountability.

The Philip C. Jessup International Court Competition, for
instance, invites law school students to consider problems
of international law. The Moot Court case recently "centered
on the jurisdiction of the new International Criminal Court

and its ability to exercise power over the nationals of states not party to the Court," said Hugo Torres, a participant from the Harvard Law School. "Specifically, the case dealt with issues of war crimes and incitements to genocide, so it had some very serious issues about the reach of the new court and who should punish such crimes."[14] Similarly, the European Law Moot Court considers significant cases of tolerance and stimulates "studies in European Law."[15]

Statutable Genocide

The Rome Statute of the International Criminal Court affirms in the preamble that "grave crimes threaten the peace" of the world, and the "most serious crimes of concern to the international community as a whole must not go unpunished." The court is determined to "put an end to impunity for the perpetrators of these crimes."

The perpetrators of serious crimes against Native American Indians have seldom been punished, and the insidious deniers of genocide protect the impunity of the perpetrators. The preamble recognizes that "grave crimes threaten the peace" of the world, and does not specifically decline consideration of past genocides. Article 24, however, provides that "no person shall be criminally responsible under this Statute for conduct prior to the entry into force of the Statute." Article 29 seems to contradict the statement of "criminal responsibility" prior to the adoption of the statute. "The crimes within the jurisdiction of the Court shall not be subject to any statute of limitations."[16]

Antonio Cassese pointed out in *International Criminal Law* that the "application of statutes of limitations to the most serious international crimes proves contrary to the very nature of international rules prohibiting such crimes. These are so abhorrent that their authors must be punished, even after the lapse of much time. Such punishment not only has a retributive effect, but also serves to deter potential perpetrators as far as possible from engaging in similar actions." Cassese observed that it "appears to be a sounder view that specific customary rules render statutes of limitation inapplicable with regard to some crimes: genocide, crimes against humanity, torture."[17]

Cassese, in a discussion of the Convention on the Prevention and Punishment of Genocide, explained that the "definition of genocide does not embrace cultural genocide," the "destruction of the language and culture of a group," an indication that cultural genocide is "rather nebulous." Obscure, imprecise, or not, the deliberate omission of cultural genocide from the treaty is worrisome in the consideration of crimes against Native American Indians.[18]

The Genocide Convention considered three categories of destruction, physical, biological and cultural. "Cultural genocide was the most troublesome of the three, because it could well be interpreted in such a way as to include the suppression of national languages and similar measures," observed Schabas. "The drafters of the Convention considered that such matters were better left to human rights declarations on the rights of minorities and they actually voted to exclude cultural genocide from the scope of the definition. However, it can be argued that a contemporary interpreter of the definition of genocide should not be bound by the intent of the drafters back in 1948. The words 'to destroy' can readily bear the concept as well as physical and biological genocide, and bold judges might be tempted to adopt such progressive constructions. In any event, evidence of 'cultural genocide' has already proven to be an important indicator of the intent to perpetrate physical genocide."[19]

The criminal court authority of enforcement would not be crucial to genocide tribunals at universities. The point of these proposed genocide tribunals is to consider native equity, moral accountability, the reasonable competition of evidence, and to create narratives of survivance. The analogies of genocide are judicial standards, principles, moral practices, and the legal examination of evidence. Native narratives of survivance are pleas for equity.

The United States voted against the Rome Statute of the International Criminal Court. John Bolton, then the undersecretary for arms control and international security, announced at the Federalist Society that the court had "unacceptable consequences for our national sovereignty." The United States, concerned about criminal jurisdiction, voted with China, Iraq, Libya, Yemen, Qatar, and Israel. Bolton argued that a "fair reading of the treaty leaves one unable to answer with confidence whether the United States would now be accused of war crimes for legitimate but controversial uses of force to protect world peace." The president and his advisors could not be "assured that they would be unequivocally safe from politicized charges of criminal liability." President George W. Bush declared, "Every person who serves under the American flag will answer to his or her own superiors and to military law, not to the rulings of an unaccountable International Criminal Court."[20]

Similar political denials, objections, and retractions might have been proclaimed by previous presidents, concerned that "charges of criminal liability" could arise from reports of serious crimes and genocide against Native American Indians. Michael Mann wrote that enlightened presidents and military officers commonly threatened genocide if indigenous families and communities did not accept deportation or removal to reservations. George Washington, for instance, "instructed his generals to attack the Iroquois and 'lay waste all the settlements . . . that the country may not be merely overrun but destroyed,' and not to 'listen to any overture of peace before the total ruin of their settlements is effected.'" Thomas Jefferson recommended the "destruction of hostile tribes" and declared that "nothing is more desirable than total suppression of their savage insolence and cruelties." Their "ferocious barbarities justified extermination." Andrew Jackson "urged his soldiers to kill women and children." The "Indian wars were the setting for all these remarks, and they helped him become president. Once in office, Jackson broke Indian treaties and launched forcible deportations. He claimed that his Removal Act of 1830 was an act of generosity, yet around 10,000 Creek, 4,000 Cherokee, and 4,000 Choctaw died along the infamous Trail of Tears."[21]

Wounded Knee

General William Tecumseh Sherman told reporters, at a press conference, December 7, 1890, in New York City, "Injins must either work or starve. They never have worked; they won't work now, and they never will work." A reporter for the *New York World* asked, "But should not the government supply them with enough to keep them from starvation?" Sherman responded, "Why should the government support 260,000 able-bodied campers? No government that the world has ever seen has done such a thing." The general deliberately falsified the appalling conditions on reservations in South Dakota. Natives were detained by the military on fraudulently reduced reservations and deprived of food and treaty provisions by corrupt federal agents. Natives were forbidden to leave the reservation without permission of federal agents.

Roger Di Silvestro pointed out in *The Shadow of Wounded Knee* that a "new government commission came to the reservation and told leading chiefs such as Red Cloud and Spotted Tail that if they did not agree to sell the Black Hills, rations for the Lakota would be cut off, and the Lakota would be removed to Indian Territory" in Oklahoma.[22] The documents and historical testimony of this actionable threat of removal from ancestral and treaty land would be considered as evidence at a genocide tribunal. Moreover, the *Chadron Democrat* published an editorial that further incited the public to racial and cultural enmity three days after the genocide at Wounded Knee Creek, January 1, 1891. "We glory in the revenge" of the Seventh Cavalry Regiment and "predict that the killing of Big Foot and his warriors will have a telling effect on the messiah craze, and will civilize more reds who are yet alone than all the power of God and education that has been pumped into them for the past 16 years."[23]

Many newspapers misconstrued the conditions on reservations and enhanced reports of violence, conflicts, and wars with Native American Indians. Some reporters wrote from a distance and rarely commented on extreme reservation poverty or the honorable resistance to venal and unscrupulous federal agents. The *New York World*, for instance, published the comments of an unnamed "experienced soldier" on December 31, 1890. "There is the strongest kind

of prejudice among officers and men on frontier stations
against Indians. Like General Sheridan, they believed 'the
only good Indian is a dead Indian.' As compared with the
white man, his life is worth almost nothing; and it is not
regarded as a crime to shoot a poor red devil for a trifling
offense."[24]

The University of South Dakota has an urgent and moral
responsibility to adjudicate by a tribunal the perpetrators of
the alleged conspiracy of genocide by certain corrupt federal agents, merchants, newspaper editors who conspired
in the incitement of racial and religious hatred, heinous
missionaries, and the military at Wounded Knee, South
Dakota. Those civilians who violated federal laws and treaties, and the officers and soldiers of the Seventh Cavalry
Regiment, should be indicted and tried, in absentia, for alleged genocide and crimes against humanity at Wounded
Knee Creek on December 29, 1890.

"The situation on Lakota Sioux reservations in 1890 was
desperate," wrote Paul Robertson in the *Encyclopedia of North
American Indians*. "Promises to increase rations, made by
U.S. officials in 1889 in order to secure signatures to reduce
Sioux treaty lands by half, and to create six separate reservations, had proved false. Instead, rations had been cut pre-
cipitously, and the people were nearly starving."[25]

Colonel Richard Dodge wrote in the *Army and Navy Journal* a "bitter indictment of government policy" just three
weeks before the genocide at Wounded Knee. The Indian,
once free and independent is now a "prisoner of war, restrained of his liberty and confined on circumscribed areas." The "Plains furnished him ample supply of food; now
he is constantly on the verge of starvation. We leave our

helpless prisoners to starve, and shoot without mercy the reckless few who, goaded to desperation by their sufferings, dare to cross the dead line of the reservation. In this horrid crime every voter of the United States is either actively or passively implicated, for it has its roots in the legislative branch of the government."[26]

On December 2, 1890, the United States Senate debated the issue of whether the government should honor treaties with natives, and considered the desperate situation on reservations in South Dakota. Rightly, a majority of the senators insisted "treaties be honored." Senator Daniel Voorhees of Indiana expressed his concern about treaty provisions based on critical reports by General Nelson Miles. "If the provisions of the resolution was to issue one hundred thousand rations and more to the starving Indians it would be more consistent with the Christian civilization than the policy we are now pursuing." General Miles stated in public interviews that the "Indians are driven into revolt—rebellion, if you please to call it so—and to the savagery of Indian warfare by starvation, it becomes inexpiable crime, in my judgment, on the part of this government to stand silently by and do nothing except furnish arms which may kill them. General Miles has stated to the public, and he has so stated to me before the publication of his interview, that these Indians are being starved into hostility and that they prefer to die fighting to being starved to death."[27]

Sitanka, or Big Foot, and other natives "had nothing on their minds except to get away from the soldiers," wrote Ralph Andrist in The Long Death. "The Sioux had hoisted a white flag in the center of their camp as an indication of their peaceful intentions and a guarantee of safety." The

Seventh Cavalry had a "splendid record, but all witnesses agree that from the moment it opened fire, it ceased to be a military unit and became a mass of infuriated men intent only on butchery. Women and children attempted to escape by running up the dry ravine, but were pursued and slaughtered."[28]

Charley Blue Arm said, "I started to the creek and on the way I saw a great number of men, women and children dead or wounded and bleeding. I went on past them down into the creek as I saw a few others running there to get protection."

Medicine Woman said, "I was wounded at the first fire, but I was so scared I did not feel it. My husband was killed there and my little girl, and a little baby boy on my back was killed by a bullet which also broke my elbow, so that I dropped the body. . . . The white men were so thick here like a whole pile of maggots."

Frank Corn, who was twelve years old at the time, said he saw "his mother Brown Ears gunned down. She told him, 'Take the Ghost shirt, put it on your back and run.'"

Edward Owl King said, "All that I remember is that I was running up this ravine trying to get away. There were some ponies, women, and children shot down and scattered; and while running I stepped on them."

Dewey Beard said, "I saw my mother standing and singing. She was waving a pistol. She told me to take it, she was dying. I cried and helped her sit down. I felt like I couldn't get up, I looked down and saw I had been shot again, in the lap. . . . I was badly wounded and pretty weak too. While I was lying on my back, I looked down the ravine and saw a lot of women coming up and crying. When I saw these

148   women, little girls, and boys coming up, I saw soldiers on
        both sides of the ravine shoot at them until they had killed
        every one of them."[29]

Natural Reason

United States tribunals in absentia are rare because defendants have a constitutional right to be confronted by witnesses. There is, however, a "rationale for holding trials
in absentia in civil law countries," noted Cassese, "since
international crimes do not fall under any statute of limitations." Furthermore, in "favor of trials in absentia one
could argue that it would be contrary to law and justice to
authorize the alleged perpetrators of gruesome crimes to
make a mockery of international justice by preventing trials through their deliberate absence."[30]

William Schabas pointed out that during the "drafting
of the Rome Statute, the issue was often presented, erroneously, as one of the principled differences with the common
law system, which does not allow for in absentia trials as
a general rule. But the fact that common law jurisdictions
make a number of exceptions, and allow for such proceed-
ings where appropriate, shows that this is not an issue of
fundamental values so much as one of different practice."
Moreover, unlike the "common law system, with its complex and technical rules of evidence, the Statute follows the
tradition of international criminal tribunals by allowing
the admission of all relevant and necessary evidence," and
it does not exclude "hearsay or indirect evidence."[31]

The University of California, Berkeley, should also establish a tribunal to consider indictments of those who allegedly murdered and participated, by government sanctions, in the wanton destruction of indigenous families and

communities in the domain and state of California. Moreover, the politicians, miners, and marketers who allegedly
conspired and purloined indigenous land to establish the
university, and other public and private institutions, should
be indicted by a genocide tribunal.

The California constitution "enshrined full white male
suffrage, the most advanced form of democracy of the age.
But it also authorized the forcible detention and placing
in indentured labor in perpetuity for any Indians who fled
the reservations or were found wandering," wrote Mann.
"This included children. The legislature authorized settler
militias to enforce the roundup." Reservations were established "on marginal land" and "could not support the Indian population." The "militias killed as many Indians as
they deported" to the reservations. "The California legislature actually opposed recognizing any Indian rights to
land in the state. But they then had to face the final consequences of such obduracy, since there was nowhere farther west to which the problem could be sent." Governor
Peter Burnett declared, "A war of extermination will continue to be waged between the two races until the Indian
becomes extinct."[32]

Ishi survived the bounty hunters. He was named by
chance, a lonesome hunter rescued by cultural anthropologists. The spirit of this native captured almost a century
ago has been sustained as cultural property. Ishi was hu-
manly secured in a museum at a time when natives were denied human and civil rights. He was christened the last of
the stone agers; overnight he became a simulation, a decorated orphan of cultural genocide, the curious savage of
a vanishing race overcome by modernity.

Ishi had endured the unspeakable hate crimes of miners, racial terrorists, bounty hunters, and government scalpers. Many of his family and friends were murdered, the calculated victims of cultural treason and rapacity. Truly, the miners were the real savages.

California natives barely survived the gold rush, the cruelties of colonial missions, racial separatists, poisoned water, and genocide. Only about fifty thousand natives, or one in five, were alive in the state at the turn of the twentieth century.[33]

Criminal Incursions

The University of Minnesota should establish a tribunal to indict state politicians, in absentia, for incitement of genocide, to consider the theft and destruction of indigenous land and resources by federal agents and state representatives, and to prosecute the Third Infantry Regiment of the United States Army for a criminal war against the anishinaabe Pillagers of the Leech Lake Reservation, Minnesota, in October 1898.[34]

Minnesota governor Alexander Ramsey declared, "The Sioux Indians must be exterminated or driven forever beyond the borders of the state," wrote Mann. Colonel Henry Sibley, a former governor, carried out a "war of extermination against the Santee Sioux."[35] The Dakota Conflict, or Sioux Uprising of 1862, was an armed resistance to the abuse and corruption of federal agents over treaty payments and provisions, and then the resistance became a rampage that lasted six weeks. Conclusive records indicate that more than a hundred soldiers and civilian settlers died in the conflict; some estimates of the total number of dead reach eight hundred. Local courts convicted 303

Dakota prisoners and sentenced them to death. President Lincoln, however, commuted most of the death sentences, leaving only thirty-eight who were executed by hanging on December 26, 1862, in Mankato, Minnesota. Those federal agents who diverted treaty provisions by fraud, theft, and misanthropy should be indicted for incitement and tried in absentia by a tribunal. The Dakota were prosecuted and thirty-eight were executed, but culpable federal agents escaped prosecution and only increased their wealth by fraud and corruption.

William Hascal Brill wrote for the *Daily Pioneer Press* and the Associated Press, on October 7, 1898, that the "battle of Leech Lake is over. The bodies of six soldiers for whom taps has been sounded for the last time and eleven severely wounded men, lying in the old warehouse near the dock in Walker, tell the story of its severity as far as the boys in blue are concerned." The Third Infantry Regiment "took part in both the battle of El Caney and that of San Juan and lost three men killed. In the battle of Leech Lake a part of one company was engaged and six men gave their lives. And yet the battles before Santiago de Cuba were called fierce once and the battle of Leech Lake was a skirmish and history will probably overlook it," wrote Brill.

"And the pity of it all is that is seems so useless. For what object, what principle did Major Wilkinson die and his men lose their lives from Indian bullets? Simply that a few Indians did not wish to go to Duluth to testify against a man that sold them whiskey. Still the authority of the government must be preserved and brave men must give up their lives in support of their oaths and allegiance."

That military oath and allegiance, at the time, conveyed

and counted criminal incursions and atrocities against Native American Indians. The soldiers stole sacred objects and destroyed native property.

The *anishinaabe* of Leech Lake complained for many years about the fraud and corruption of federal agents and speculators who stole timber from their land and built dams that flooded the wild rice. Roger Pinckney pointed out in his story about the war that "Minneapolis flour millers persuaded Congress to regulate the flow of the Mississippi by building a series of dams on lakes at the headwaters of the river." The rising water flooded native communities and, without notice, "drowned beds of wild rice, and washed the bones of Indian dead upon the shore."[36]

The Pillager warriors, outnumbered more than three to one, routed the soldiers of the Third Infantry Regiment in a single day, October 5, 1898. The Pillagers reported no casualties. The army casualties were six dead and eleven wounded, a certain defeat seldom mentioned in military histories.

Rights of Perception

"What breaks into language in light of the disaster is not some content that eludes language but unsayability itself," observed Edith Wyshogrod in *An Ethics of Remembering*. "How is such unsayability to make its way into the work of a historian who crafts a film or a narrative about the past?"

The actual victims of genocide are dead, and the stories of their death and historical absence are the causes of justice in human rights tribunals. The stories of genocide are established by archives, witness testimony, diverse narratives, remembrance, hearsay and indirect evidence, and by those imaginative storiers who have the right of consciousness and survivance. Genocide is understood by documents and narratives, and, in part, by the gravity of the atrocity, the number of dead and the comparative, abstract representations of victimry. The testimony and historical narratives by human rights advocates and prosecutors provide an argument for indictments, in absentia, of alleged perpetrators and those who incited and were associated with the perpetrators of genocide. The victims of genocide are represented in tribunals by remembrance, historical testimony, and documents, a presence, in absentia, to summon and accuse alleged perpetrators of crimes against humanity. Equity is another consideration of genocide tribunals, the recovery of ruin and detriments for crimes against ancestors: slavery, for instance, the confiscation of property and arbitrary internment of Japanese citizens during the Second World War, and the art and property stolen from the ancestors of Jews.

Historians have published admirable accounts and reliable interpretations of the tragic "massacre" at Wounded Knee. These narratives, and grave numbers, however, do not alone provide a persuasive prosecution of the alleged perpetrators of genocide. Many documents and other historical evidence are misconstrued by falsifiers, and deniers, who would otherwise misrepresent documents to serve, pardon, or condemn governments and federal agencies for various extreme political causes.

The Convention on the Prevention and Punishment of Genocide provides that "genocide whether committed in time of peace or time of war, is a crime under international law." Robertson pointed out that the intention of genocide "must be to destroy human beings on account of their race."

154   Surely, intentions and incitements by elected politicians
and military leaders to exterminate indigenous families
and communities is a crime of genocide. "The Convention
defines genocide as the committing, with the intention to
destroy in whole or in part a national, ethnic, racial or religious group, or any of the following five acts: (a) killing
members of the group; (b) causing serious bodily harm or
mental harm to members of the group; (c) deliberately in-
flicting on the group conditions of life calculated to bring
about its physical destruction in whole or in part; (d) impos-
ing measures intended to prevent births within the group;
(e) forcibly transferring children of the group to another
group."[37]

There is substantive testimony, historical documents, an-
ecdotal and indirect evidence to create a conclusive narrative
that the five acts of genocide were perpetrated, at various
times and locations, against Native American Indians.

Lethal pathogens are the colorable agents of colonial
conquest, occupation, and dominance. Direct evidence that
diseases were widely used as a weapon is unresolved, neither persuasive nor conclusive. The colonial and military
destruction of native communities was vast and criminal,
but most natives died by the millions in several waves of
diseases first delivered inadvertently by native traders, and
then by missionaries, colonists, and emigrants.

Ward Churchill declared in various tenet piques of historical revisionism that the military distributed infectious
trade blankets to the Mandan at Fort Clark on the Missouri
River. Churchill, by mode of victimry, pronounced that the
blankets had been exposed to smallpox, the very cause of
the disease that devastated native communities.

Guenter Lewy, and many other scholars, countered the view of intentional dissemination of disease by the military. "The United States did not wage biological warfare against the Indians; neither can the large number of deaths as a result of disease be considered the result of genocidal design," he wrote in "Were American Indians the Victims of Genocide?"[38]

The epidemics "weakened the Indian economic systems and dispirited the people, whose world order seemed to have collapsed in the face of unknown forces," observed Francis Paul Prucha in The Indians in American Society.[39] "Some tribes almost entirely disappeared as a result of disease and conquest," wrote Robert Berkhofer Jr. in The Frontier in History. "Such severe demographic decline had profound implications for tribal leadership succession and the nature of governance, economic subsistence and patterns of survival."[40]

Russell Thornton observed in American Indian Holocaust and Survival that smallpox was the most "destructive during the nineteenth century." President Thomas Jefferson, in 1801, "caused the first American Indians to be vaccinated, rather than just inoculated."[41]

Inherent Dignity

The Universal Declaration of Human Rights provides, in thirty articles, the "inherent dignity" and "inalienable rights of all members of the human family." These rights are the "foundation of freedom, justice and peace in the world."[42]

Native American Indians have been consistently denied the inherent "inalienable rights" of the declaration in a constitutional democracy. The reality of human rights provisions is more literary irony than protection. Yet, the

156   declaration is a profound source of endurance in native
stories, creative literature, and the everlasting narratives
of survivance.

The first three articles are romantic contradictions as
natives on reservations were seldom entitled to ordinary
"rights and freedoms" provided by the declaration. Genocide tribunals should consider, for instance, the Mystic
River Massacre of the Pequot in 1637, the Gnadenhütten
Massacre of the Christian Delaware in 1782, and the Black
Hawk War in 1832. "Like the soldiers of My Lai, the militia at Gnadenhütten destroyed unarmed men, women, and
children and did so out of some strange reflex of fear and
resentment toward people they felt were not quite human,"
wrote the historian Page Smith.[43]

The next six articles of the declaration prohibit slavery,
cruel, inhuman punishment, legal recognition, equal protection against incitement and discrimination, arbitrary
detention, and the right to remedies by national tribunals.
The provisions of these articles were not practiced by federal agents or protected by government laws or policies in
the nineteenth century. Consider the Seminole Wars of 1818,
the racial exclusion and hatred of runaway slaves, maroons
and Black Seminoles. General Andrew Jackson led an invasion against the black warriors in Florida.

The last twelve articles of the declaration provide for
an entitlement of full equality, a right to the presumption
of innocence, freedom of movement and residence, and
to leave the country; a right to nationality, property own-
ership, thought, conscience, peaceful assembly, equal access to public services, social security; and the right to freedom of expression. These declarations of rights and specific

provisions have been denied on reservations, at different
times and states, by the arbitrary authority of federal agents.
Many state governments once deferred ordinary rights and
services, such as residency, medical services, and voter reg-
istration, to the federal government because natives were
separate trust tenants on treaty reservations. Consider, in
the context of these situational provisions, the massacre of
natives in California: Winnemem Wintu in 1854, the Wiyot
in Humboldt County in 1860, and the Keyesville Massacre
in Kern County in 1863. Moreover, consider the Bear River
Massacre of natives in Idaho Territory in 1862, the Sand
Creek Massacre in Colorado Territory in 1864, and the genocide at Wounded Knee Creek on December 29, 1890.[44] The
historical documents, testimony, and indirect evidence of
these massacres of natives could create a substantive narrative in a genocide tribunal.

Universities in every state should establish genocide tribunals to consider crimes against Native American Indians. Scarcely any federal agents, public officials, military
leaders, newspaper editors, or land speculators have ever
been brought to justice for alleged genocide of native women
and children, racial incitement, or for crimes against humanity. Many of the very perpetrators of genocide appro-
priated the ancestral land and property of murdered, removed and exiled Native American Indians.

7. Ontic Images

Native American Indian personal and cultural identities have always been strategic maneuvers, and in that sense modernist, names and singularity that arise from, and are created by both communal nominations, collective memories, and by distinct individual, visionary experiences.

Consider the analogies of native visionary, totemic images, and the photographic representations of *postindian* identities, or those ontic, imagic moments that follow the invention and occidental simulations of the *indian* in the Americas.

Analogies in this sense are visual and move to a "tentative harmony," as Barbara Maria Stafford observed in *Visual Analogy: Consciousness as the Art of Connecting*. "This uncanny visual capacity to bring divided things into unison or span the gap between the contingent and the absolute illustrates why analogy is a key feature of discernment." She wrote to "recuperate analogy, then, as a general theory of artful invention and as a practice of intermedia communication."

Similitude, however, "is not identity since the prototype—whether in art or biology—undergoes continuous development from its original conception through subsequent incarnations as a consequence of the environments or gestures through which it passes."[1]

Native American Indians no longer turn eager, romantic boys into loyal scouts, or fantastic warriors by special merit badges, or with obscure metaphors turn tourists wobbly over the wise tease of animals, birds, and nature in tricky stories.

The native myths and simulations that once connected tourists to the obscure, and to the diversions of the racial and cultural other, are now best overturned by liberal irony, a romantic liberation in modernist native literature. Bourgeois tourists, the new bohemians of cultural adventures and discoveries, wobble more over the mundane chance of becoming a winner at a reservation casino and helping the native poor at the same time. And there are hundreds of native casinos dedicated to that common transmutation of retired, loyal scout mothers and leaders into romantic, lazy gamblers.

Native myths and simulations are much richer by the tease of stories, by the natural, tricky associations of humans and animals, than by any combination of casino numbers or turn of cards. That sense of natural chance may be seen in creative art, photographic images, and heard in tricky stories, but hardly in the click and whir of a machine, or the crash of coins. Native stories, in this sense, are modernist by chance, totemic associations, and by analogy; casinos are mundane, monotheistic dissimulations of native stories and collective memory.

Storiers of Modernity

Native American Indians are the originary storiers of this continent, and native stories are the arcane creations of a

real existence that arise in a customary modernity. Native
stories of totemic associations, visionary, imagic moments,
or those tacit images of an ontic sense of presence, and survivance, are the actual turns of native modernity.

"Cultural changes, such as the one that gave birth to the
modern age, have a definitive and irreversible impact that
transforms the very essence of reality," wrote Louis Dupré
in *Passage to Modernity*. "Not merely our thinking about the
real changes: reality itself changes as we think about it differently. History carries an ontic significance that excludes
any reversal of the present."

Dupré explained that a "nominalist theology" and an ar-
chaic, creative humanism are the "border stones" of modernity. The divine was separated from nature in the late
fourteenth century, and, at the same time, the stories of
creation changed. Cultural meaning was converted by this
"removal of transcendence." Consequently, he argued, instead of "being an integral part of the cosmos, the person became its source of meaning." Reality was separated
into two spheres, nature, of course, and the human mind
as the source of meaning. This, he pointed out, "marks a
new epoch of being."[2]

Natives are not premodern in the sense of primitive, medieval cultures. Such peevish notions were presented by the
monotheists, polytheists, the separatists of manifest destiny, and by colonial dominance. Clearly, natives are the
storiers of natural reason on this continent, and their stories are, as they have always been, the imagic moments of
cultural conversions and native modernity.

"One of the glories of being a Plains Indian," observed
Larry McMurtry in *Crazy Horse*, "was that one didn't have
to stay put."

Crazy Horse, for instance, who was born near the Belle
Fourche River, "was an Oglala who spent a lot of time with
the Brulés (his mother's people), some time with the Chey-
ennes, and, later in his life, at least a little time with the
Hunkpapas."[3] Natives have always been on the move, by ne-
cessity of sustenance and over extensive trade routes. Motion is a natural right, and the stories of visionary *transmotion* are a continuous, distinctive sense of sovereignty.

The *indian*, of course, has no real referent, no actual native ancestors. The simulation of that name is a colonial
enactment. The *indian* is the absence of natives. The name
is an ironic noun, a simulation of dominance that trans-
poses native memories, imagic moments, and stories of
survivance.

Natives have resisted empires, negotiated treaties with
their enemies, and, as strategic visionaries and emissar-
ies, embraced the very simulations of their absence to secure the chance of a decisive presence in the historical narratives of colonial and constitutional democracies. Native
resistance to manifest manners and dominance is an undeniable trace of presence, but even these ironic, imagic
moments, and stories of survivance on the continent are
wrongly cast as narratives of absence and victimry.[4]

Natives must create their own stories; otherwise, the
sources of their identities are not their own. Natives are the
actual authors of the politics of resistance and cultural conversions on this continent, a distinctive, literary modernity.
Native identities likewise bear the traces of renunciation
and absence of connections to traditions, the racialist *indian* suits, documents of modiation, and the tricky cues of
dominance in the occidental theaters of tragic victimry.

The sources of native identities considered in this es- say are imagic moments, the traces of natural reason. The prudence and origin of place, cultural conversions, and, since the representation of natives in pictures and as published authors in the eighteenth century, ontic traces that give rise to a distinctive literary modernity. The poseurs of *indian* identities are constrained by their own simulations; the anecdotes of their past paradoxically isolates them in the politics of dominance and a folkloric futurity.

Native identities are created in names, stories, the teases of remembrance, and natural traces of the seasons. Cranes, bears, cedar waxwings, and other totemic creatures are active characters of my memories and imagic moments. My father, grandmother, and other native relatives are a presence not an absence in my stories, and now that sense of presence is in the book. The creation of my native identities is in the book. My resistance to simulations and cultural dominance is in the book, and that is the ontic significance of a literary modernity.

"Identity is not so much apprehending a face as winning it over," wrote Edmond Jabès in *The Little Book of Unsuspected Subversions*.[5] The author created an imagic moment that waits to be heard in the book; that moment is a visionary presence, a literary modernity. "Our very existence consists in our imagination of ourselves," wrote N. Scott Momaday. "The greatest tragedy that can befall us is to go unimagined."[6]

Native identities are stories that arise in the common tease of cultures, a sense of presence, and the obscure traces of traditions. Personal identities are created in the eminence of remembrance and extended families, not in that wicked hush of racial politics and separatism. Native identities are visionary and literary.

"The world exists because the book does. For existing means growing with your name," wrote Edmond Jabès in *The Book of Questions*. "To be able to say: 'I am in the book. The book is my world, my country, my roof, and my riddle. The book is my breath and my rest.'"[7]

Native stories are sources of survivance and, at the same time, the chance that racial associations are coercive. Consider the absence of natives in histories, the burdens of arbitrary federal policies, the deceptions of public documents, the tedious celebration of cultural revisions, racialist modiations of blood, and yet, natives create stories of survivance, a sense of presence and distinctive identities in the very midst of these many contradictions and contingencies. Natives are in the world of the book, and natives are the imagic moments of a literary modernity.

Certificates of Presence

"Every photograph is a certificate of presence," wrote Roland Barthes in *Camera Lucida*. The "certificate," he argued, "is the new embarrassment which its invention has introduced into the family of images."[8] Natives, of course, are twice the discountenance in "ethnographic" photographs: the first is the simulation of *indians* as cultural representations; the second is the certification of *indian* poses as authentic. Moreover, the *indian* "certificates of presence" soon became museum objects in the "archive fever" of preservation.[9]

Edward Curtis, for instance, a pictorial photographer of the late nineteenth century, actually altered some of his pictures to preserve the poses of indian "traditions." The simulations of his "certificate" indians have become the real, the faux evidence of a "vanishing race," and the simulations are a discountenance of native modernity.

"Curtis concentrated on representing 'traditional' ways, even to the extent of issuing wigs to cover shorn hair, providing costumes, and removing signs of the mechanistic twentieth century," observed Mick Gidley in Representing Others.[10] These pictorial photographic images and representations of indians disavowed imagic moments, cultural conversions, and the actual presence of natives.

Many natives once posed in the aura of these romantic, sepia simulations of the "traditional" past. Dennis Banks, Russell Means, and others were once vested as the representations of commonly known photographs. How ironic that the poses of certain radicals were the specious simulations of premodern indian cultures. The poseurs maintain the obvious, a cultural dominance that denies real native pictures, cultural variations, conversions, and modernity.

Clearly, the "wonder and illusion of representation is different from the wonder and illusions of reality," wrote David Freedberg in The Power of Images. "Representation is miraculous because it deceives us into thinking it is realist, but it is only miraculous because it is something other than what it represents."[11]

Pictures are a paradox of native identities. The images in photographs are not the real, and not the actual representations of time or culture. The stories of photographic images create a sense of both absence and presence: simulations are the absence, and stories of actual family images are an obvious sense of presence. The easy perception of indian simulations, the absence of natives, is not the same as the stories of a native sense of presence in the imagic moments of pictures. The simulations of absence are tragic victimry, and the stories of a native presence are survivance, a native literary modernity.

Picture Discourse

W. J. T. Mitchell considers a "pictorial turn" in the academic discourse on pictures, an anxiety over "visual representation" and modernity. "What makes for the sense of a pictorial turn, then, is not that we have some powerful account of visual representation that is dictating the terms of cultural theory, but that pictures form a point of peculiar friction and discomfort across a broad range of intellectual inquiry." Mitchell cited the connections of "spectacle" by Guy Debord and "surveillance" by Michel Foucault, and argues in Picture Theory that "we still do not know exactly what pictures are, what their relation to language is, how they operate on observers and on the world, how their history is to be understood, and what is to be done with or about them."[12]

What do we see that is native, and how do we create identities in the imagic moments of pictures? How can there be a sense of native *self*, a discoverable identity, in a picture of someone else? How can that tacit sense of self in a picture ever be defined or described as a method of perception and identity?

The sense of discovery is not the same as tacit perception, and the mirror image of the self is not the same as a picture, or the image of countenance. The perception of selfsame traits in a photograph, for instance, could be the

image of the self once recognized in the mirror, a mimetic
conversion and paradox of identity.

Photographs "turn the past into a consumable object,"
wrote Susan Sontag in *On Photography*. "As photographs
give people an imaginary possession of a past that is un-
real, they also help people to take possession of space in
which they are insecure." She pointed out that photographs
acknowledge but do not explain the image. "The primitive
notion of the efficacy of images presumes that images possess the qualities of real things, but our inclination is to attribute to real things the qualities of an image."[13]

Recently, two authors, Greg Sarris and W. S. Penn, told
stories about how they came to perceive and understand
the traces of their native identities in pictures, the marvelous, imagic moments of literary modernity.

Greg Sarris, the author of *Watermelon Nights*, traces his native identity to an imagic moment in a common high school
yearbook. *People* magazine reported that Sarris, at age nineteen, "learned from a doctor how his unmarried mother,
a rebellious girl" from a wealthy family, died at age seventeen "after giving birth to him in a horribly botched delivery." Nine years later he discovered a picture of his father,
a student at the Laguna Beach High School in California.
"'My heart leaped, and I just knew,' says Sarris. 'He was my
father. He was darker than me—but that smile.'"[14]

Sarris perceived a selfsame countenance in that high
school photograph, an imagic moment, and "discovered
that he is descended from the Native American Miwok tribe,
whose members not only embraced him, but in 1992 elected
him their modern-day chief. It is a transformation that Sarris himself marvels at."

Sarris perceived an imagic moment in a picture, the smile of his father, Emilio Hilario. That moment was native, a pictorial trace of ancestors, not an *indian* simulation. Bunny Hartman, his mother, was pictured in the same high school yearbook. "Still more pieces fell into place when Sarris tracked down a friend of his mother's, who remembered Bunny and Emilio's three-year high school romance." Emilio was Filipino and Miwok. "After tracking down Hilario relatives in the Laguna phone book, Sarris learned that his father, a salesman, had died just seven months before of heart failure." That originary moment, a trace of native identity, and sense of presence in a picture, came long after his adoption and adverse experiences as a youth in suburban Santa Rosa, California.[15]

Sarris is the author of many books and once taught literature at the University of California, Los Angeles. *People* reported that he was a "troubled, streetwise adolescent" who went on to earn a doctorate at Stanford University. His imagic moment of identity in a picture is an instance of literary modernity.

"I want a History of Looking," asserted Roland Barthes. "For the Photograph is the advent of myself as other: a cunning dissociation of consciousness from identity." He argued that his photographic image is "heavy, motionless, stubborn," and "never coincides" with his sense of self. The action of seeing oneself "differently from in a mirror" has, he suggested, caused something of a disturbance to civilization. Previously, before the development of photography, a painted portrait was a "limited possession" that represented a certain social status.[16]

Sarris perceived his own smile, a mirror image, in a

picture of a high school student who would become his father, the creation of a native self in the very countenance of the other. That "cunning dissociation of consciousness" was the creation of a native sense of identity.

Natives "know that identity is found in a lonely vision," wrote W. S. Penn in *All My Sins Are Relatives*. Solitary, indeed, but not forsaken. An unusual native presence in the very silence of a picture. The vision "may come on you slowly" as a mixedblood construction, "a beautiful jigsaw of self which is just slightly out of synch with the ways of the majority of people around you." He mused on native literature and traces his own identity to the Nez Perce and Osage. Penn taught literature at Michigan State University.

"Growing up, we knew we were Indian. There was, after all, Grandfather, and he told us stories no one else wanted to. But we did not know how Indian. It was a piece of laundry disguised or hidden from us," wrote Penn. That indian laundry, at the time, was a simulation, the absence of native ancestors. Then, "by luck," he "discovered a picture" in the archives at the Brooklyn Museum, "a picture of me taken in 1877 in Osage, Oklahoma." Naturally, the reader would pause to ponder that date, and wonder if the author had lost a century. No, the date was correct. Penn had perceived a curious, arcane me, a selfsame image in an archive picture. The image of the self as other, an imagic moment, acknowledges a countenance but does not explain the picture. The actual me of that imagic moment was named Albert Penn. He is pictured with two other natives in a backlighted studio. Albert, the other in the picture, has become a trace of native identity.[17]

"Whatever it grants to vision and whatever its manner, a

photograph is always invisible: it is not it that we see," observed Roland Barthes.[18] The imagic moment, or vision, is the story of the picture, and for these two native authors, that moment is a source of identity. The imagic moment is the creation of an ontic sense of presence, another connection in a picture.

"In the past, a discontent with reality expressed itself as a longing for *another* world," argued Susan Sontag. "In modern society, a discontent with reality expresses itself forcefully and most hauntingly by the longing to reproduce *this* one. As if only by looking at reality in the form of an object—through the fix of the photograph—it is really real, that is, surreal."[19]

W. S. Penn, the author, created a sense of native presence in the phenomenal image of the other, a literary modernity. Albert Penn is archival, a tenuous ancestor, but the author created an imagic moment in that picture and boldly announced a surname connection to the Osage of Oklahoma.

"Mother once devised a kind of family tree for me, a tree laddered with question marks and dead ends," wrote Penn. "It was her nature and her upbringing to want us not to be Indian." She "meant well when she made up the family tree," but now the image of "Albert Penn standing in colorful silk shirt and neckerchief and high-waisted pants, his perpendicular ears disguised (thought not hidden) by his long hair, the extent of Mother's wishful thinking in compiling that tree becomes astounding."[20]

Greg Sarris and W. S. Penn discovered selfsame images, a native connection in photographs. They put themselves into pictures to *potentiate* a latent, imagic moment by their language and literary actions. The inimitable stories of their imagic moments and sense of native presence are pictorial conversations, a literary modernity.

"One says that a person 'puts himself into' his acts, or that he is *not* 'in' what he says or does," wrote R. D. Laing, the revolutionary psychiatrist, in *Self and Others*. "He may seem to be 'full of himself' or 'beside himself' or 'to have come to himself' again after 'not being himself.' These expressions are attributions about the person's relations to his own actions, and are used quite naturally as the language of the 'man on the street.' In them all the issue is the extent to which the act is seen or felt to *potentiate* the being or existence of the doer, or the extent to which the action makes patent the latent self of the doer."[21]

Daniel Burston considers Laing's "philosophical anthropology" and "concepts of selfhood and identity" in *The Wing of Madness*. Laing, he argued, "endorsed the thesis" that the "experience of personhood, of an 'I' as a locus of experience of and action on the world, presupposes a 'Thou,' an other, in terms of whom one's own existence is understood. Whether we exist in a close, distant, complementary, or adversarial relationship, self and other are always reciprocally constituted. So one's sense of identity is never simply a product of unmediated introspection, but a selective synthesis of refracted self-appraisals, elements of the self that are expressed in dialogue (and in conflict) with others."[22]

Sarris traces his sense of native presence to a paternal smile in a high school yearbook. Later, the stories of that imagic moment became a real connection to native ancestors. Penn discovered a selfsame countenance in an archive photograph and created an imagic moment of a native, literary identity. The pictorial conversion is vested "in colorful silk shirt and neckerchief," a new *me* in an archive instance of literary modernity.

Patricia Penn Hilden, elder sister of the author, wrote in her memoir *When Nickels Were Indians*, "This meant that we were all much more Indian then we had known—a mixture of Osage *and* Nez Perce. Furthermore, some records indicate that the Osage part married a Mexican part as well as an English part at some point."[23]

Greg Sarris and W. S. Penn created a sense of native presence by pictorial conversions and by stories of an imagic moment, but not, to their credit as literary artists, by racialist simulations. The politics of race and color, of course, is one of the most spurious cultural codes of a native presence. Genetics deconstructs the notions of race, but genetic codes alone do not account for imagic moments or a native sense of presence and survivance.

Racial Escorts

Marge Anderson, once the distinguished chief executive of the Mille Lacs Band of Ojibwe Indians in Minnesota, observed that Ojibwe or *anishinaabe* "tradition speaks of peace among the four colors—red, white, yellow and black—which represents the four races on earth. Sadly, some people in this world don't show respect for all races, and they hurt others through their lack of understanding."[24]

Sadly, rather than begetting a sense of peace, the notion of four racial colors perpetuates a crude separation of humans and cultures. Marge Anderson, a generous native leader, surely never intended to advertise racialism and theories of phrenology. The four colors notion, and dubious native tradition, insinuates polygenesis, or the partite creation of humans advanced in the past century.

William Warren, the *anishinaabe* historian, observed more than a century ago that some native creation stories were told as a courtesy to missionaries. "These tales, though made up for the occasion by the Indian sages, are taken by his white hearers as their bona fide belief, and, as such, many have been made public, and accepted by the civilized world," he wrote in *History of the Ojibway Nation*. The Great Spirit, in one of these stories, created three races: white, black, and the red race. "To the first he gave a book, denoting wisdom; to the second a hoe, denoting servitude and labor; to the third, or red race, he gave the bow and arrow, denoting the hunter state." These tricky creation stories were translated and treasured by missionaries at the time. "We have every reason to believe that America has not been peopled from one nation or tribe of the human family, for there are differences amongst its inhabitants and contrarieties as marked and fully developed as are to be found between European and Asiatic nations—wide differences in language, beliefs, and customs."[25] Warren in his history, and the *anishinaabe* in their stories and tease of creation, sustained a sense of native, literary modernity.

The scientific theories of cardinal colors were advanced more than two centuries ago. Johann Friedrich Blumenbach studied crania and named "five basic races": "Mongolian, American, Caucasian, Malayan, and Ethiopian." "Through his observations of skulls he identified the Caucasian as the original type from which other races have degenerated," wrote Robert Bieder in *Science Encounters the Indian*. He pointed out that early nineteenth-century phrenologists "claimed that the brain was the organ of the mind; that the brain was composed of individual faculties that controlled personality, thought, and moral action; that the strength of these faculties could be determined by protuberances on the skull; and that each race manifested its cultural traits through the shape of the cranium. Thus, phrenologists believed, each race possessed a typical, or national, cranium."[26]

Samuel Morton, for instance, determined race by brain size. He filled crania with "mustard seed" and weighed the seeds to name the race. Morton, in *Crania Americana*, concluded that "Indian crania were radically different from Caucasian, African, Mongolian, and Malayan crania." Indian crania, he observed, were smaller by volume, and that represented savagism. "They are not only adverse to the restraints of education, but for the most part incapable of a continued process of reasoning on abstract subjects."

Bieder wrote that *Crania Americana* "provided a scientific foundation for a polygenetic racial history of man."[27] Polygenism, the theory of a separate creation of the races, was a political favor to slavers. Morton and other scientists of the time reasoned that savages were "more animal than human." The monogenists maintained that there was a unity of creation, or monotheism, and reasoned that ordinary human differences could be explained by experience and environments.

Carolus Linnaeus, the eighteenth-century naturalist, created a binomial nomenclature for plants and animals, and he also classified humans. He "found five natural categories of humans, four of which were geographically based," writes Barbara Katz Rothman in *Genetic Maps and Human Imaginations*. Linnaeus named and characterized five basic human groups: *Homo sapiens Americanus,* red, harsh face, wide nostrils, scanty beard, obstinate, free, and ruled by custom; *Homo sapiens Asiaticus,* yellow, melancholy, greedy, haughty, severe, and ruled by opinion; *Homo sapiens Afer,* black, lazy, flat nose, silky skin, ruled by caprice; *Homo sapiens Europaeus,* white, serious, strong, blond hair, blue eyes, active, very smart, inventive, ruled by laws; *Homo sapiens Monstrosus,* those curious and strange humans.[28]

Linnaeus represented three categories of the modern human species with racial detractions, ruled by custom, opinion, and caprice; those ruled by laws, the sapiens white, he vested with care and fair countenance. The last category was monstrous.

The United States Immigration and Naturalization Service provides five similar categories to determine the "race" of applicants for citizenship: American Indian or Alaskan Native, Asian or Pacific Island, Black, White, and Unknown.

Russell Means, the brave dancer, radical spiritualist, errant reservation politician, presidential candidate, *postindian* movie actor, and cruces of *indian* simulations, has his own notions of race, reason, and culture. "Humans are able to survive only through the exercise of rationality since they lack the abilities of other creatures to gain food through the use of fang and claw," he pointed out in his autobiography *Where White Men Fear to Tread.* "But rationality is a curse since it can cause humans to forget the natural order of things in ways other creatures do not. A wolf never forgets his or her place in the natural order. American Indians can. Europeans almost always do."

Means argued that he does not care about skin color, and at the same time, he noted that white is a race and "one of the sacred colors of the Lakota people—red, yellow, white and black. The four directions. The four seasons" and the "four races of humanity." He described the brew of four colors as a fifth race. "Mix red, yellow, white and black together and you got brown, the color of the fifth race. This is a natural ordering of things."[29]

Race is a simulation, and the "science" of race is political not biological; human differences are genetic, and the notions of four races are faux traditions and detractive science.

"We are not separate species," argued Rothman. "Race was a liquid concept," but the once common metaphor of *blood*, as blood will tell, blue, red, hot, cold, thicker than water, has lost significance. "No longer visible, no longer divisible, race has moved inward from body to blood to genes; from solid to liquid to a new crystallization. Blood no longer tells. Race is now a code to read; the science of race is the science of decoding."[30]

Genetic Storiers

Families, genetic codes, and imagic moments, not racial colors or the size of crania, are the sources of native identities. Stories create the names, the memorable scenes, and sense of presence; actions and ancestors are the contingencies of recognition in native communities.

Daniel Burston observed that common cultural categories and situations shape our sense of self and that "we can go further and say that *individual identities are syntheses of these social categories and inclusion, and to that extent they are social constructions.*" Many of these "categories of inclusion that the individual internalizes are categories of exclusion

as well."[31] Race, residence, and gender, for instance, are
three constructions and contingencies of identity.

Native stories are also wise, tricky, ironic, and delusions
of solidarity. For instance, the stories of native nicknames
are imagic moments, and the names are memorable experiences in many communities. Customarily, the tease of nicknames is an inclusive notice, the sanction of a presence in
stories; likewise, the ironic turn of nickname stories is an
act of native survivance and literary modernity.

The tease of nicknames and imagic moments might be
the tricky metaphors of genetic codes in native stories, as
the stories, ironic or otherwise, are "written into our bones
and skin and hair, there to be read by anyone who knows
the code," observed Rothman.

She noted that communities are "organized around the
question of what constitutes a person. That question is
asked at the borders of life, at birth and death, but it also is
asked at the borders between people." Race, she pointed out,
chooses the person. "Race is a code written upon the body.
Historically and consistently that code has been used as a
weapon. People read race to exclude, to identify the other,"
she wrote. "Knowing the code let people pick up runaway
'mulatto' slaves, catch Jews with false papers, identify the
'halfbreed' moving into town."

The genetic code is not "what unites us: we unite ourselves," she argued in the context of communities. "Identity politics is a rallying cry for people whose identity is imposed and devalued. We unite from below, and try to use
the messages that have been written on our bodies not to
separate, not as weapons against others, but as the threads
from which we can weave a community."[32]

The stories of imagic moments are inclusive and reciprocal, a native sense of presence and an "ontic significance" that cannot be reversed by the deceptive actions of racial separatists. Native names, stories, visions, trickster conversions, and connections to new communities are in the world of the book, a literary modernity.

8. Anishinaabe Pictomyths

The *anishinaabe* created by natural reason a sense of imagic presence and mythic survivance in the painted and incised pictures of animals, birds, and miniature characters on birch bark, wood, and stone. These images, or pictomyths, were venerated and carried into every native season, experience, and sacred histories.

The pictomyths on wood, bark, hide, and stone were created by visions and sustained by stories. Some photographs of ancestors are stories, the cues of remembrance, visual connections, intimations, and representations of time, place, and families, a new native totemic association alongside traditional images and pictomyths.

"Drawings were also made in the soft, dry ashes of a fire or on the dry earth," wrote Frances Densmore in *Chippewa Customs*. "The drawings in the ashes or in dry earth were usually a map, an illustration or a narrative, or a delineation used in the working of a charm."[1]

Densmore observed that the "figures included crude illustrations of men, animals, birds, and other material objects, and in the *midewiwin* symbols representing the sky, earth, lakes, and hills, as well as sounds and 'spirit power.' A simpler symbolism was used in messages and casual records, including signs to represent days, direction, and duplication of numbers."

The *anishinaabe midewiwin*, or Ojibwe Grand Medicine Society, "picture writing could be used to represent the name of a person," and the image of a dream might be represented "by a symbol painted" on a "blanket, or on the hide" of a wigwam.[2]

The figures painted on stone, on the face of granite, are more fantastic than any representations of natural motion or naturalism. There is no trace of face or hands in some visions and dream images, but explicit lines that show sound, voice, and heart. The "artist was groping toward the expression of the magical aspect of his life, rather than taking pleasure in the world of form around him," noted Selwyn Dewdney and Kenneth Kidd in *Indian Rock Paintings of the Great Lakes*. Essentially "the origin and purpose of these deceptively simple paintings remain a mystery."[3]

The *anishinaabe* pictomyths, transformations by vision and memory, and symbolic images, are totemic pictures and not directly related to emulsion photographs; yet, there is a sense of survivance, cultural memory, and strong emotive associations that bears these two sources of imagic presence in some native families.

The *anishinaabe* convene familiar cultural pictures, images and photographs of family, friends, and honorable political and historical figures. Native families rarely decorate the walls of their houses on reservations with pictures of strangers, or posters of classical or modern art; however, copies of expressionist paintings by George Morrison, David

Bradley, Frank Big Bear, Patrick DesJarlait, and many other native artists are appreciated in native homes.

Color photographs of President John F. Kennedy, and copies of portrait photographs of Geronimo, Chief Joseph, Sitting Bull, Bear's Belly, American Horse, Qahatika Girl, and many other distinguished natives photographed by the inimitable Edward Curtis, are not uncommon in many reservation homes.

Everlasting Sky, John Kakageesick, was not photographed by Edward Curtis, but he was a notable native at home in Warroad, Minnesota. Kakageesick is forever pictured in a simulated bright orange headdress on color postcards sold at the Warroad Historical Society.

Everlasting Sky was probably 124 years old at the time of his death in December 1968. I was a journalist for the *Minneapolis Tribune* at the time and reported the funeral ceremonies. By native tradition he would have been buried in his finest buckskin clothing, with his knees bent toward his chest, leaving the world in the same position of his birth, but the local mortician dressed the body of Kakageesick in a blue suit and white shirt enhanced in a fluffy satin metal coffin. He was buried, after a traditional honoring ceremony, in the Highland Park Cemetery.[4]

The Warroad Village Council publicly declared May 14, 1844, the estimated date of birth to celebrate his presence in the town. Everlasting Sky lived on a land allotment on Muskeg Bay, Lake of the Woods, and his personal experiences and memory reached beyond the establishment of the state and reservations. He was an adult at the time of the Civil War, and probably heard stories about President Abraham Lincoln.

Bruce White presented two photographs of Everlasting Sky in his memorable study of photographs of the *anishinaabe* in Minnesota. Kakageesick wears an elaborate headdress with a beaded headband in the postcard picture, and in the second photograph he wears a striped flannel shirt and holds a ceremonial pipe. Everlasting Sky "continued to live on his land south of the city until his death," wrote White. "He was a familiar figure in Warroad throughout his life. Postcards with his face on them came to symbolize the city's history and heritage."[5]

The Kodak Brownie, first introduced as an inexpensive cardboard box camera in 1900, provided a new and original source of native stories, the ready, arrested images of friends and family. The spare meniscus lens captured natives in ordinary scenes, and in common, untouched poses at home and at work, gathering wild rice and berries, curing hides, and preparing maple sugar.

The Brownie scenes of friends and family were almost always casual, and at times fortuitous in contrast to the studio photographs a generation earlier. The studio poses were formal, often ceremonious natives and families, in sharper focus, serious, retouched poses in front of ethereal backdrops. The box camera, however, inspired a new perception and consciousness of the real, of humans and nature, a new expressive, wondrous world of black, white, and grey eyes and hands in distinctive, arrested motion.

The eyes and hands are metaphors of presence in photographs, a sense of presence and right of natural stories in arrested expressions and gestures. The eyes are emotive, and some eyes seem to insinuate a moment of truth, rage, shame, a verity, even in the black and white shadows. Many native bodies are cultural object, dressed at times for the studio, and with the simulations of traditional vestments.

That sense of presence is evident in many verbal references to people and scenes in photographs. The present tense, more often than not, is used descriptively, and that creates a sense of presence. Mary Wind, for instance, wears high heel shoes in one photograph, rather than the past tense, she *wore* high heeled shoes. The present tense continues the sense of motion, presence, and survivance.

The Brownie Camera overturned the disposition of studio poses and masters of portraiture. The inexpensive box camera could easily be carried anywhere, and for that reason the photographs were more common, customary scenes, and sometimes the images inspired more personal stories. Studio and box camera pictures are equally and rightly treasured, nonetheless, and create a sense of presence in native memories and stories.

The Brownie Camera was a prelude to individuality and modernity, and yet the pleasure and practice of taking photographs scarcely superseded the direct traditional connection to stories about native images on bark, wood, and stone.

"Photography evades us," declared Roland Barthes in *Camera Lucida.* "Whatever it grants to vision and whatever its manner, a photograph is always invisible: it is not it that we see." The photograph "represents that very subtle moment when, to tell the truth, I am neither subject nor object but a subject who feels he is becoming an object."[6]

The *anishinaabe*, by their visionary practices, were always original, individualistic, and embraced with ironic confidence most industrial technologies of modernity, inexpensive telephones, automobiles, electrical power, refrigeration, and yet continue their stories that create a unique sense of cultural presence and survivance.

Bruce White presents in *We Are at Home: Pictures of the Ojibwe People* narrative portraits, studio and box camera photographs, of several *anishinaabe* generations. "In the 1850s photographers in St. Paul recorded Ojibwe leaders in their studios," observed White. "In these photographs Ojibwe leaders were recorded in the artificial surroundings of the studio, or 'gallery,' in poses that resembled European portraiture, wearing clothing sometimes not their own, holding objects that they did not own, but ones which fit the stereotypical views of whites."

"The process of understanding Ojibwe photographs departs from simplistic, surface interpretations enforced through stereotypical presentations and opens the photograph to new possibilities," wrote White.[7]

The photographs in the first chapter on *dikinaaganan*, cradleboards, show domestic scenes and situations, children, and infants in cradleboards near *waaginaagan*, a wigwam, "constructed of birch bark and woven mats." Decorative beadwork is pictured on other cradleboards, and there are scenes of native women at work with infants in cradleboards on their backs, resting against a tipi, and at peace in a hammock.

One photograph shows two native women standing on a wood plank sidewalk in front of a store, Confections and Tobacco's. One woman has her back turned to the camera to show her child and the decorative cradleboard. Nearby, a man watches the photographer from inside the store. He wears a white shirt and tie, and seems to be amused. The two women wear dark clothes. The man in the window is a distraction, and not the subject of the photograph taken about 1910 in northern Minnesota.

Roland Barthes described in *Camera Lucida* his "general, enthusiastic commitment" to photographs as *studium*, an appreciation and participation in the figures, faces, gestures, and actions. Likewise, a general appreciation of the *anishinaabe* in photographs is *studium*, a familiarity of the images of natives.

"To recognize the *studium* is inevitably to encounter the photographer's intentions, to enter into harmony with them, to approve or disapprove of them, but always to understand them, to argue them within myself," observed Barthes. Culture, the very source of *studium*, "is a contract arrived at between creators and consumers."[8]

The picture of the two native women, one with her back turned to show a cradleboard to the photographer, in front of Confections and Tobacco's, is appreciated by this theory of *studium*, a common cultural curiosity that animates the scene and photographic practice.

The concentration of this distinctive picture, and the apparent intention of the photograph to focus on a decorative cradleboard, is broken by the face of a man inside the store. The man is not part of the native scene, and, in fact, he seems to be amused by the entire situation and presence of the photographer.

Barthes used the word *punctum* to designate a break in the concentration and intention of the photographer. The *punctum* is a "wound," the photograph is "punctuated" by accident or chance. The face of the man inside the store, in this sense, is *punctum*, a "bruise" or "wound," in the concentration of the scene. The focus of the picture is punctuated by chance, a surprise that may arouse another interest in the picture. Barthes declared that *punctum* has the "power of expansion," or the power of one image or scene to change or expand the association of another.[9]

Harry Ayer photographed an *anishinaabe* couple, Tom and Mary Wind, and their baby, in front of Miller's Tea Room, Wigwam Bay, at Lake Mille Lacs about 1925. Mary wears a print dress, silk stockings, high heel shoes with leather strap, and carries a baby wrapped in a quilt on her back. Tom Wind wears a wool driving cap, long sleeve shirt, and rubber hip boots. There is no trace of native traditions. Mary's slip and Tom's waders are the only apparent *punctum* is this photograph.

Bruce White presents a wide range of photographs of *ogimaag* leaders and provides a cogent discussion of the conditions of leadership and political authority in communities. The "earliest photographs of Ojibwe leaders resembled paintings, following styles of portraiture perfected by centuries of European artists," wrote White. "These photographs generally included the face, arms, and torso of their subjects, each subject wrapped in a blanket, sometimes holding a few symbolic objects such as pipes and weapons."[10]

Joel Whitney, a prominent pioneer photograph of *anishinaabe* leaders, established a portrait studio more than a century ago on Third and Cedar in Saint Paul, Minnesota. Whitney photographed many native leaders who were in the city to meet with "government officials at the Territorial and later State Capitol." White pointed out that these "Indian portraits do not appear to have been done for the

Indians themselves, but rather to be sold to white customers. Among these photographs are at least thirty portraits of Ojibwe leaders."[11] Whitney sold many of these photographs as *cartes de visite* portraits mounted on cards.

Whitney photographed Naganab, or Foremost Sitter, in his studio. Naganab was active in the fur trade and a leader at Fond du Lac in Minnesota. "Naganab was known for his diplomatic eloquence," observed White. He wore a presidential peace medal and was a representative at several treaty conferences with the government of the United States. "We think the time is past when we should take a hat and put it on our heads just to mimic the white man, to adopt his custom without being allowed any of the privileges that belong to him. We wish to stand on a level with the white man in all things," Naganab told government officials. "I call upon all the commissioners to use their influence that our place shall be made as permanent as the north star, which never changes its location."[12]

"Nindabimin, We Are at Home" presents pictures of various structures, ceremonial, grave houses, and family houses of the *anishinaabe*. The *waaginaagon*, wigwam, for instance, was covered by birch bark, *wiigwaas*, over a dome structure of tamarack. The birch bark structures were replaced by log and frame houses in the nineteenth century. "Certainly fur traders had been building log structures of various designs among the Ojibwe for hundreds of years," wrote White. "When the United States government sought to move Ojibwe people from throughout Minnesota to the White Earth Reservation, one promise made was that a log or frame house would be built for those who moved."[13]

Edward Bromley, a newspaper photographer, visited

the White Earth Reservation more than a century ago and photographed George Lufkin, his wife, and three children standing on the porch of a frame house with glass windows. George wears a black fedora, four-button coat, and leather boots. His wife wears a stylish blouse, long dress with checked patterns, pleated at the hem, and she holds a child in a striped shirt. The two other children wear school uniforms, double-breasted black coats, caps, and high top leather shoes. The eldest boy wears an oversized coat, the sleeves hang almost to his knees, the *punctum* in this picture. The great coat punctuates the experiences of a child at federal school, and the expansion of fugitive stories in the picture.

Robert G. Beaulieu lived and practiced photography about a century ago on the White Earth Reservation. He was probably the first professional native photographer. Beaulieu's photographs are memorable, high contrast communal scenes and events, including the White Earth Band. Augustus H. Beaulieu, his older brother, and his cousin, Theodore H. Beaulieu, established the first newspaper on the White Earth Reservation. *The Progress* was first published on March 25, 1886.

Bugonaygeshig, or *bagone giizhig*, Hole in the Day, an eminent native warrior, was photographed by James S. Drysdale, Walker, Minnesota, shortly after the war at Sugar Point, near Bear Island in Leech Lake. The Third Infantry had invaded the reservation, in search of Bugonaygeshig, on October 5, 1898. The Third Infantry was surrounded overnight, and with no provisions. The Pillagers, only nineteen warriors, defeated more than seventy immigrant soldiers and won the war in one day.[14]

Hole in the Day, the Pillager warrior, is pictured in a structure of a maple sugar lodge. He wears a fedora, an ammu-
nition belt, and cradles a Winchester rifle on his arm. The
most memorable *punctum* in this photograph is the heavy
necklace, a collection of spent rifle shells fired by the army
at Sugar Point. The necklace is an ironic remembrance of
native survivance.

"*Biboonagad*, A Year Goes By" presents photographs of
natives at work in the four seasons. The *anishinaabe* hunt,
fish, gather *manoomin*, wild rice, pick berries, prepare hides,
maple sugar, and build various structures. There are several
photographs of the stages of building a birch bark canoe.
These active, communal scenes are seldom seen in studio
photographs. The inexpensive box camera made it possible
to photograph natives fully occupied in almost any activity.
White provides a precise narrative about the many seasonal
activities of the *anishinaabe*. The women, for instance, sew
the birch bark to the cedar frame. Once the birch bark was
sewn to the cedar, the women "coated the bottom of the
canoe with a pitch" made of boiled spruce resin.

"From the earliest photographs of Ojibwe people taken
by whites it is hard to find adequate and balanced representations of people's lives," declared Bruce White. "Studio
portraits of people standing alone against a painted back-
drop usually give few clues to the relationship of people pictured to other people, how they lived their lives, their spiritual beliefs, the values that mattered to them."[15]

White overturns the simulations of stoical, isolated natives in studio portrait photographs in "*Bimaadiziwin*, The
Circle of Life." He presents a diverse natural domain of natives in active, communal situations. There are pictures of

190   spiritual leaders, unique characters, families, ceremonial
associations, singers, drummers, and dancers. Many of
the scenes pictured in this chapter provide a visual continuity of communal activity. The photograph of the White
Earth Reservation dance on June 14, 1924, is an annual ceremonial event today. The United States flag is at the center of the dance grounds, and the dancers circle the Stars
and Stripes. The thousands of native men and women who
served their country during many wars, and those who lost
their lives, are honored at the annual dances.

"*Anishinaabeg*, The People" presents "individual stories
and experiences of the people photographed," wrote White.
"When examined in this context, Ojibwe photographs are
one part of a rich record of struggle, survival, and triumph
though many generations."[16] These are pictures and stories
that inspire a sense of native presence and survivance.

9. Edward Curtis

Kevin Gover, the assistant interior secretary, apologized for the many transgressions of the Bureau of Indian Affairs. "This agency set out to destroy all things Indian," he said at an anniversary celebration of the agency, according to David Stout of the *New York Times*. "The legacy of these misdeeds haunts us," said Gover. "Our hearts break."[1]

Gover is a member of the Pawnee Tribe. He was born in Lawton, Oklahoma, graduated from Princeton University, and the University of New Mexico Law School. His career and native feats are singular; yet, his nominal regrets are ironic after more than a century of federal policy deceits, chicanery, manifest manners, and cultural dominance.

The native story, however, is not only in the text of his apology; the story is in the visual analogies of the large photograph above the news article. Gover is pictured in a decisive pose near a framed portrait of Bear Bull. The Blackfoot was photographed by Edward Curtis, who first visited the tribe at the end of the nineteenth century with George Bird Grinnell.

Gover looks almost to the left in the newspaper photograph. Bear Bull looks to the right of the scene, a pensive, pictorialist profile. Gover bears a studied smile; he is pictured as an approachable native lawyer who wears spectacles, a white shirt, dark necktie, and long hair. Bear Bull is an ancient image, a man of great creases, evident traditions, and coarse braided hair. His lips, slightly parted, are close to a whisper, and his eyes seem to be focused in the distance.

These two natives, a lawyer and a traditionalist, separated by four generations, reservations, and distinctive cultures are aware of the camera. Credibly, they are both about their survivance poses in the presence of photographers; they are bound by native analogies and the common history of the camera. Gover was photographed by Carol Powers for the news story in the *New York Times*. Bear Bull was captured forever in a picture by Edward Curtis. The analogy of these native images is pictorialist, a double reference to the native past and futurity.

Gover is native, but his apology for the agency was ironic, not cultural; rather, a plaintive, political simulation of the past that should have been made by someone other than a native. Bear Bull stands alone, close to the camera, an aesthetic, pictorial pose, the intended image and idea of the vanished race by Edward Curtis.

Curtis pictures may, in fact, be the choice of more natives than any other photographer. This association, in my view, is aesthetic, not ethnographic; natives, at last, may stand with the visual analogies of artists more than with the language of social scientists.

Curtis, however, presented his photographs, notes, and

cultural observations as ethnographic. He argued against those detractors who petitioned the government that he was not a trained ethnographer, and that his work was not decisive. Three generations later the native heirs choose his photographic images for reasons other than the politics of the social sciences. Perhaps natives praise the visual analogy.

Why would natives pose to create a portrait simulation, a pictorial image not their own, for photographic adventurists who later nominate their pictures as the *real*, and the ethnographic documents of a vanishing race?

Perhaps for the money and tricky camera stories.

Why, several generations later, would natives embrace these romantic pictures as real moments of their own cultural memories?

Perhaps the images create a sense of native presence, a visual analogy. Or, perhaps it is a cult of native remembrance. "In photography, exhibition value begins to displace cult value," wrote Walter Benjamin in *Illuminations*. "But cult value does not give way without resistance. It retires into an ultimate retrenchment: the human countenance. It is no accident that the portrait was the focal point of early photography. The cult of remembrance of loved ones, absent or dead, offers a last refuge for the cult value of the picture."[2]

Richard Kearney argued in *The Wake of Imagination* that the "human ability to 'image' or 'imagine' something has been understood in two main ways throughout the history of Western thought." The first is a "*representational* faculty which reproduces images" of some reality; the second is a "*creative* faculty which produces images" that stand alone.

"These basic notions of imagination" refer to "everyday experience" and "artistic practices."[3]

The modernist constructions of culture, with natives outside of rational, cosmopolitan consciousness, are simulations by separation, a sense of native absence over presence in history. The absence of natives was represented by images of traditions, simulations of the other in the past; the presence of natives was tragic, the notions of savagism and the emotive images of a vanishing race. The modernist images of native absence and presence, by creative or representational faculties, are the rational binary structures of the other, an aesthetic, ideological disanalogy.

The absence of natives is the simulated presence of the other in the narratives of cultural dominance. The actual presence of natives is ironic in ethnography. "The absence of the Other from our Time has been his mode of presence in our discourse—as an object and victim," observed Johannes Fabian in Time and the Other. "That is what needs to be overcome; more ethnography of Time will not change this situation."[4]

The modernist possession of the other, however exotic the fugitive poses, objective reason, and creative images, has no obvious, comparable humanistic worth as an absence, because notions of discovery, theories of evolution and material culture, and other simulations of indians, must be new, forever hyperreal even as cultures vanishes, otherwise the captured images and museum artifacts would be rated as no more than "courteous kitsch." Ironically, kitschy simulations somehow "authenticate" the bourgeois worth of secular kachinas and doorstop coyotes.[5]

The distinctions and discrepancies of pictorial, ethnographic, and detractive visual images of natives are not easily resolved by cultural evidence, censure, or the politics of identity. Crucial to the resolution of these vagaries of photographic esteem is a visual method of interpretation; a choice of metaphors and visual reason that does not separate natives as the other in an eternal academic disanalogy.

Barbara Maria Stafford argued in *Visual Analogy* for the recuperation of the "ancient and intrinsically visual method of analogy for modern times." Analogy is the "human desire to achieve union" with the other. She pointed out that the "visual arts are singularly suited to provide explanatory power for the nature and function of the analogical procedure."[6]

Edward Curtis created pictorialist images of natives, but most of the interpretations are ethnographic. The creation of visual images, in other words, is represented by linguistic authority. Pointedly, photographic images are bound by the structures of language. Stafford argued that language is a "godlike agency in western culture," and to free "graphic expression from an unnuanced dominant discourse of consumerism, corruption, deception, and ethical failure is a challenge that cuts across the arts, humanities, and sciences."[7]

Semir Zeki likewise observed in *Inner Vision* that "language is a relatively recent evolutionary acquisition, and it has yet to catch up with and match the visual system in its capacity to extract essentials so efficiently."[8]

Analogy is an active, aesthetic, creative connection in the visual arts, and in the sense of natives, analogy is a desire to achieve a human union in visual images, rather than a cultural separation in language. Analogy absolves

196   the distance and discrepancies of pictorialist and ethnographic pictures of natives by restoring a sense of visual
reason. Bear Bull and Kevin Gover come together by choice
and cameras, and by the metaphors of similitude in the adventures of native poses.

Analogy "demands that we take seriously the problem
of correlation," wrote Stafford. Analogy "is central both
to ancient religions and to a modern anthropology of the
senses." Analogy is a creative, visual process, but it was "sup-
planted by the elevation of atomistic difference: the obsession with unbridgeable imparity and the hieratic insistence
on insurmountable distance between the material and spiritual realms." Analogy "has the virtue of making distant
peoples, other periods, and even diverse contemporary con-
texts part of our world." Stafford wants to "recuperate the
lost link between visual images and concepts, the intuitive
ways in which we think simple by visualizing."[9]

Consider the learned theories and studied pictures of natives as the "hieratic insistence" on disanalogy. Ethnology,
for instance, became a sacred association in the studies of
native cultures. William John McGee, the "ethnologist in
charge" at the Bureau of American Ethnology in the late
nineteenth century outlined the goals of his agency in this
way: "Ethnologists, like other good citizens, are desirous
of raising the Indian to the lofty plane of American citizenship; but they prefer to do this constructively rather than
destructively, through knowledge rather than ignorance,
through sympathy rather than intolerance," wrote McGee.
Ethnologists "prefer to pursue in dealing with our immature race the course found successful in dealing with the
immature offspring of our own flesh and blood."

Curtis announced similar racialist notions that natives were comparable to children. The notion of natives as immature was a common theory of evolution at the time. Many scientists were involved in a harsh debate over monogenism, a single origin, and polygenism, many origins. These notions of creation were used to explain distinctive native cultures, and native resistance to cultural dominance.

Early in the nineteenth century many "critics began to question the monogenetic assumptions, set forth in the Bible, that all mankind shared the same origin," wrote Robert Bieder in *Science Encounters the Indian*. "Increasingly they began to explain Indians' recalcitrant nature in terms of polygenism. To polygenists Indians were separately created and were an inferior species of man."[10]

Natives were first simulated as savages in the common cultural binaries of savagism and civilization. Then, by chicanery, federal treaties, and military means natives were removed to reservations and nominated the vanishing race at the end of the nineteenth century.

American civilization was a cultural manifest, and a religious covenant over bogus savagism. The "Indian was the remnant of a savage past away from which civilized men had struggled to grow," wrote Roy Harvey Pearce in *Savagism and Civilization*. "To study him was to study the past. To civilize him was to triumph over the past. To kill him was to kill the past. History would thus be the key to the moral worth of cultures." American civilization progressed from "past to present, from east to west, from lower to higher." Pearce pointed out that those "who could not journey to see Indians in person could see them pictured in numerous collections of Indian sketches and portraits."[11]

Edward Curtis was born in Wisconsin in 1868. Naturally, he grew into the popular simulations and tragic narratives about natives. He likely read or was aware of dime novels, captivity narratives, and the sensational newspaper stories of the evanescence of the transient savages. As a young man he must have seen sketches of natives and reproductions of portraits by George Catlin and Charles Bird King. Curtis was curious, no doubt, and eager to understand the history and literature of his time.

Curtis opened a photographic studio shortly after he moved with his family, at the end of the nineteenth century, to Puget Sound. Curtis lost his father, and while he assumed the responsibilities of his family, his circumstances improved as a photographer. At the same time, natives lost their land, human rights, a sense of presence, and were pictured as the tragic cultures of a vanishing race. Sitting Bull had been shot by soldiers, and then, two weeks later, hundreds of Ghost Dancers were massacred by Seventh Cavalry soldiers on December 29, 1890, at Wounded Knee. Curtis was a man of nature, a mountaineer and adventurist, but surely he could not have been unaware of newspaper stories about these native miseries. His first pictures must have drawn him into many conversations about natives. Curtis was motivated, after all, to pursue a photographic record of the last natives, and he did so with romantic, pictorial images that ran against the popular notions of the savage.

Many American newspapers created and promoted stories of savagism and the vanishing race. The Civil War, and later the telegraph, changed journalism and the way news was reported. Press associations and "cooperative news gathering" were inspired by the telegraph. War "increased newspaper readership and stimulated new competition between urban newspapers," observed John Coward in *The Newspaper Indian*. Editors "discovered that they could increase their profits when they published stories about major battles," including, of course, conflicts with natives.[12]

Journalists, at the time, were too close to the western adventures of the army, and many thought that native cultures "could be easily known and explained by simple observation," noted Coward. "The 'vanishing Indian' theme was especially popular in the nineteenth century, when native cultures did seem to be fading before the westward rush of white settlement." Clearly, "newspapers played a major role in creating and maintaining popular Indian identities in the nineteenth century." The press, however, was not alone in the promotion of the savage. George Catlin and many other artists, photographers, politicians, and an entire cultural system created the image and historical idea of the tragic savage at the vanishing point.[13]

Sitting Bull, the Lakota healer, for instance, was known largely through simulations and "newspaper representations," especially in the sensational stories on the Battle of the Little Bighorn. The *New York Times* raised a catch question about Sitting Bull: Was he "an extremely savage type, betraying that bloodthirstiness and brutality for which he has so long been notorious?" Sitting Bull was a native humanist; however, the image of the savage was created by newspaper reporters, readers, strangers. "The Sitting Bull of the papers and the man himself were often worlds apart."[14]

Luther Standing Bear, the author and actor, had graduated from the Carlisle Indian Industrial School and was working at John Wanamaker's department store in Philadelphia

when he read in a newspaper that Sitting Bull was sched-
uled to lecture in the city. "The paper stated that he was the
Indian who killed General Custer! The chief and his people
had been held prisoners of war, and now here they were to
appear" in a theater, Standing Bear wrote in *My People the
Sioux*. "A white man came on the stage and introduced Sitting Bull as the man who had killed General Custer," which
was not true. "Sitting Bull arose and addressed the audience in the Sioux tongue, as he did not speak nor understand English. He said, 'My friends, white people, we Indians are on our way to Washington to see the Grandfather,
or President of the United States. I see so many white people and what they are doing, that it makes me glad to know
that some day my children will be educated also. There is
no use fighting any longer. The buffalo are all gone, as
well as the rest of the game. Now I am going to shake the
hand of the Great Father at Washington, and I am going to
tell him all these things.' Then Sitting Bull sat down. He
never even mentioned General Custer's name." His lecture
was translated as the story of the massacre at the Little Big
Horn. The white man "told so many lies I had to smile,"
wrote Standing Bear.[15]

Curtis created his picture "The Vanishing Race" in 1904.
The photogravure, published three years later in the first
of his mighty twenty-volume *The North American Indian*, de-
picts a column of natives lost in the shadows, a sentimental
evanescence. Mick Gidley rightly argues in *Edward S. Curtis
and the North American Indian, Incorporated* that the "ideological thrust of the heritage of photographic pictorialism in
Curtis's images worked, almost synergistically, to disguise,
even deny, what was, in fact and effect, a seemingly almost

endless series of damaging political and economic deci-sions."[16] These decisions based on agency policies and new federal laws, such as the allotment act that reduced native treaty land by more than half, were carried out in the presence of Edward Curtis.

"The thought that this picture is meant to convey is that the Indians as a race, already shorn of their tribal strength and stripped of their primitive dress, are passing into the darkness of an unknown future," Curtis wrote in the caption to "The Vanishing Race." About the same time he wrote in Scribner's Magazine that the "relationship of the Indians and people of this country is that of a child and parent. We will stand convicted for all time as a parent who failed in his duty." He declared that natives were "being ground beneath the wheel of civilization, and though we may be able to justify our claims that advancement and progress demand the extermination of the Indians, we can scarcely justify the method used in this extermination."[17] Curtis, of course, would always be the master of the pictures.

Remarkably, this haunting photograph, "The Vanishing Race," was created less than a decade after he first aimed a cumbersome view camera at Princess Angeline, the native daughter of Chief Seattle. "I paid the princess a dollar for each picture made," wrote Curtis. "This seemed to please her greatly and with hands and jargon she indicated that she preferred to spend her time having pictures made than in digging clams."[18]

Curtis paid natives to pose; he selected ornaments, vestments, played the natural light, tone, picturesque reflections, and the solitary nature of natives in his pictures. The pictorial images of pensive warriors are simulations of the real; transmuted in visual analogies. The aesthetic poses of natives countered the cruelties of reservations and binaries of savagism and civilization.

"In terms of pictorialist aesthetics, posing contributed positively to the final image," observed Christopher Lyman in The Vanishing Race and Other Illusions. "In terms of ethnography, posing did 'injustice to scientific accuracy.'"[19] Curtis paid natives to pose and dance in several simulated ceremonies, but he may not have understood native resistance or the actual tricky scenes he captured. The motion picture of Navajo Yebechai Prayer, for instance, was probably transposed by chance, but many natives believe that the dance was reversed as an act of resistance, and to protect the sacred. The dancers held rattles in the wrong hand.

Curtis, however, may not have been at the actual ceremonies that he simulated in his pictures. He staged the dances out of season. "Navajo sensibilities" clearly were not his "primary considerations." Curtis used "not only 'phony' costumes, additions, and poses," observed James Faris in Navajo and Photography, "but, indeed, in some cases, actual phony Navajo."[20]

Curtis is lauded as a pictorialist, but not favorably reviewed as an ethnographic photographer. Yet his pictures are rarely mentioned in historical references to the pictorialists, or Photo-Session, at the turn of the twentieth century in New York City. Curtis was not of the salons or societies that established the aesthetic, pictorial arts of photography; his focus was more ideological, a photographic rescue artist. He posed as an ethnographer out to capture the last images of a vanishing race. To do this, of course, he paid for native poses, staged, altered, and manipulated his pictures to create an ethnographic simulation as a pictorialist. Clearly, he was an outsider, too far removed from the photographic salons to court or count on ready shows and reviews that had instituted pictorialist photography. Curtis, moreover, had received a five-year endowment from the financier John Pierpont Morgan to produce twenty volumes of *The North American Indian*. The project actually lasted more than twenty years.

Alfred Stieglitz founded the Photo-Session, a group of pictorialist photographers dedicated to expressive, picturesque images and the aesthetic art of creating pictures. "Stieglitz was himself a proponent of what came to be known as 'straight photography,'" noted Christopher Lyman. The "straight" school "asserted that photography had its own pure aesthetics which should not be diluted by extensive manipulation of its process."[21]

Gertrude Käsebier and other pictorialists had once experimented with ethnic and native images, but they soon focused on other subjects. Curtis, on the other hand, was dedicated to natives and the politics of the vanishing race. He visited more than eighty distinct native communities, some more than once, and created more than forty thousand photographs. Most notably, he published twenty volumes of his photogravures, *The North American Indian*.

Stieglitz and the Photo-Session associated as aesthetic, modernist photographers to advance pictorialist expression, to support the art practice, and to hold exhibitions of pictorial images. Photographic salons were established in several cities, and both "straight" and pictorialist pictures were presented in exhibitions. The *New York Times*, in a review of an exhibition of photographs at the Montross

Galleries in New York in 1912, noted that the "advocates of pure or 'straight' photography feel that by manipulating a print you lose the purity of tone which belongs especially to the photographic medium in trying to get effects that can be more satisfactorily obtained with the painter's brush."[22] Stieglitz was a "straight," photographic impressionist; at the same time he advanced the artistic practices of the pictorialists. These practices countered the common snapshot of popular culture.

John Tagg wrote in *The Burden of Representation* that photography was rather "common as to be unremarkable" in the late nineteenth century. Pictorialists reacted and sought "to reinstate the 'aura' of the image and distinguish their work aesthetically from that of commercial and amateur photographs." He argued that the revolution was not pictorialist, but a new means of political control. "It was no longer a privilege to be pictured but the burden of a new class of the surveilled," wrote Tagg.[23]

Curtis created simulations of surveillance, the pictorialist pose of ethnographic images. He removed parasols, suspenders, wagons, the actual traces of modernism and material culture in his pictures of natives. Curtis was a pictorialist, but his removal practices were ideological, a disanalogy. He created altered images of the vanishing race at the same time that thousands of native scholars graduated from federal and mission schools. Luther Standing Bear had returned to the reservation as a teacher. Charles Eastman returned as the first native medical doctor on the Pine Ridge Reservation. Curtis may not have noticed native resistance or survivance. Clearly he was an adventurist, sometimes blindsided by his own vanity, debts, and the

politics of ethnography. He pursued pictures of an undoc-
umented vanishing race.

"Curtis was concerned about criticism of *The North American Indian* by professional ethnologists," noted Christopher Lyman. "He explained away their skepticism, however, as a reaction to inflated accounts of his work in the popular press." Curtis "was selling images to a popular audience whose perception of 'Indianness' was based on stereotypes."[24] He was motivated, of course, to remain in the favor of ethnologists.

Curtis created the picture "Ogalala War-Party" at a time when natives were starving on reservations. Surely he was not insensitive to the adversities of natives, but his pictures reveal only the simulations of the vanishing race. He paid natives to pose as warriors at a time when their rights were denied, and their treaties were scorned and evaded by federal agents and the military. Curtis was a dedicated pictorialist, but he assuredly miscarried the ethics of his vested situation on reservations and in native communities. Yes, he was indeed answerable for his time with natives, not by historical revisionism, but because he boldly advanced his career in the presence of native torment and worried hearts.

Lyman noted that Curtis, "like that of most people of the period, seemed preoccupied with images of Dakota 'hostility.' The caption for 'Ogalala War-Party' explains, 'Here is depicted a group of Sioux warriors as they appeared in the days of intertribal warfare, carefully making their way down a hillside in the vicinity of the enemy's camp.'" Curtis created a simulation of a native absence and an ethnographic presence.

The photogravure "In a Piegan Lodge," published in *The*

North American Indian, was retouched by the crude removal of a clock. The original negative pictures the clock in a small box on the ground between two natives. Curtis removed the clock to save a simulation of traditional authority. The picture with the clock has a curious elegance and inspires a visual analogy. The retouched photogravure without the clock is fakery and disanalogy.[25]

Dino Brugioni outlined "four distinct kinds of faked photographs" in *Photo Fakery*. The first two are the removal and insertion of details, and the other two are photomontage, and false captions. Curtis was clearly a photographic faker by his removal and insertions of details, and by false captions.

"Photography transcends natural boundaries and verbal language and is probably the most important vehicle for advancing ideas, and ideals, throughout the world," wrote Brugioni. "When a photo is manipulated in any way, truth is compromised; when truth is compromised, distrust begins. Distrust produces a lack of faith in the media," he noted, but photography "has always been manipulated."[26]

Curtis created by strategic manipulations pictures of native disanalogy. Presumably, he was a likable, lonesome adventurist in native communities. He wrote about a sense of natural peace at campsites, but he had been weakened by time, promises, many debts, and the dubious praise of politicians.

Curtis simulated natives as the absolute absence of civilization and modernity. He was a cultural separatist, and a racialist of his time. Yet, his ethical demerits as a photo faker are not ours. Today, the natives in his pictures, but not the simulated *indians* of his photographic missions, await the recuperation of visual analogy.

10. George Morrison

George Morrison is a man of natural light, an eternal, elusive shimmer on the "endless space" of a horizon. I am inspired by his native vision and sense of liberty, and admire his dedication to the creation of marvelous expressionist landscapes.

I first told him that some thirty years ago. He was always modest, even shy. He was gracious and diverted my praise with an invitation to share a bottle of imported red wine. George was a connoisseur of art and fine wine. We talked about expressionism in art and literature, the sentiments of native art, and the politics of aesthetic resistance, that spring afternoon at his spectacular home, a restyled church in Saint Paul. At the time he was a professor of studio art at the University of Minnesota. I was a journalist, an editorial writer for the *Minneapolis Tribune*.

George was amused by the thought that we might have met and become friends in Greenwich Village in 1955. I was a military veteran and a first year student at New York University that same year he drank with Franz Kline, Willem de Kooning, and other good friends and artists at the Cedar

Street Tavern near Washington Square. He was thirty-six years old at the time, the first native artist to achieve international recognition as an abstract expressionist.

George Morrison has inspired and influenced many native artists and creative writers. I honor his courage as a creative artist, and might have found my confidence as a native writer much earlier if we had become friends that year in Greenwich Village. Morrison was a perceptive apostle of native liberty.

Horizon Lines

George Morrison teased the elusive hues and mighty blaze of colors, the rise and weave of wood, and the ancient creases of stone. He envisioned an eternal horizon in his memorable creations, an aesthetic meditation on the tones of nature and natural liberty.

"The basis of all art is nature," he told Margot Fortunato Galt in *Turning the Feather Around*. The North Shore of Lake Superior "was subconsciously in my psyche, prompting some of my images."[1] Morrison was nurtured in the true presence of indigenous sounds and light created by the seasons of the lake. He conceived of these images in the abstract rush of colors and memory, not in the mere academic representations of the natural world. Clearly he perceived that nature was never silence, but a brace of color and music.

Morrison was inspired by expressionism, an art movement already underway at the time of his birth, September 30, 1919, in Chippewa City, Minnesota, a native village located near the Grand Portage Reservation. He was born at home, a descendant of the Raven totem of the *anishinaabe*, otherwise known as the people named the Chippewa.[2] His

surname marks a union of curious voyageurs, the fur trade,
and cultural transcendence.

Morrison was carried as an infant, or *abinoojiiyens*, in
the language of the people, by his mother in a *dikinaagan*,
a cradleboard, crafted in the traditional way by his father.
"I was wrapped in buckskin of cloth decorated with beadwork by my mother," he wrote in *This Song Remembers*. "There
were twelve children in our family, crowded into a small
frame house without electricity or plumbing. We were often hungry and sick."[3]

Morrison learned the words and stories of primary colors in two languages, a source of envisioned tone, concentration, and intuitive artistry. The *anishinaabe* word *inaazo*,
an animate verb that means, in translation, "colored a certain way," traces the native sensibilities of his expressionist art. The word *misko*, "red," for instance, is a preverb of
visual memory, as in *miskomin*, "raspberry," *miskwaawaak*,
"red cedar," *miskwi*, "blood," and in *miskwazhe*, "to have
measles." He likely observed the tricky tone of *ozhaawashko*,
a word that means blue and green, the transcendence of a
bruise, *ozhaawashko aniibiish*, "green tea," and *ozhaawashko
bineshiinh*, "bluebird." The preverb *ozaawi* signifies the color
brown and yellow, as in *ozaawikosimaan*, "pumpkin," *ozaa-
windibe*, to "be blond" or "have brown hair," and *ozaawi
bimide*, "butter."[4]

"I believe in going back to the magic of the earth and
the lake, the sky and the universe. That kind of magic. I
believe in that kind of religion," he declared. "A religion
of the rocks, the lake, the water, the sky. Yes, that's what
I believe in."[5]

Morrison was given two sacred names, Turning the Feather Around and, Standing in the Northern Lights, at a healing ceremony. These names inspired a sense of a native presence and survivance. "Walter Caribou did a healing ceremony for me. I was very ill, and living here at Grand Portage facing the lake," said Morrison. Caribou "dreamed two names—one dream, two names. Maybe I was on my way to recovery. Maybe what he did helped to make me well. You never know."[6]

Morrison survived several serious medical conditions and then in his sixties he was diagnosed with a rare disease of the lymphatic system. As a child he was disabled by tuberculosis of the hip and treated for more than a year at the Gillette State Hospital for Crippled Children in Saint Paul, Minnesota. "Actually, it was kind of a good period. I was eleven, doing a lot of reading, and then there was a lot of interaction with the other kids," he reminisced with characteristic liberal irony. "I was able to exchange ideas with other children. The hospital had a good program. I went to school there, was active with art projects, did a lot of reading and became more introspective."

"After the operation I was able to walk for the first time in almost a year, but I had a stiffer leg. The doctors had fused the hip."[7] He returned to high school in Grand Marais, Minnesota, and was the first in his family to graduate. He was encouraged by his teachers to study at the Minneapolis School of Art.

"I found myself naturally inclined to draw. Doodling is another word for making some kind of images on paper," he said. "When I started going to school, I got things from kids by swaps. I used to make illustrations for some of the town kids, for their schoolwork. Then they would give me a swap—a jackknife or something."[8]

He studied advertising, at first, because he had started in commercial art; later he transferred to fine arts at the Minneapolis School of Art. "There were a lot of design courses and color courses. Color came naturally to me. I fell right into it; I did well," said Morrison. "Everybody did much the same thing. Everybody drew the figure. And everyone's figure was pretty much the same. From that time at art school, there are only a few of my paintings still in existence." The *Dirt Track Specialist*, a "fairly realistic" portrait, was done with a palette knife, "but very fine, exacting work. Not a slick painting like the kind the academics were teaching. They were very slick. I guess certain students, including myself, were reacting against the academicism."[9]

Morrison matured with a physical disability, in dire poverty, and at an insurmountable cultural distance, one might surmise, from the princely salons of modern art that once shunned and later celebrated the subjective tease and prompts of abstract expressionism. Morrison, however, would continue the visionary practices of native artistry, probably unaware of that singular association at the time, with his own creations in wood, and in his paintings, waves of brilliant, layered pigment.

The *anishinaabe* painted and incised subjective, surreal pictures on wood and stone. Many centuries later similar images were renewed on spiritual scrolls, beaded patterns on clothes, ceremonial objects, and in contemporary art. Surely the ancient pictures are atavistic expressions, the intuitive course of nature on a mythic horizon.

Morrison, in an interview, endorsed the "influence of

surrealism" in his horizon pictures. "There is no evidence of sentiment" and "no literal translation of people, sky or water." He pointed out that the "landscapes, by definition, are the horizon lines," and the bright, thick colors are "more surreal than literal or realistic."[10]

Morrison circumvented academicism, or traditional, artistic formularies at the Minneapolis School of Art. He was never a "slick" painter, and his surreal, artistic expressions served no social or cultural possession of nature or satiny landscapes. Likewise, nature was neither a genre nor an object of cultural sentiments in his early landscapes.

"One might put this even more simply," observed John Berger in *Ways of Seeing*. "The sky has no surface and is intangible; the sky cannot be turned into a thing or given a quantity. And landscape painting begins with the problem of painting the sky and distance."[11] Morrison absolved these naturalistic teasers with the shimmer of horizon lines.

Morrison imparted a common, personal, and always communal manner. He was liberal, an advocate of certain radical native causes, and, at the same time, an elusive visionary. He justly resisted the notion that there was an essential connection between traditional culture and creative art. He argued that the identity of the artist does not decide the meaning or determine the merit of the art. The *anishinaabe* and other native artists create more than the mere simulations, primitive silhouettes and masterly slogans of discovery cultures.

"I never played the role of being an Indian artist. I always just stated the fact that I was a painter, and I happened to be Indian. I wasn't exploiting the idea of being Indian at all, or using Indian themes," he told Margot Fortunato

Galt. "But as my work became better known, some critics would pick up on my Indian background, and they'd make something of it. I guess they were looking for a way to understand my work."[12]

Morrison created small pictures at the end of his career, at a time when he was recovering from the lymphatic disease. The horizon pictures are visionary, surrealist expressions of color, contours, textures, traces of light, and many images afloat. Mottled, mythic creatures, for instance, are buoyant, suspended over the shore in the pencil and ink picture *Landscape/Seascape with Surrealist Forms: Red Rock Variations*, 1984. The earth is burnt orange, the water is dark, the creatures are red, and the horizon line is a primeval union, a natural transcendence of time, distance, and memory.

"I can see the lake change by the hour, from blue to yellow and rose" outside the studio windows at Grand Portage. "Dramatic things happen in the sky, with clouds and color," said Morrison. "The basic thing in all the paintings is the horizon line which identifies each little work as a broad expanse of a segment of the earth." He created abstract figures of nature with layers of primary colors. At times he used a muted palette to "catch a range of light after sunrise or before sunset." The one "thing that makes the little paintings vibrant is the layering of colors. I might start with red, then stipple on the opposite or complement of that, blue, then come back to red, then another cold color. The color way underneath comes through to the surface and gives the sensation of shimmering movement."[13]

Nature is a natural shimmer, a bounce of light and chance of colors. Philip Ball pointed out in *Bright Earth* that "nature had more hues than the artist." Morrison decidedly perceived the variations of natural light and created a dance of hues by layers of primary, saturated pigments. Ball noted that the "picture is never finished," because the colors change evermore with time. "No artist has ever painted an image frozen in time; all painting is a perpetual process, with every scene destined to rearrange its tonal contrasts as time does its work on the pigments."[14]

Morrison said he was "fascinated with ambiguity, change of mood and color, the sense of sound and movement above and below the horizon line," and therein "lies some of the mystery of the paintings: the transmutation, through choosing and manipulating the pigment, that becomes the substance of art."[15] The Minnesota Museum of Art exhibited sixty-one of his small paintings in 1987.

Sam Olbekson noted in *Akwe:kon* that the horizon line "seems to twist and turn along its length due to variations in the color and brightness of the water and sky," and this "calculated tension between water, sky, and horizon along with the energetic use of color and texture creates a sense of receding space and invites the viewer into the work, and into the mind of the artist." Morrison has "created a world of imagery that speaks of the subtle tension, yet beauty in an environment changed by external forces."[16]

Morrison explained many times that he was obsessed with the horizon because he was born and matured near the shore of Lake Superior. Elizabeth Erickson asked him in an interview about his use of the words "mystery" and "magic" as an artist. He answered that the horizon series "has been an obsession with me, now and for perhaps most of my life. And that, in itself, has a particular magic that maybe I'm trying to interpret." The "magic of nature" is the sound of waves on the shore, the ambient light, and the constant changes of the horizon outside his studio window. "Someone mentioned the haunting quality of the texture" in the horizon series, said Morrison. "Then hidden underneath the pigment is some kind of magic that one can't describe that is part of the artist trying to bring out the potency of nature."[17]

"I think of the horizon line as the edge of the world, the dividing line between water and sky, color and texture. It brings up the literal idea of space in painting," said Morrison. "From the horizon, you go beyond the edge of the world to the sky and, beyond that, to the unknown." He returned to the lake at the end of his life, and from his studio above the shoreline watched the inimitable colors of the horizon forever change with the light. "I always imagine, in a certain surrealist way, that I am there. I like to imagine it is real."[18]

Endless Space

George Morrison was an introspective, meditative artist who was liberated from racialism and poverty by chance, by his singular imagination and ambition, by his painterly associations, and by memorable revolutions in aesthetics. Clearly, his creative deliverance was by nature, literature, light, color, latent visions, and by the analogies of horizon lines and "endless space."

Morrison praised a high school teacher who encouraged his interest in literature, especially the novels of Charles Dickens. A Tale of Two Cities was his favorite novel, and he once cited the first lines, "It was the best of times, it was the worst of times." Rightly, these crucial, comparative sentiments might have described his situation as a student in public school, a Native from Chippewa City. The sentiments continue, "It was the age of wisdom, it was the age of foolishness, it was the epoch of belief, it was the epoch of incredulity," and more, "in short, the period was so far like the present period, that some of its noisiest authorities insisted on its being received, for good or for evil, in the superlative degree of comparison only."[19] The French Revolution of the novel, a time of chance, great conversions, injustice, and betrayal was not an obscure metaphor for his own adventures and native survivance as an artist in the shadow of the Great Depression in America.

He completed his studies at the Minneapolis School of Art in 1943, and, with an Ethel Morrison Van Derlip scholarship, continued at the Art Students League in New York City. Expressionism, cubism, surrealism, and other art movements were eminent and unmistakable influences at the time. Jackson Pollock and other painters had studied at the same art school.

Morrison painted abstract expressionist figures and landscapes that were exhibited in several galleries with the work of other young artists. *Three Figures*, his gouache and ink on paper, for instance, was a radical departure from the academic portraiture and realism taught at the Minneapolis School of Art.

The figures were elongated, "very somber works, with dark colors," he explained. He ascribed the latent source of the figures to a complicated romantic association with an art student, Cicely Aikman. "Our relationship lasted until" her former boyfriend "returned from the war." Morrison was exempt from military service because of a disability.

He explained that the "paintings contain the symbolism   217
of three people; one of them is me."[20]

Morrison encountered Jackson Pollock, Willem de Kooning, Franz Kline, and other abstract expressionist painters
at the Cedar Street Tavern in Greenwich Village. "The bar
wasn't a showy place with art work on the walls. It was just
a common bar. Dark wood and booths. Bland would be a
good word for it," he reminisced. "Though they were the
'big boys,' gestural painters at the height of their notori-
ety, the camaraderie was such that they didn't walk around
and act superior. They were friendly to everyone."[21] Morrison, at the time, lived in a studio nearby on East Ninth
Street near Cooper Union.

"The Cedar was the cathedral of American culture in the
fifties," observed a painter in Republic of Dreams, a history
of Greenwich Village by Ross Wetzsteon. "But the critic
Leslie Fiedler saw it differently. 'In all that aggression and
machismo there was always a trace of hysterical desperation.'" The "Cedar became a kind of intersection between
the first and second generation of abstract expressionists"
after the tragic death of Jackson Pollock.[22] Morrison was an
inspired expressionist painter, but he was never consumed
by chauvinism, desperation, or frenzy.

Morrison summered with other artists at Provincetown
on Cape Cod in Massachusetts. The town reminded him of
Grand Marais on Lake Superior. He was aroused by the natural light and many moods of the ocean. The great curve
of the beach became a source of driftwood, the natural
start of his intricate, found and prepared wood collages. He
called the constructions "paintings in wood," the "texture
of oil painting." The wood landscapes were connected to

the earth, and yet "come from the water. I realize now that in making these I may have been inspired subconsciously by the rock formations of the North Shore."[23]

He received a Fulbright grant in 1952 to study in France. He sailed on the *Queen Mary* with his wife, Ada Reed, an art student, and Kobi, a black poodle he secured in an art trade, and enrolled at the Ecole des Beaux-Arts in Paris. Later that year he was at the University of Aix-Marseilles. "In Europe I did a lot of things on paper, some with wash and ink, some gouache," but "very few oils because of the bulk."[24]

Morrison received an Opportunity Fellowship from the John Hay Whitney Foundation the following year, and moved from the Côte d'Azur to Duluth, Minnesota. "Maybe I wanted to be back in Minnesota or back with my family, I'm not sure. With the fellowship, I had money to live on without having to work."[25] Assuredly, by that time his work was widely exhibited, favorably reviewed, and acquired by collectors and museums. His painting *Construction* was purchased by the Walker Art Center, for instance, and was pictured in a feature story in the *Duluth News-Tribune*. Morrison was reasonably secure as an artist, but he and his first wife would soon separate and divorce.

Walter Chrysler, a celebrated collector of expressionist art, bought *Aureate Vertical* and two other paintings by Morrison. The vertical character dominated his work in the late fifties. "You could say paintings like *Aureate Vertical*," a large golden painting on canvas, had "structures within a landscape space." These works were described as "endless space" and with no horizon line. The expressionistic space reached outside the canvas. The notion of untold, boundless space "struck some people as explosive and destructive," in other words, destructive of the "objective in painting, not showing a literal subject matter."[26]

Hans Hofmann, Willem de Kooning, and other abstract expressionists presented their work with unrenowned artists at minor galleries. Morrison was included in many of these shows, and soon became part of the art scene. Hofmann was an influential artist and teacher who advocated an escape from "the tyranny of reality," observed Ross Wetzsteon, and "to integrate the natural world with an individual temperament." Hofmann "saw art as a spiritual quest, and scornfully rejected psychological subtexts or ideological preconceptions—his gospel was the purity of painting."[27]

Morrison had anticipated these sentiments of nature in his expressionistic art. Clearly, he lived in a constant, creative space, through his travels, painterly associations, and the camaraderie of Greenwich Village. By then his work had been acquired by the Whitney in New York, the Joslyn in Omaha, the Minneapolis Institute of Arts, and many "other museums in Philadelphia, Atlanta, Richmond, Utica, and Rochester, New York."[28] Morrison would return from the "endless space" of his work to the more familiar abstractions of nature, the horizon lines of Lake Superior.

He taught at his alma mater, the Minneapolis School of Art, for a short time in 1959, and while he was there the Kilbride-Bradley Gallery sponsored a special show of his recent paintings. John Sherman reviewed the show in the *Minneapolis Tribune*. "Morrison over the years has edged away from figurative painting and now is almost entirely devoted technically, to pattern and texture, in a rich repertoire of colors." His "pieces project as visual music in various keys and harmonies.

"The paintings seem to originate in a deep composure rather than stirred by external excitement, and they strike inner chords while pleasing the eye. They are animated by different schemes. In some there is a calm vertical flow, in others there is a blazing centripetal movement," observed Sherman. An "art of sensitivity and range, essentially lyrical and subjective. It discloses an experienced skill in setting up the counterpoint and tensions which induce you to gaze for a long time, seeking out the secrets imbedded there."[29]

Morrison was invited to teach at the School of the Dayton Art Institute, Ohio, in 1960. There he continued to paint large vertical structures in bright, emotive colors, and included an abstract expression of an urban landscape. Hazel Belvo, an art student, read about his work in the *Dayton Daily News* and attended his painting class. They married a few months later and returned to New York. Briand Mesaba, their son, was born on April 9, 1961. Franz Kline was named the godfather.

Morrison taught painting at Cornell University and at Pennsylvania State University two years later. In 1963 he was appointed an assistant professor at the prestigious Rhode Island School of Design in Providence. Morrison and his family continued their summer visits to Cape Cod. He found driftwood on the beach for collage "paintings." Some of the wood had "bits of paint" washed gray by the waves, rust stains, and the aesthetic texture and color of nail holes. "There was an interesting history in those pieces," a trace of "who had touched them, where they had come from."[30]

"I selected colors at random for a given spot on the collage," as in "my abstractions," explained Morrison. "I clustered little pieces of wood alongside bigger ones. But unlike the abstractions, the wood collages are clearly based on landscape." Sam Sachs, director of the Minneapolis Institute of Arts at the time, bought the first abstract wood "painting." Morrison sold his wood collages on commission to several corporations, and never had one of his own. "Whenever I finished a piece, it was already sold."[31]

Morrison received an honorary master of fine arts degree from the Minneapolis School of Art in 1969. The following year he resigned from the faculty of the Rhode Island School of Design and accepted a position in American Indian Studies at the University of Minnesota. "I wanted to come back to the Indian connection, to Minnesota and my family," he explained. "I felt an inner need to come back, not realizing the consequences of what I was doing. I felt the need to put certain Indian values into my work."[32] The following year he accepted a permanent position in the Studio Arts Department.

The Walker Art Center, in 1974, sponsored a show of his pen and ink drawings, textured lines that revealed elements of cubism and surrealism. The drawings show a horizon line, and one "represents a tree coming through from the bottom to the top of the drawing. That was very subconscious."[33] Philip Larson observed an "analogy to landscape" in the drawings and, in an interview, asked Morrison about the horizon line. "There was one thing I started out with in each drawing," responded Morrison. "I'd draw a pencil line one quarter from the top to indicate the horizon line. I wanted to make that very evident," and that "gives it the tangible evidence of landscape, the top sky plane, and the lower water or land plane."

Larson asked, "Do you think there are still figurative or referential elements in your art?" Morrison equivocated, "They are remote and hidden. Only an organic suggestion remains. The abstract context takes over" in the drawings. The curved lines denote "any kind of figurative element, like breasts, sexual organs, plants, water or clouds. In the new drawings, it went into a more pure state and the overall textural surface became more formal. The drawings are laid out with precise straight and curved lines, all the same distance apart, and the whole surface is evenly textured. There is an effect of shallow cubist depth made with overlapping lines, and a sense of indefinite space extending outwards from all four sides." The "illusionistic qualities come from the lines."[34]

Most of his pen and ink drawings create illusions, or surrealist, cubist perceptions, but the virtual motion of the lines in others is a mirage of nature, not merely an inaccurate perception. The intricate lines seem to move, as in the natural motion of the wind. Morrison created virtual analogies of landscapes in the "endless space" of his large vertical expressionistic paintings, and in horizon lines, the shimmer of nature and memory. Analogies are "inherently visual," a natural move to "tentative harmony," declared Barbara Stafford in *Visual Analogy*. She would "recuperate analogy," an eternal, natural harmony, "as a general theory of artful invention" and practice.

"Today, however, we posses no language for talking about resemblance, only an exaggerated awareness of difference." The world is "staggering under an explosion of discontinuous happenings exhibited as if they had no historical precedents." Stafford argued that without a "sophisticated theory

of analogy, there is only the negative dialectics of difference, ending in the unbreachable impasse of pretended
assimilation."[35]

Morrison was born and raised in the presence of visual
analogies of nature, color, and the shimmer of horizons,
a "magic of the earth." He resisted, as his native ancestors
had done, the cursory disanalogies of nature, the insular
notions of realism, naturalism, and academicism in the
course of his abstract expressionist paintings, wood collages, and line drawings. He never lost the visual analogies
of nature and the hues of a horizon.

Morrison retired from the University of Minnesota in
1983. He was honored with a special exhibition, George
Morrison: Entries in an Artist's Journal, at the University
Gallery. "It was like putting my private diary on public dis-
play," said Morrison. "Throughout my career the sketch-
book or journal has been an intimate source of personal
expression." The journal was a narrative of surrealist expressions, creative ideas, and "automatic drawing techniques to record an inner solitude and loneliness."[36]

Shortly after his retirement, he built a house and studio on the Grand Portage Reservation. The Lake Superior
shoreline was only twenty-four steps below the deck of his
studio. The sound of the lake was constant, the color of
the horizon protean. At about the same time, he was diagnosed with Castleman's disease of the lymphatic system.
"I started to think about summing up my life, about legacies," he told Margot Fortunato Galt. "I wanted to work on
more sculptural ideas and do more drawings. I wanted to
have a big show, a lifetime show that would pull my work together. I didn't know if I would have the time." His immune

system had been weakened by the disease, and by "radiation and chemotherapy treatment." Morrison created small horizon paintings during his treatment and recovery. "The basic thing in all the paintings is the horizon line which identifies each little work as a broad expanse of a segment of the earth."[37]

Morrison painted in a "small format" because of his disease. "During his convalescence he began painting on small panels, most about six by eleven inches," noted Charleen Touchette in *American Indian Art*. The paintings varied by hues and saturation of color, "tone, texture and application of paint." Sixty-one of these inspired landscapes comprise the series Red Rock Variations: Lake Superior Landscape.[38]

Mark Rollo wrote in *The Circle* that Morrison was modest about his eminence as an artist, and he was not sentimental about "growing old." Morrison said it "would be 'kind of nice' to have his ashes scattered in the big water" of Lake Superior and the Atlantic Ocean. "One always wants to live longer, of course. You feel that your life is just beginning and you need more time. You wish you had another lifetime."[39]

Morrison was honored by a retrospective of his creative work in 1990. The Minnesota Museum of Art in Saint Paul and the Tweed Museum of Art in Duluth sponsored the exhibition, Standing in the Northern Lights. The name of the retrospective was one of his sacred names. Sixty-seven works, including four wood collages, expressionistic paintings, and horizon scenes, were presented. The exhibition also traveled to the Plains Art Museum in Moorhead, Minnesota. The Rhode Island School of Design awarded him an honorary doctorate of fine arts in 1991.

Red Totem I, a twelve-foot-high stained, intricately designed cedar sculpture, was included in the 1997 exhibition Twentieth Century American Sculpture at the White House: Honoring Native America. Morrison created Red Totem I in 1980. The White House presentation honored native artists and the fine arts movement in Native America.[40]

"My art is my religion," declared Morrison in This Song Remembers. "I've tried to unravel the fabric of my life and how it relates to my work. Certain Indian values are inherent— an inner connection with the people and all living things, a sense of being in tune with natural phenomena, a consciousness of sea and sky, space and light, the enigma of the horizon, the color of the wind."[41]

George Morrison died at age eighty on April 17, 2000, in Grand Marais, Minnesota. Mary Abbe reported in the Minneapolis Star Tribune that Morrison was "one of Minnesota's most distinguished and beloved artists." She noted that like "Claude Monet's famous Impressionist paintings of the Seine River, Morrison's abstractions reflected" Lake Superior's "ever-changing moods. Their common motif is a horizon that burns fiery red, flares pink or modulates to dusky blues and dappled greens depending on the season, weather and time of day."[42] Morrison, though, created a more memorable horizon line that shimmered with the magic of nature not impressions of the city. He is also honored for his public works in Minneapolis, including an enormous wood mural at the American Indian Center, a totem in the LaSalle Plaza, and an abstract stone mosaic sidewalk on the Nicollet Mall.

George Morrison wore the seasons of survivance and crucial waves of culture on his face. He was wounded by

226   disease, and sustained by an eminent artistic vision. There were abstract traces of winter on his brow, the intricate light of spring and autumn in his eyes, and the blaze of summer colors in his stories. He is forever at the "edge of the world" in my memory.

George was a generous, cosmopolitan native artist, and his spirit endures on the horizon of Lake Superior. David Bradley, Frank Bigbear, Kent Smith, and many other distinguished, contemporary native artists have been inspired by his vision, creative integrity, and native liberty.

11. Bradlarian Baroque

David Bradley is a master of narrative art. He creates distinctive painterly scenes in bold, memorable colors, a marvelous communal and particular presence of ironic characters in the protean traditions and practices of native storiers.

Bradley is a storier with paint.

The Bradlarian baroque is a unique narrative art style. Bradley creates figures that are slightly contorted, whimsical, wittingly eccentric, and freaky at times, and with a conceivable sense of ironic motion in the bright colors, composition, and painterly features. *Indian Market*, for instance, shows a gathering of zany characters, a native clown on a skateboard with a watermelon, dogs, birds, a buffalo head, a ghostly arm reaching out of a manhole for money, decorative cowboy boots under a table, a satirical tease of *DUH Magazine*, an ersatz Sikh and four people queued with fists of money to buy native pottery, and other simulated, ironic characters muster one afternoon at the Plaza in Santa Fe, New Mexico. The mountain hues and a perfect rainbow crown the mystical scene.

The *End of the Santa Fe Trail*, *The Immaculate Assumption*,

Canyon Road Cantina, Pueblo Feast Day, The Last Supper, and *The Elaine Horwitch Indian Market Party,* and other communal scenes in his masterly paintings are native allegories, baroque by composition, figuration, and coloration, an original painterly style that invites the viewer to the elusive satire of trickster stories on canvas.

Bradley reveals in the composition of his paintings the ironic signatures of open doors and windows, paper money, electrical outlets, power cords, dogs, birds, torn wallpaper, exposed adobe bricks, video cameras, and the visionary presence of familiar characters in the fantastic art world of Santa Fe. *Pictures at an Exhibition,* for example, shows a mariachi band, a bird, squirrel, monkey, mask, paper money on the floor, and several paintings by David Bradley on the gallery walls. *Indian Pow-Wow Princess in the Process of Acculturation* is mounted over a power outlet, and the scene outside the open green door is one of his paintings. Diego Rivera and Frida Kahlo are poised in front of the Lone Ranger and Tonto. Georgia O'Keeffe stands alone, forever a solitary signature character. An apparent religious figure has a bird on his shoulder and a squirrel on his back. A chubby woman and short stocky man are dancing, reminiscent of painterly scenes by Fernando Botero.

"David Bradley's paintings offer an invitation to enter into a world within a room," wrote Elizabeth Sasser in *Southwest Art.* "'The room,' Bradley says, 'is a stage and the wall is a curtain.' Windows cut openings into that 'curtain' and frame a different kind of reality. . . . 'People,' the artist observes, 'sometimes mistake my windows for paintings. But paintings and windows are synonymous—a painting is a window.'" Sasser noted that the "torn paper is a recurrent motif in Bradley's rooms. He explained that when the paper is stripped away 'there's a hole and you can see the plaster and board. That's the real wall.' Lower down the wall is an electrical plate and with a cord which moves out of the picture plane. It too is present in many of Bradley's interiors; he describes it as 'a kind of signature.' To Bradley, the introduction of electricity was a landmark in the lifestyle of the Indians." The artist explained that the power cords reach into a new and "different dimension."[1]

Native tricksters are a trace of the marvelous, a visionary presence in stories. The *anishinaabe*, otherwise known as Chippewa or Ojibway, named their cultural trickster Naanabozho and delighted in the stories of an utmost priapic, elusive, undefined character of transformation, conversion, and trickery. *Anishinaabe* trickster stories heal the heart by native irony, humor, and by the images of survivance and sovereignty.[2]

"Some people say why not be more serious," Bradley said in a personal interview. "My response is, Life is humor, life always has mysteries, beauty, chaos, elements of theater, comedy, tragedy, and the tease of a trickster. My art is about life."[3]

Bradley is aware that some viewers are uncertain about the ironies and sentiments of humor in narrative art, and mainly the incongruities of native trickster stories. He composes distinctive characters in both simulated and ordinary situations. The Lone Ranger, Tonto, and Georgia O'Keeffe, for instance, are cast in the same market scene. The irony is perceived in figures, the integrity of color, and in the curious unity of painterly motion in the communal scenes.

"I think every ethnic group has its own unique brand of

humor," said Bradley. "As an artist, I try to deal with all the human condition. Humor breaks down social barriers and brings people together."[4]

Bradley creates narrative art with a visionary practice that is similar to the inspired stories about native tricksters. The viewer is stimulated to appreciate the painterly characters and sense of presence as the listener might imagine the marvelous scenes in trickster stories. Naanabozho is an elusive, ironic creator, and, at the same time, the trickster is a contradiction of creation. Tricksters are imagined, and only imagined in stories and narrative art.

Bradley, in his early career as a sculptor, molded a ceramic Naanabozho, a foot high figure with a small head, thick bound braids, and enormous hands, corpulent shanks, and huge moccasins. The trickster sculpture is baroque, a native trace of visionary stories. Jim Lenfestey acquired *Naanabozho* about thirty years ago at the Judith Stern Gallery in Minneapolis.

"David is right to call his life and art a symbolic vision quest, but both his vision and quest are as real as they are symbolic," wrote Suzan Shown Harjo in *Restless Native: David Bradley*, a publication of the retrospective exhibition at the Plains Art Museum in Moorhead, Minnesota. "Both involve an ideal of and search for justice and beauty, with just enough belly-laughs to keep things lively. . . . David has a great talent for seeing more than most people see, politically and visually."[5]

Bradley mentioned in various interviews that he was inspired and influenced by other painters and sculptors from the late George Morrison, Patrick Desjarlait, Fritz Scholder, Grant Wood, Robert Rauschenberg, and Diego Rivera, to folk artists in Haiti, and Fernando Botero. Bradley's *Homage to Botero*, for example, is a lithograph of a stout native with a pot on her head. The composition is a new native baroque, a signature style of robust figures similar to those created by Botero.

Bradley was exposed as a young man to the ironic characters in trickster stories, the baroque representations of the sacred, depictions of spirits, masks, and native ceremonies, and the audacious renditions of war scenes. Botero was introduced to the baroque interiors of churches in Medellín, Columbia. Neither Bradley nor Botero were exposed as young students to the mighty muse and genius of famous artists in museums.

"The drama of the baroque style was not aimed as aesthetic enjoyment, but as a religious experience that would have a lasting impact on the beholder" wrote John Sillevis in *The Baroque World of Fernando Botero*.

"To be called 'a baroque artist' could mean an artist who is willing and able to break the classical rules of art," observed Sillevis. "Another aspect of the baroque is the play of light and shadow, enhancing the tangibility of the subject. Color, texture, and brilliance all contribute to this effect. Emotions are expressed by the human figure with a strong physical presence in which such qualities as opulence, and sensuality are most conspicuous."[6]

Bradley evades the practice of academism and the cultural sentiments of classical art. He surely teases realism and commercial representations by irony and native coincidence, a narrative art that reveals the fantasies and pretensions of acquisitive cultures and art markets. The play of bold colors enhances a sense of presence, and the diverse

characters in his painterly scenes, either particular in a
landscape or communal at an art gallery, are associated
by native irony and the unity of visionary motion in primary colors.

"Colour is something spiritual, something whose clarity
is spiritual, so that when colours are mixed they produce
nuances of colour," asserted the philosopher Walter Benjamin. "When colour provides the contours, objects are not
reduced to things but are constituted by an order consist-
ing of an infinite range of nuances. Colour is single, not as
a lifeless thing and rigid individuality but as a winged crea-
ture that flits from one form to the next."[7]

Bradley clearly creates nuances of colors in character and
narrative scenes, a unique sense of native presence and motion by visual perception. Only a clever colorist can turn the
nuance of nature and painterly figures into a narrative art
with incongruity and irony.

The concept of a native baroque is borrowed and used
in the general sense of ornamentation, elaboration, bold
coloration, whimsy, and the distortion or conversion of authenticity. Botero's painterly figures are rotund distortions
of reality, and yet there is always a recognizable actuality in
the grotesque. Bradley creates diverse characters in elaborate visionary conversions of the real, the traces of the actual in the ironic narrative art of native survivance.

Bradley is a meticulous painter; even so he has created
and sold several hundred paintings, abstract collages, sculp-
tures, and lithographs in the past thirty years since he was a
student at the Institute of American Indian Art in Santa Fe,
New Mexico. Museums and individual collectors treasure
his narrative market scenes, individual portraiture, ironic

images, signature collages, and a series of double portraits
named the American Indian Gothic. Bradley first studied art
and painting at the College of Saint Thomas in Saint Paul,
Minnesota, the University of Arizona at Tucson, and then
from 1975 to 1977 he served in the Peace Corps.

Bradley is *anishinaabe*, a registered citizen of the White
Earth Reservation in Minnesota. He bears the common
native bruises of ethnic encounters, hues of fosterage and
family memories, the tricky humor and politics of gallery
associations, and the incongruities and ironies of native
survivance. The recollections of his youth, a curious, visionary sense of native stories, his unique personal experiences, and several remarkable teachers provided a natural cause to become an artist. Bradley easily adapted to
the style of instruction at the Institute of American Indian
Arts. "They gave me a canvas and some paint and told me
to start painting."[8]

Nicole Plett interviewed Bradley, early in his career, for
Art Lines in Santa Fe. She asked about his training as an artist. "I went to some universities, and the art classes were
lousy and I dreaded school," said Bradley. At the Institute
of American Indian Art, however, Bradley said he was "re-
born again or something, because it was just perfectly ac-
commodating in the way I worked and the way I think. It
didn't go against the grain like some of the other schools.
So from that point on, that's what I really count as getting
a serious art education." Bradley returned many years later
to teach at the Institute. You "really become aware there. If
your identity may have been in doubt before, after two years
and the people you meet and the things you go through,
why, it clears it up. It did for me. It was like a rebirth. And it

was just like I started me whole life over again. And that's where my art is coming from right there."[9]

Bradley was truly inspired by the work of the late *anishinaabe* artists George Morrison, an abstract expressionist, and Patrick Desjarlait, a folk art impressionist. Bradley created a diptych in their honor for an exhibition at the Ancient Traders Gallery in Minneapolis. He told a reporter that he did not want to "come home without paying homage to those two giants who influenced all of us."[10] He was not, however, directly influenced by abstract expressionism. Morrison, Hans Hoffman, Franz Kline, Willem de Kooning, Jackson Pollack, and many other renowned abstract expressionists were master painters in a previous generation. Morrison was an apostle of expressionism and native liberty. Desjarlait provided the direction of an artistic style that was understandable. Bradley was influenced, more precisely, by the social realism of Diego Rivera, and the baroque narrative art of Fernando Botero. Bradley turns to expressionism in his abstract collages, and, at the same time, he is pleased to proclaim that he is also inspired by the narrative folk art of Haiti.

Bradley served for two years in the Peace Corps. The first year he initiated a subsistence agricultural program to provide vegetables for natives in the Dominican Republic near the border with Haiti. There, he was inspired by the narrative folk art, the portrait and communal compositions in bright, primary colors by untutored artists. The second year he was invited to serve in rural Guatemala where he established a livestock extension program. "I lived with a Mayan family, and they were terribly poor but with great strength and integrity," he said in an interview.[11] The "Mayan Indians gave me a new sense of vision."[12]

Bradley merged his personal native influences and experiences with the untutored folk art style several years later at the Institute of American Indian Art. The outcome of his early impressions is a unique, baroque narrative style of art, communal scenes in bold colors with a sense of whimsy and native irony.

"Colour, above all, and perhaps even more than drawing, is a means of liberation," declared Henri Matisse. "Liberation is the freeing of conventions, old methods being pushed aside by the contributions of a new generation. As drawing and colour are means of expression, they are modified. Hence the strangeness of new means of expression, because they refer to other matters than those which interested preceding generations."[13]

Haitian art schools in the early nineteenth century encouraged portraiture. Most painters, however, were not recognized until the founding, some sixty years ago, of the Centre D'Art by DeWitt Peters. Hector Hyppolite, a "voodoo priest," was one of the "greatest natural painters" in the "history of the art movement in Haiti."[14]

Dorothy Dunn established formal art instruction at the Santa Fe Indian School in 1932. She encouraged native traditions, for instance, those derived from early native art practices of Winter Counts and Ledger Art, and advanced the naturalistic, or narrative style of art at the school. The native students, however, soon insisted on more liberty of artistic spirit, passion, and expression than the sanctions and practices of naturalism. Allan Houser, Joe Herrara, Pablita Velarde, Oscar Howe, and many other eminent native artists attended the school. The Studio at the Santa Fe Indian School was the foundation of the Institute of American Indian Arts.

Bradley was inspired by many native artists who had studied at the Studio in Santa Fe, and by the bright compositions of narrative folk art in Haiti. Sooner or later he would have discovered the "passion and color" of these untrained painters of "mundane existence,"[15] but fortuitously his service in the Peace Corps, more than thirty years ago, immediately preceded his studies at the Institute of American Indian Arts. He was ready by experience, by passion, and by coincidence to start his career as an artist and sculptor.

Grant Wood posed his daughter and a dentist for the prominent double portrait *American Gothic*. Wood was evasive about the intended satire of his painting, but unintended is no less a satire. Many painters and photographers since then have mimicked the composition and the puritanical characters. Gordon Parks, for example, photographed a woman holding an upright mop in one hand and a broom in the other in front of the Stars and Stripes. Satire is clever and tricky in literature and art, and some photographs are comic teasers, but the extremes can be crude and spiteful, such as "Goth American Gothic" and "Plastic Surgery American Gothic."

Bradley salutes *American Gothic* by Grant Wood with a brilliant painterly satire of a baroque narrative double portrait of Georgia O'Keeffe and Alfred Stieglitz. Susan Moldenhauer, in an essay for the exhibition "David Bradley: Postcard from Santa Fe, at the University of Wyoming Art Museum," wrote that Bradley's "masterful *American Gothic: O'Keeffe and Stieglitz Meet Tonto and the Lone Ranger* is exemplary. This classic double portrait reminiscent of Wood's best known masterpiece presents Georgia O'Keeffe, her signature initials as an adornment and canvas and paint brushes in hand, and her husband, photographer Alfred Stieglitz." The "Lone Ranger stands in the doorway of his Silver Bullet Bed and Breakfast, a brothel of sorts with Marilyn Monroe peering from the upstairs window. A weathervane depicting James Earle Fraser's signature sculpture, *The End of the Trail*, is perched above."[16] Tonto clutches paper money in both hands. The Silver Bullet has a vacancy.

The iconic farmwoman in *American Gothic* by Grant Wood wears a cameo necklace, a colonial print apron with a rickrack border, and a Peter Pan collar. The puritanical farmer wears a striped Gatsby shirt with no collar, overalls, and a sport coat, and holds a hayfork with three tines.

Georgia O'Keeffe in *American Gothic* by Bradley wears an identical colonial apron with a rickrack border, and collar, but the necklace is a thick silver cross with turquoise. Stieglitz wears the same Gatsby shirt and overalls but with paper money tucked in the chest pocket. Steiglitz carries a camera, not a hayfork. Painterly signatures abound, puffy clouds, exposed adobe brick, jewelry and curios on sale, and paper money. Bradley creates many ironic cues in the composition. Stieglitz, for instance, rolls his eyes upward in disgust or arrogance. *Tanto Curios* means "as much" in Spanish and "too much" in Italian, an ironic variation on the name Tonto, an "idiot" in Spanish.

Bradley has painted several other double portraits in his series American Indian Gothic. *Ghost Dancers, Dorothy and Richard Nelson on the Shores of Gitchi Gami, Paul Bunyan and Babe, Sitting Bull and Wife, Indian Self Rule*, and there are many other double portraits in the series. *Abiquiu Afternoon* is a variation of the American Indian Gothic, a double portrait of R.C. Gorman, the distinguished artist from Canyon de Chelly on the Navajo Nation, and Georgia O'Keeffe, seated outside at a round table. A signature cat is in one corner and paper money in the other. O'Keeffe is a caricature of *Whistler's Mother* by James McNeill Whistler.

Family scenes include *Buffalo Dance Feast Day*, *Chippewa Family*, and many individual portraits, *Georgia O'Keeffe* as *Whistler's Mother* with paint and a palette, *Pow Wow Princess*, *Pueblo Morning*, *Sleeping Indian*, *Dream Near Santa Fe*, *Homage to Crow King*, *Pueblo Madonna*, and hundreds more, including four color image variations, *Homage to Warhol*. Bradley created several satire portraits. *Land 'O Bucks* is a buxom woman in a tight fringe dress. She holds paper money over a sign that reads, "The Wantobe Tribe, Authentic Indian Art and Crafts." Bradley also painted several cowboy scenes, for instance *True Grit* and *How the West Was Lost*.

Mary Abbe reviewed the exhibition Restless Native in the Ancient Traders Gallery and wrote in the *Minneapolis Star Tribune* that "Bradley evidently thinks of himself as something of a tumbleweed, rootless and impatient. . . . Colorful, witty and meticulously rendered, his paintings, collages and mixed-media pieces depict the world with amused detachment, noting its hypocrisies and foibles but also honoring good people, respecting history and celebrating long friendships. In an often cynical age, his work has a guileless intelligence that's terrifically appealing."[17]

Bradley never hesitates to pronounce that art is liberty. "Art is about freedom, and an artist must follow his heart," he has said in many interviews.[18] Bradley follows his heart, and his art heals with humor and liberates with compassion and irony.

12. Mister Ishi of California

Ishi was never his native name.

Ishi was named by chance, not by vision, a lonesome hunter rescued by cultural anthropologists. Native names are the rise of collective memories, but his actual names and sense of presence are obscure; yet, his museum nickname, more than any other archive nomination, represents to many readers the tragic victimry of Native American Indians in California.

Ishi by Archive

The spirit of this native hunter, captured almost a century ago, has been sustained as cultural property. Ishi was humanely secured in a museum at a time when natives were denied human and civil rights. By another suit of cultural dominance his remains have been repatriated to an ancestral scene; united with great sorrow, worried hearts, and political penitence, his ashes and brain have been buried at last in a secret place near Mount Lassen.

"He is the last of his tribe," wrote Mary Ashe Miller in the *San Francisco Call*, September 6, 1911. "Hunting has been his only means of living and that has been done with a bow and arrow of his own manufacture, and with snares. Probably no more interesting individual could be found today than this nameless Indian."[1]

Sheriff Webber secured a "pathetic figure crouched upon the floor" of a slaughterhouse, the *Oroville Register* reported on August 29, 1911. "The canvas from which his outer shirt was made had been roughly sewed together. His undershirt had evidently been stolen in a raid upon some cabin. His feet were almost as wide as they were long, showing plainly that he had never worn either moccasins or shoes. In his ears were rings made of buckskin thongs." The sheriff "removed the cartridges from his revolver" and "gave the weapon to the Indian. The aborigine showed no evidence that he knew anything regarding its use. A cigarette was offered to him, and while it was very evident that he knew what tobacco was, he had never smoked it in that form, and had to be taught the art."[2]

Alfred Kroeber read the newspaper reports and contacted the sheriff who "had put the Indian in jail not knowing what else to do with him since no one around town could understand his speech or he theirs," wrote Theodora Kroeber in *Alfred Kroeber: A Personal Configuration.* "Within a few days the Department of Indian Affairs authorized the sheriff to release the wild man to the custody of Kroeber" at the museum of anthropology. Ishi was housed in rooms furnished by Phoebe Apperson Hearst.[3]

Ishi was christened the last of the stone agers; overnight he became the decorated orphan of cultural genocide, the curious savage of a vanishing race overcome by modernity. He was alone but never contemptuous, servile, or the romantic end of anything. His stories were never given to victimry. He was a native humanist in exile, and a storier of survivance.

Ishi had endured the unspeakable hate crimes of miners, racial terrorists, bounty hunters, and government scalpers. Many of his family and friends were murdered, the calculated victims of cultural treason and rapacity. Truly, the miners were the savages.

California natives barely survived the gold rush, the cruelties of colonial missions, partitionists, and poisoned water. Only about fifty thousand natives, or one in five, were alive in the state at the turn of the twentieth century.

Ishi never revealed his sacred name or any of his nicknames, but he never concealed his humor and humanity. Lively, eager, and generous he told tricky wood duck stories to his new friends. This gentle native, rescued by culturologists, lived and worked for five years in the museum of anthropology at the University of California.

Ishi "was to be photographed in a garment of skins, and when the dressing for the aboriginal part began he refused to remove his overalls," reported Miller in the *San Francisco Call*. "He say he not see any other people go without them, and he say he never take them off no more," said the native translator Sam Batwi.[4]

"Ishi was photographed so frequently and so variously that he became expert on matters of lighting, posing, and exposure," wrote Theodora Kroeber. "Photographs of him were bought or made to be treasured as mementos."[5]

Alfred Kroeber, the eminent academic humanist, pointed out that Ishi "has perceptive powers far keener than those of highly educated white men. He reasons well, grasps an idea quickly, has a keen sense of humor, is gentle, thoughtful, and courteous and has a higher type of mentality than most Indians."[6]

Ishi was at "ease with his friends," wrote Theodora Kroeber. He "loved to joke, to be teased amiably and to tease in return. And he loved to talk. In telling a story, if it were long or involved or of considerable effect, he would perspire with the effort, his voice rising toward a falsetto of excitement."[7]

Saxton Pope, the surgeon at the medical school located near the museum, wrote that Ishi "amused the interns and nurses by singing" his songs. "His affability and pleasant disposition made him a universal favorite. He visited the sick in the wards with a gentle and sympathetic look which spoke more clearly than words. He came to the women's wards quite regularly, and with his hands folded before him, he would go from bed to bed like a visiting physician, looking at each patient with quiet concern or with a fleeting smile that was very kindly received and understood."[8]

Thomas Waterman, the linguist at the museum, administered various psychological tests at the time and told a newspaper reporter that "this wild man has a better head on him than a good many college men."[9]

The Bureau of Indian Affairs sent a special agent to advise Ishi that he could return to the mountains or live on a government reservation. Kroeber wrote that Ishi "shook his head" and said through the interpreter that he would "live like the white people from now on. I want to stay where I am. I will grow old here, and die in this house." And by that he meant the museum.[10]

Ishi died of tuberculosis five years later, on March 25,

1916. His brain was removed during an autopsy, and the rest of his cremated remains were stored in a cinerary urn at the Mount Olivet Cemetery in Colma, California.

Kroeber was in New York when he learned that Ishi was gravely sick. He wrote that he would consent only to a "strict autopsy" to determine the cause of death. "If there is any talk about the interests of science, say for me that science can go to hell. We propose to stand by our friends." His letter and cautionary advice, however, arrived too late. Ishi had died at the museum and his brain had already been excised as a racial artifact. "Besides, I cannot believe that any scientific value is materially involved. We have hundreds of Indian skeletons that nobody ever comes near to study. The prime interest in this case would be of a morbid romantic nature."[11]

Edward Gifford, a curator at the museum, explained why the brain had been removed. "The matter was not entirely in my hands." What "happened amounts to a compromise between science and sentiment with myself on the side of sentiment." Ishi had earned the respect, favor, and sentiments of scientists at the time, but not enough to secure his spirit at the autopsy. "The remains are to be placed in a niche in the columbarium at Mount Olivet Cemetery." The ashes were placed in a "black Pueblo jar, more appropriate than the onyx urns." "The funeral was private, and no flowers were brought."[12]

Ishi was missed by the public. Many letters were received, "expressing affection for him and sorrow that he was gone." Some of those letters "blamed the staff for not having taken better care of him: a museum was not a proper home, they said; there had been carelessness in allowing Ishi to be exposed to infection; he should have been taken back to his old home and natural environment." A group of high school students from Kansas City "who knew of Ishi from one of their teachers who had spent some time with him at the museum before he was ill," held a memorial meeting for him.

"Meanwhile, within the museum walls there lingered a numbing sense of loss, and an unwonted silence no longer interrupted by the soft-voiced inquiry, *Evelybody hoppy?*"[13]

Theodora Kroeber noted that his estate was divided between the state and the hospital. The dean of the Medical School "received two hundred and sixty half dollars," she wrote in *Ishi in Two Worlds*. His treasure, in this way, "continues to contribute its bit to the science of healing, a science for which Ishi himself had so great a curiosity and concern."[14] Clearly, greater care was taken to fairly disperse his salary savings than to protect his brain and the journey of his spirit in the world.

Orin Starn, professor of anthropology at Duke University, recently discovered a letter in the Bancroft Library written by Alfred Kroeber to Ales Hrdlicka, who was then the curator of physical anthropology at the Smithsonian. "I find that at Ishi's death last spring his brain was removed and preserved," Kroeber wrote to Hrdlicka. "There is no one here who can put it to scientific use. If you wish it, I shall be glad to deposit it in the National Museum Collection."

Kroeber was not sentimental enough and anthropology was not ethical enough at the time to consider the spiritual presence, the stories, natural unity, and repatriation of his good friend, the native humanist he had named Ishi.

Ishi by Exile

Ishi created a sense of natural presence in his stories, a native presence that included others. He was a visionary, not a separatist, and his oral stories were scenes of liberty. This native humanist was amused by the silence of scripture. He was a tricky storier in exile.

Ishi was in exile by name, by racial wars, and by the partisans of cultural dominance. He was a fugitive in his own native scenes, pursued by feral pioneers and malevolent miners; yet he endured without apparent rancor or mordancy and created stories of native survivance, the analogies of leave, deliverance, and sovereignty.

The pioneers were separated from animals and natural reason by monotheism and the biblical covenants of human dominion over nature. Ishi was a humanist more at home in nature than a museum; clearly, he was a man of natural reason, a mature storier and healer, and, unlike the pioneer predators, he seemed to embrace the merits of a true democratic and civil society.

Ishi was "remarkably talkative" with those he trusted, and his "temperament was philosophical, analytical, reserved, and cheerful," observed Saxton Pope in his essay "The Medical History of Ishi." Moreover, he "probably looked upon us as extremely smart. While we knew many things, we had no knowledge of nature." Pope, a medical doctor, wrote that his "affability and pleasant disposition made him a universal favorite."[15]

Ishi weathered his exile without an obscure cause of cultural or national liberty. He lived by the natural right of seasons not museums, but at the end he was evermore alone, his spirit exiled by an autopsy in the city.

Albert Camus, the novelist and philosopher, and Ishi the native humanist and storier, both lived in exile. Camus created a literature of separation and exile. Ishi created songs and stories of natural reason, survivance, and liberty. Nature was his source of presence and actuality. Ishi and Camus were more at ease in nature, the rush of sun and seasons, than in the causes and measures of history.

Camus "exults in the sensation of being fashioned by wind and sun to the pattern of the burning countryside stretching before him. He feels his blood throb in rhythm to the pulsations of the sun and the zenith," observed John Cruickshank in *Albert Camus and the Literature of Revolt*. "Whereas the pantheist seeks escape from himself through identification with a spiritualized nature, Camus is at pains to emphasize the strictly physical reality of natural objects and of his own presence in nature."[16]

"Camus lived in the permanent purgatory of exile—physical, moral, intellectual," wrote Tony Judt in *The Burden of Responsibility*. Always "between homes (in metaphor and reality alike) and at ease nowhere." Judt asserted, "Just because you are from somewhere does not mean you cannot be an exile there, too," a point made by other writers. "Nonetheless, if Camus had a place of his own at all it was Algeria."[17]

Ishi was a fugitive of natural, ancestral scenes, and an outsider in a museum of manifest manners and cultural history. Evermore he is discovered in the ironic traces of ethnographic archives. Camus was at home in his memories of nature, his ancestors, and in his stories of Algeria. Ishi was at home in natural reason and his stories. Conversely, they were exiles by sound and silence, by oral stories and scripture.

Camus never mentioned native oral stories in his essays, but he shared an obvious vision of nature with Ishi. They were betrayed by nations, by cultures, but not by nature. These storiers of exile were not weakened by the absence of ancestral scenes; rather, they created by nature a visionary sense of liberty.

Camus, all his life, "remained true to the convictions that man fulfills himself completely, lives a total reality, insofar as he is in communion with the natural world and that the divorce between man and nature mutilates human existence," wrote Mario Vargas Llosa in *Making Waves*. "Perhaps it is this conviction, the experience of someone who grew up at the mercy of the elements, which kept Camus apart from the intellectuals of his generation." Camus, and his love for nature, is a "permanent aspect of his work." The "sun, the sea, the trees, the flowers, the harsh earth or the burning dunes of Algeria are the raw material for description or the starting point for reflection, they are the obligatory reference points of the young essayists when he attempts to define beauty, celebrate life or speculate on his artistic vocation."[18] Vargas Llosa might have made a similar observation of Ishi. Always, the anthropologists were separated from natural reason by their count and comparative measures of culture and history.

Ishi and Camus were exiled from distinctive landscapes, and yet their stories consecrate a primordial sense of nature. Camus was moved by nature, and yet he "was a provincial for better or worse, above all for better in many respects," wrote Llosa. "First, because, unlike the experience of men in large cities, he lived in a world where landscape was the primordial presence, infinitely more attractive and important than cement and asphalt."[19] Nature was solace by memory and metaphor; separation was minded in history.

"History explains neither the natural universe which came before it, nor beauty which stand above it," wrote Camus in "Helen's Exile," an essay in *Lyric and Critical Essays*. "Consequently it has chosen to ignore them." Nature, however, is always there. "Her calm skies and her reason oppose the folly of men."[20]

Ishi was exiled from traces of the seasons, the scent, sound, and vision of a natural presence in the mountains; he was driven from these ancestral scenes by the predators of culture and history. He was an artist secured in a museum, an obscure native under surveillance, but that was not an absolute separation from natural reason or his creative stories of survivance and liberty.

"Both the historical mind and the artist seek to remake the world," wrote Camus. "But the artist, through an obligation of his very nature, recognizes limits the historical mind ignores. This is why the latter aims at tyranny while the passion of the artist is liberty."[21]

Ishi was fortunate, in an ironic sense, to have an audience of dedicated, humane, and curious listeners for his stories of native liberty. He lived by natural reason and the tease of seasons. Today, almost a century later, the audience has increased and the listeners are even more dedicated to understand in translation the sense of native presence and survivance of his wood duck stories.

Ishi by Litigation

Harken Lucero reached into the niche and seized the black cinerary urn that contained the remains of Ishi. Lucero, a gushy sculptor, raised the urn as a video camera operator

moved closer to capture another scene in the eternal stories of a native exile.

"I can feel the spirit of Ishi in my hands, his spirit is moving through my body," said Lucero. His hands trembled,
a vulgar pose and pretension, but not enough to lose control of the cremains. Lucero anticipated the audience and
surely staged an incredible performance in the columbarium at the Olivet Cemetery in Colma, California, near San
Francisco.

I was at this kitschy spectacle, along with Caitlin
Croughan, an independent fundraiser who had introduced
me to the sculptor; Lorna Fernandes, a correspondent for
the San Francisco Chronicle; the assistant director of the cemetery association; the maintenance man of the niches; and
several other spectators. Alas, if a judge and jury had been
present that afternoon at the columbarium they would have
observed the ironic presentiments of the sculptor and decided post hoc to set aside a money suit against me, the
fundraiser, and the University of California, Berkeley.

Lucero is a dedicated sculptor who easily noted his identity as an Indian. He was also determined to convince a jury
that he should be awarded fifty thousand dollars for his preliminary work on a monument to honor Ishi.

Lucero removed the black, polished cinerary urn from
the niche to make a rubbing of the precise inscription on
the curve.

ISHI
THE LAST YAHI INDIAN
1916

His "hands trembled as he held tightly to the urn," wrote
Fernandes. Another artist tried to cover the urn with butcher

paper to make an impression of the words, but the paper was too thick to leave a charcoal representation. The comic scene was recorded by video and later played in county court as evidence in a lawsuit.

Lucero assumed that he had been commissioned to create a sculpture for Ishi Court in Dwinelle Hall on the campus at Berkeley. And he pretended that the comical butcher paper image would be used to make an engraving on a memorial plaque at the entrance to the courtyard.

The maintenance man at the columbarium watched the artist struggle with the thick paper on the curve of the urn, and then, in almost a whisper, he offered thin, rubbing paper made for that exact purpose. Finally, a charcoal representation was made of the incised words on the pottery.

The assistant director of the cemetery boldly announced to the audience that the pot was thrown, and the very words carved by Ishi the last Yahi Indian. Fernandes wrote as much in her notebook, a mundane romantic notion of a native premonition of death. I leaned closer and evenly told the reporter than the cemetery official was either a sentimentalist, stupid, or misinformed. Fernandes resisted my intervention at first, but later she was convinced that the letters incised on the curve of the urn were in perfect serif type, closer by design to a roman typestyle that to the cursive hand of a Yahi named Ishi. Furthermore, he was a hunter not a potter. Most of these comic scenes were video recorded as a documentary.

I proposed in October 1985 that the architectural extension to Dwinelle Hall should be named Ishi Hall. My proposal won wide support from students and faculty, and was unanimously endorsed by the student union at the University of California, Berkeley.

Simply, my proposal focused on the significant contributions that Ishi had made to the University of California. Alfred Kroeber noted that "he had mastered the philosophy of patience." Saxton Pope pointed out that Ishi "knew nature, which is always true," and that he had the mind of a philosopher.

Ishi served with distinction the curatorial interests of the new Museum of Anthropology. He endured without rancor a museum nickname and was, after all, vested as the first native employee of the University of California.

None of this information, however, fairly impressed the faculty committee that first considered my proposal. Ishi, in name and service, was denied a byword presence on the campus by the Dwinelle Hall Space Subcommittee. The final decision, after a hearty discussion of toilets and closet areas in the building, could not be overturned by any other committee

Ishi was twice denied a presence by name, but seven years later my direct petition to the chancellor resulted in an acceptable compromise. The actual decision, however, had more to do with the politics of federal funds, criticism of repatriation policies on the campus, and, because of that, an urgent interest to favor native issues and academic programs.

Chancellor Chang-Lin Tien reminded me that "the process of naming, or renaming, a campus building involves review at several levels on the campus and at the Office of the President." Chancellor Tien received my letter of appeal on

June 2, 1992, to "consider the sense of resentment and anger
that you might feel if your reasonable initiatives to honor a
tribal name and emend institutional racism were consigned
to the mundane commerce of a campus space subcommittee." I pointed out that hundreds of Native American Indians had been "invited to 'reclaim' the campus," which was
located on stolen native land, during the Columbus "quin-
centenary celebrations, a demonstration that would be worthy of academic, public, and media consideration."

Several months later the director of space management on
the campus presented a compromise to me that the central
courtyard of Dwinelle Hall could be named Ishi Court. The
concessions were honorable, but the original documents
that supported the decision were lost; several months later
the case was regenerated and copies were conclusively trans-
mitted to the Regents of the University of California.

Ishi Court was dedicated on May 7, 1993. Gary Strankman, justice of the First District California Court of Appeal,
said the ceremony "concerns naming, the act of giving to
that which existed before and which will exist after a verbal symbol." He pointed out an irony of memorial names,
that for "every student or visitor who can give you some personal history of Wheeler, Boalt, Sproul, or Dwinelle, I can
find a hundred, no a thousand, who can tell you the story
of Ishi. Without a name he has achieved a fame and a respect that they can only envy."[22]

Caitlin Croughan was inspired by the dedication and
thereby proposed to raise money to create a monument in
honor of Ishi. She invited me to meet with a native sculptor
whose work she admired, and later to observe the spectacle

of the niche at the columbarium. That sculptor, of course, was Harken Lucero.

Croughan, an honorable fundraiser, became a casual agent for the sculptor, and, based on that camaraderie, she set out to find money in the name of Ishi. Lucero, meanwhile, assumed that such notice and his documented pose at the niche was an oral commission to create a memorial sculpture. No promise or parole contact had ever been made; rather, the creative representations of his sculpture were not suitable, in my view, as a memorial in Ishi Court.

Lucero alleged in a "complaint for damages for breach of contract," filed on August 2, 1995, that the defendants, Gerald Vizenor, Caitlin Croughan, and the Regents of the University of California, "entered into an oral contract" to design and sculpt a statue of Ishi and that the defendants would pay fifty thousand dollars to Lucero.

The story became a comic epitome of scammers.

Ishi, the native in exile, was teased by name in an incredible sculptural association with Mahatma Gandhi. Brashly, the manifest scammers arrived in silky suits to propose fundraiser strategies.

Yogesh Gandhi, then the director of the Gandhi Memorial Foundation of Orinda, California, insisted that we meet to discuss Ishi and Native American Studies. He suggested a sculpture giveaway, a fundraising tactic that worked in his foundation. He had commissioned the creation of a miniature bronze sculpture of Mahatma Gandhi. Bronze copies of the spiritual leader were then given to potential contributors. Ishi, likewise, could be cast in bronze and given away to raise money in his name. I resisted his foundation strategies, but not his interest in Native American Studies.

Croughan considered but declined an invitation to work as a fundraiser for the Gandhi Foundation. Lucero, at about the same time, presented a stone sculpture to Gandhi. Later his name was mentioned as the very sculptor who could create a bronze giveaway miniature of Ishi.

Yogesh Gandhi, a few months later, attended a reception on the campus for Vibert de Souza, the minister for Amerindian affairs, Republic of Guyana. Gandhi grandly toured Ishi Court and then visited briefly with Chancellor Tien. Gandhi was soon distracted by the presidential election and seemed to lose interest in fundraiser strategies for Native American Studies.

Gandhi, we later learned, had been charged with federal mail fraud as part of a campaign spending investigation conducted by the Justice Department. The *San Francisco Chronicle* reported on March 6, 1998, that Gandhi was arrested "in connection with two American Express credit card applications he allegedly signed with another man's name."

The *New York Times* reported on November 8, 1996, that the Democratic National Committee returned a large contribution solicited by John Huang. The contribution "initially appeared to come from Yogesh K. Gandhi, a great-grandnephew of Mohandas K. Gandhi who runs a California foundation that honors the Indian leader's memory. Yogesh Gandhi made the donation during a fundraising event in May in a Washington hotel at which he and an associate, a Japanese spiritual leader named Hogen Fukunaga, gave President Clinton a peace award." Gandhi, however, a few months later told a court in California "that he had no assets or bank accounts in the United States." Moreover, "relatives more closely related to Mohandas Gandhi have complained that Yogesh Gandhi has improperly exploited his family name and does not represent its true interests."

Lucero lost his case in judicial arbitration, and a month later, on February 27, 1997, after three days of trial, he lost in San Francisco County Superior Court. The jury rendered a verdict in favor of Gerald Vizenor and the University of California. Fred Takemiya, university counsel, pointed out in a letter to the vice chancellor that the jury "could not reach the necessary consensus for a verdict" in the case of Caitlin Croughan. "Some of the jurors apparently felt that she should have taken more clear, affirmative steps to stop Lucero's efforts at creating a model of his concept of the statue." The court declared a mistrial in her case.

Ishi by Names

"Mammedaty was my grandfather, whom I never knew," wrote N. Scott Momaday in his memoir *The Names.* "Yet he came to be imagined posthumously in the going on of the blood, having invested the shadow of his presence in an object or a word, in his name above all. He enters into my dreams; he persists in his name."[23]

Ishi is not his native name, but we imagine his presence by that museum nickname. Ishi is in our visions, and he persists by that name in our memory. We bear his exile as our own, and by his tease and natural reason we create new stories of native irony, survivance and liberty. My stories are an expiation of our common exile in this culture of tricky giveaways.

13. Haiku Traces

The essence of haiku is a tease of nature, a concise, intuitive, imagic moment. Haiku is a mood of creation, an elusive, ironic, sense of place, motion, and impermanence; a tricky fusion of nature, emotion, ethos, culture, and survivance. The aesthetic creases, or the precise turns, traces, and cut of words in haiku, are the shadows of experience, inspiration, and memory.

The imagic moments in haiku scenes are virtual, the fugitive turn of the seasons, an interior motion, and a continuous sense of presence in nature.

Haiku was my first poetry, the original imagistic associations of underived experience in the natural world. The metaphors of my haiku scenes were teases of nature and memory. The creases of the words cut to the seasons, not the mere cosmopolitan representations or rumination of an image in a mirror.

Pine Islands

Matsushima, by chance of the military, was my first connection to a haiku scene, the actual place the moon rose over those beautiful pine islands in the *haibun*, or prose haiku, of Matsuo Bashō.

"Much praise had already been lavished upon the wonders of the islands of Matsushima," Bashō writes in *The Narrow Road to the Deep North*, translated by Nobuyuki Yuasa. "Yet if further praise is possible, I would like to say that here is the most beautiful spot in the whole country of Japan. . . . The islands are situated in a bay about three miles wide in every direction and open to the sea. . . . Islands are piled above islands, and islands are joined to islands, so that they look exactly like parents caressing their children or walking with them arm in arm. The pines are of the freshest green, and their branches are curved in exquisite lines, bent by the wind constantly blowing through them."[1] I was there, in that same *haibun* sense of place, almost three centuries later in the motion of experience, and tried my best to envision the presence of Bashō.

> water striders
> master bashō wades near shore
> out of reach

The United States Army, by chance, sent me to serve first on Hokkaido and then at a post near Sendai in northern Japan. I was eighteen years old at the time. Haiku, in a sense, caught me out on the road as a soldier in another culture and gently turned me back to the seasons, back to the tease and native memories. The turns and imagistic scenes of haiku were neither exotic nor obscure, because nature is a sense of presence, not a tenure of experience, or pretense of discovery.

Haiku scenes are similar, in a sense, to the dream songs and visionary images of the *anishinaabe*, Chippewa or Ojibwe. I was inspired by these literary connections at the time. The associations seem so natural to me now. Once, words and worlds apart in time and place, these poetic images came together more by chance than fate, and later by intuition and consideration.

Many *anishinaabe* dream songs are about the presence of animals, birds, and other totemic creatures in experience, visions, and memory. The same can be said about haiku scenes, that the visions of nature are the perceptions and traces of memory.

Yosa Buson wrote haiku poems that suggested a longing for home. These poems are so "poignant that he has come to be knows as 'the poet of nostalgia' in recent decades," wrote Makoto Ueda in *The Path of Flowering Thorn*. Buson, who was born some seventy years after Matsuo Bashō, traveled to the pine islands and wrote at least one poem about Matsushima.

> in matsushima
> a man gazing at the moon
> empty seashells

There, at Matsushima, "Bashō was so overwhelmed by the moonlit scenery that he was not able to compose. The moon view in Buson's hokku may well be Bashō, who became 'empty' like a pair of seashells on the shore and could not write. Or the man may represent all visitors to Matsushima, Buson himself included, who are too dazzled by its scenic beauty to find words to express it. And those speechless admirers are numberless like seashells on the shore of Matushima."[2]

Haiku Moment

"The essence of all nature poetry is animism," R. H. Blyth points out in *A History of Haiku*. "Haiku is an ascetic art, an artistic asceticism. Of the two elements, the ascetic is more rare, more difficult, of more value than the artistic."[3] Likewise, *anishinaabe* animism, that sense of natural presence, an imagic moment, is an artistic union of nature, intuition, and emotion, or natural reason.

Kenneth Yasuda writes in *The Japanese Haiku* that haiku is an aesthetic experience, and that sense of a "haiku moment" is eternal. "Every word, then, in a haiku, rather than contributing to the meaning as words do in a novel or sonnet, is an experience." That eternal moment is natural reason in a haiku scene. "A haiku moment is a kind of aesthetic moment—a moment in which the words which created the experience and the experience itself can become one."[4]

Haiku scenes and native dream songs are imagic moments, and, in that sense, the actual experiences of nature are an aesthetic survivance. The *anishinaabe* dream songs are visions of motion and perception, and, at the same time, tease nature. Haiku scenes and *anishinaabe* dream songs are created by natural reason.

Many haiku scenes, even in translation, aroused in me a sense of natural presence. That intuitive moment, a *haiku moment*, was natural reason: the images of leaves floating silently beneath a waterfall, sunrise on the wings of a dragonfly, the slow march of a blue heron in the shallows, the great shadows of sandpipers on the beach, cracks of thunder in the ice, and the return of the juncos to a bare birch tree. These are scenes of motion, the unities of natural reason and survivance.

Haiku scenes are accessible in nature and culture, the subject and object of perception and experience, and that alone was more than any poetry had ever given me in the past. Haiku from the start turned my thoughts to chance, and impermanence, the very tease of a real and aesthetic presence in nature.

"I knew well it was no use to cry, that water once flown past the bridge does not return, and blossoms that are scattered are gone beyond recall," Kobayashi Issa writes about the death of his daughter in The Year of My Life. "Yet try as I would, I could not, simply could not cut the binding cord of human love."[5] Sato, his daughter, is remembered in this poignant haiku translated by Nobuyuki Yuasa:

> the world of dew
> is the world of dew
> and yet. . .
> and yet. . .

I first read haiku as the evocative memory of nature, and yet the scenes, the imagic moments, connections, and associations, were ironic traces of my impermanence in nature. Haiku created a sense of presence, and, at the same time, reminded me of a nature that was already wounded, desecrated, removed, and an absence in many places on the earth. Nature is a presence not a permanence, and a haiku moment is an aesthetic survivance. My very first literary creations were haiku scenes, and since then, that imagistic sense of nature has always been present in my writing. I may never know if my haiku are right by nature, only that the scenes are my best memories. In this way, my sense of presence, experience, and survivance is in nature and the book.

Yosa Buson, the son of a farmer, was born more than two centuries ago, and yet we met by chance and nature in the book. He was a cultural dilettante and, at the same time, a brilliant haiku poet. Buson writes with wit about the seasons and teases his own sense of transience in the world. He was never devoted to nature, as other poets were, but he created memorable imagic *haiku moments.* R. H. Blyth translated this haiku scene by Buson:

> winter rain
> a mouse runs
> over the *koto*[6]

I head the natural music of that scene two centuries later and wrote this haiku back to him one early winter in Bena, Minnesota, on the Leech Lake Reservation.

> cold rain
> field mice rattle the dishes
> buson's *koto*

Blyth noted that the "aim of haiku, according to Buson, is to express in ordinary language the inner poetical philosophy of all sublunary things. That is to say, the most delicate feelings and profound meanings of things are to be portrayed as though they were every-day occurrences."[7]

A haiku is "not explicit about what has been going on in the mind of the author," Daisetz T. Suzuki writes in *Zen and Japanese Culture.* "He does not go any further than barely enumerating, as it were, the most conspicuous objects that have impressed or inspired him. As to the meaning of such objects . . . it is left to the reader to construct and interpret it according to his poetic experience or his spiritual intuitions."[8]

Donald Keene, in *Japanese Literature,* similarly observes that a "really good poem, and this is especially true of haiku, must be completed by the reader. It is for this reason that

many of their poems seem curiously passive to us, for the
writer does not specify the truth taught him by an experience, nor even in what way it affected him."⁹

Dream Songs

The *anishinaabe* dream songs and tricky stories of creation
that bear the nature, elusive ironies, and tragic wisdom of
natives were traduced and depreciated by the hauteur of discovery, the cruelties of monotheism, and the literature of
dominance. The *anishinaabe*, my paternal ancestors, were
removed to the White Earth Reservation in Minnesota, and
named the Chippewa. They were wounded in spirit, but always dynamic, and in the early years of the reservation my
relatives published *The Progress*, a newspaper that was critical of federal policies. The visions, oral stories and dream
songs of the *anishinaabe*, however, had already been translated and compared as static, passive cultural evidence, for
the most part, by ethnographers, rather than as the creative
scenes of nature by native artists.

"The sky loves to hear me sing," is one heartened invitation to nature in an *anishinaabe* dream song. The poet
singer listens to the turnout of the seasons, and then puts
the words of his song directly to the wind and sky. The gesture, in part, is ironic, a native tease of nature.

"With a large bird above me, I am walking in the sky," is
the translation of another avian vision by an *anishinaabe* poet
singer who was heard more than a century ago in northern Minnesota.

Frances Densmore, the honorable recorder of native songs
and ceremonies, translated these *anishinaabe* dream songs
at the turn of the last century. Densmore observed, "Many

of the songs are taught only to those who pay for the privilege of learning them, and all the songs are recorded in mnemonics on strips of birch bark. This record serves as a reminder of the essential idea of the song and is different in its nature from our system of printing. The Indian picture preserves the idea of the song, while our printed page preserves the words which are supposed to express the idea but which often express it very imperfectly."[10] The songs are imagic moments, similar to the tease of nature in haiku scenes.

> as my eyes
> look across the prairie
> I feel the summer
> in the spring

> overhanging clouds
> echoing my words
> with a pleasing sound

> across the earth
> everywhere
> making my voice heard[11]

The *anishinaabe* "ability to dream was cultivated from earliest childhood," writes Densmore in *Chippewa Customs*. Dreams were a source of wisdom, and children were encouraged to remember the stories of their dreams. "Thus the imagination was stimulated, and there arose a keen desire to see something extraordinary in sleep." The *anishinaabe* "say that in their dreams they often returned to the previous state of existence." Some dreams had such great power "that a man had been known to assume the form which had been his in a previous existence, and which

had formed the subject of his dream." The stories of great
dreams secured a sense of "protection, guidance, and assistance."[12] Clearly, the imagic moments of native dreams,
in the sense of the *anishinaabe*, were stories of survivance,
not possessive or passive, but active and visionary.

My introduction to haiku, by chance of the military,
made it easier to understand natural reason and the survivance of native dream songs and literature. How ironic
that my service as a soldier would lead to a literary association of haiku, and an overture to *anishinaabe* dream songs.
Truly, haiku enhanced my experiences of the native dream
songs, and consideration of native reason and comparative philosophies.

"On the one hand there is the disposition of things—
their condition, configuration, and structure. On the other
there is force and movement," François Jullien observed
in *The Propensity of Things*. "The static versus the dynamic.
But this dichotomy, like all dichotomies, is abstract. It is
a temporary means for the mind to represent reality, one
that simplifies as it illuminates." What, then, really exists,
"stranded between these two terms of the dichotomy," the
static and dynamic? "How can we conceive of the dynamic
in terms of the static, in terms of 'disposition'?"

The Chinese concept of *shi* is a critical disposition of dynamic literature, and the efficacy of philosophy. Jullien wrote
that Liu Xie, a sixth-century literary philosopher, "offers
us a fine image for the dynamism at work in a literary text:
when one sets down the brush at the end of a paragraph, it is
like feathering an oar while rowing. The boat continues to
drift forward just as, at the completion of a passage, the text
continues to progress. A 'surplus of *shi*' carries it forward,

leading to the point where it will link up with its own continuation. A text exists not only through its 'order' and 'coherence,' but also through its 'flow' and unfolding.'"

The text flows by the cultural strategies of tone and dynamic rhythms, and by an interior sense of natural reason. Many haiku scenes have *shi*, and the disposition, the temperament, inclination, the mood and aesthetic tendencies, or imagic moments, continue to move in nature and in our memories.

Jullien noted in his introduction that the "term *shi* is the same as the word *yi*, which is believed to represent a hand holding something, a symbol of power." Xu Shen, the second-century lexicographer, "thinks that what is held in the hand is a clod of earth." The diacritic radical *li*, or force, was added to the character later.[13]

"Aesthetics plays an exceedingly important role in Chinese writing, more so than in any other system of writing. Calligraphy has been elevated to an artform," wrote John DeFrancis in *The Chinese Language*. Xu Shen compiled an etymological dictionary of more than nine thousand characters in some five hundred "semantic keys," or "significs." The significs are otherwise named "radicals," or the basic, significant, semantic elements of characters. "Most striking of all is the fact that the Chinese chose a semantic basis rather than a phonetic one for their system of classification."[14]

Jullien considered *shi* a "touchtone" character, and, as an imprecise word, *shi* both semantic and more than a concept; *shi* is a poetic disposition and "intuition of efficacy."

The poem "must be conceived all at once, from start to finish, as a continuous *variation*," wrote Jullien. "In poetry, as in every thing else, dynamism must be renewed, through internal contrasts and shifts from one pole to the other, in order to be continuous." The "poetic *shi*," or the "*dispositional propensity* born of that emotion," becomes the visionary *transmotion* of the expression and imagic moment.

Jullien wrote that a poem is "a single surge of internal energy" and quotes Wang Fuzhi that a poem is "not like 'a melon,' which can be 'divided into slices.'" The "continuity is intrinsic."[15]

Kitaro Nishida, the Japanese philosopher of experience and reality, observed in *An Inquiry into the Good*, "What people usually refer to as *nature* is what remains after the subjective aspect, the unifying activity, is removed from concrete reality. For this reason, there is no self in nature." He wrote "that it is not that experience exists because there is an individual, but that an individual exists because there is experience. I thus arrived at the idea that experience is more fundamental than individual differences, and in this way I was able to avoid solipsism." By solipsism, he means "the theory that the self can know only its own experience," or the idea that the self is the only source of reality.[16]

Any hint of the self is absent in most haiku scenes, but even when subjective experience is mentioned it is not solipsistic or the self of nature. Issa, for instance, is moved by nature, and includes references to himself in his haiku scenes. "Issa's whole life was a tragedy," Blyth wrote in *Haiku: Eastern Culture*. "He was one of those men who attract failure and misfortune." Issa was moved by a sense of fate. "Life goes along joyfully and painfully, with ecstasy and anguish, and Issa goes with it. He does not praise or condemn."[17]

> for you fleas too
> the night must be long
> it must be lonely

"Issa's sympathies were always with small and weak animals, perhaps because he identified himself with them, as the victim of his stepmother's cruelty," Donald Keene wrote in *World Within Walls*.[18]

> skinny frog
> don't be discouraged
> issa is here

Issa must be here too, in the motion of translation and in the consideration of readers. I first read his haiku two centuries after he cajoled that skinny frog and created this scene at Lake Itaska, Minnesota:

> tricky frogs
> croak a haiku in the marsh
> skinny issa[19]

Likewise, the *anishinaabe* created an elusive self in their dream songs, but not the self of nature. "The sky loves to hear me sing," and, "With a large bird, I am walking in the sky," are the voices of visionaries, the motion of intuition, and transformation of the self, not the subjective, solipsistic estates of nature.

> the first to come
> epithet among the birds
> bringing the rain
> crow is my name

This *anishinaabe* dream song is about the arrival of spring and the crows, a natural motion of the seasons. The singer

269

has taken the name of the crow and teases a shamanic, visionary voice of nature. The crow, or *aandeg*, is a sign of wisdom, maybe even tragic wisdom.

> overhanging clouds
> echoing my words
> with a pleasing sound
> across the earth
> everywhere
> making my voice heard[20]

The shamanic voice is a summer storm. Frances Densmore wrote that the singer "hears the reverberations of the thunder and in his dream or trance he composes a song concerning it." Again, the voice is created in nature, the visionary sound of the storm, but is not a subjective voice of nature. The *anishinaabe* do not have a word for the concept of nature. The native tease of the seasons is distinct, direct, and visionary.

> from the half
> of the sky
> that which lives there
> is coming
> and makes a noise

Densmore noted that the singer of this dream song imagines that the thunder *manidoo*, or spirit, "sometimes makes a voice to warn him of its approach." The voice is the *manidoo*, not a mere representation of the spirit. "The idea which underlies the song is, that which lives in the sky is coming and, being friendly, it makes a noise to let me know of its approach."[21] The *anishinaabe* word for thunder is *biidwewidam* and means to "come making noise." The voice of thunder is in motion, a dynamic sound, not subjective, or passive mimicry.

The self, or voice, in haiku scenes and *anishinaabe* dream songs are dynamic and visionary; the dispositions of *mani-doo* and *shi* are imagic moments in nature, but not the subjective voices of nature. The presence of a visionary voice carries the moment of the image, the dream song, and haiku scene into nature. The voice and tone continue as cultural strategies into the text of this discussion.

"Only when there is a unifying self does nature have a goal, take on significance, and become a truly living nature," wrote Kitaro Nishida. "The unifying power that is the life of such nature is not an abstract concept artificially created by our thought but a fact that appears in our intuition." He pointed out, "Artists are people who most excel in this kind of intuition."[22] The imagic moments and intuition of haiku scenes create the experiences, memories, and aesthetic survivance of nature.

Suzuki wrote in *Zen and Japanese Culture* that haiku, "like Zen, abhors egoism in any form of assertion. The product of art must be entirely devoid of artifice or ulterior motive of any kind. There ought not to be any presence of a mediatory agent between the artistic inspiration and the mind into which it has come. The author is to be an altogether passive instrument for giving an expression to the inspiration."[23] The visionary voices in haiku and native dream songs are intuitive, a dynamic presence that only appear to be passive because it is not the ego or self that discovers and owns nature in poetry. The voices of thunder and a crow are intuitive, neither passive nor possessive. Suzuki abhors egoism, but the visionary pronouns of nature are intuitive, not a ruse of devotion or the tricky asceticism of Zen Buddhism.

Philosophy, religion, and literature are inseparable in many cultures. Characteristically, haiku and *anishinaabe* dream songs are more intuitive than demonstrative, more shadows, suggestions, and concise images than the metes and bounds of abstract literature.

"The thought process underlying this nondemonstrative approach does not simply rely on language but rather denies it," observed Masao Abe in the introduction to *An Inquiry into the Good* by Nishida. "This separation from language and rational thought is typically found in Zen, which conveys its basic standpoint with the statement, 'No reliance on words or letters; a special transmission apart from doctrinal teaching.' The same attitude appears in Confucius, who proclaims, 'Clever talk and pretentious manner are seldom found in the Good.' We encounter it in ink drawings that negate form and color, Noh theater with is negation of direct or external expression, and Japanese *waka* and *haiku* poetry."

Abe wrote that to "generate a creative synthesis of Eastern and Western philosophy, one must include but go beyond the demonstrative thinking that is characteristic of the West and both arrive at unobjectifiable ultimate reality and give it a logical articulation by conceptually expressing the inexpressible." That, the "unobjectifiable ultimate reality," is a tease of nature, and a crease of names. The imagic moments are haiku scenes, native dreams, and the visionary.

"Thinking and intuition are usually considered to be totally different activities, but when we view them as facts of consciousness we realize that they are the same kind of activity," argues Nishida. "At the base of thinking there is always a certain unifying reality that we can know only through intuition."[24]

Haiku Scenes

Haiku scenes ascribe the seasons with shadow words, the light that turns a leaf, a bird, a hand. Shadow words are intuitive, concise, the natural motion of memories, and the seasons. Blyth wrote that "haiku is the result of the wish, the effort, not to speak, not to write poetry, not to obscure further the truth and suchness of a thing with words, with thoughts and feelings." And yet, we read and write with pleasure in the motion of nature and literature. Blyth asserted that a "haiku is not a poem, it is not literature; it is a hand beckoning, a door half-opened, a mirror wiped clean. It is a way of returning to nature, to our moon nature, our cherry blossom nature, our falling leaf nature, in short, to our Buddha nature."[25]

Matsuo Bashō as born in 1644 at Ueno, near Kyoto. He was troubled, ridden by doubts as a youth, and later turned to Taoism and Zen Buddhism, wrote Makoto Ueda in *Bashō and His Interpreters*. Bashō decided on "*fuga*, an artist's way of life, a reclusive life devoted to a quest for eternal truth in nature." He pursued *fuga* with sincerity; nonetheless, "he had lingering misgivings about its redemptive power. To his last days, he did not seem able to merge poetry with belief completely."[26]

Haruo Shirane pointed out in *Traces of Dreams* that "Bashō initially went to Edo in order to become a haikai master, a marker who could charge fees for grading haikai." However, he soon turned his back "on the most lucrative aspect of haikai. Even as a marker in Edo, Bashō apparently was reluctant to charge fees. Most of his disciples also avoided the profession of a marker." The name of a marker, or grader, was the same as a haikai master. The haikai, from *haikai no renga*, was a comic, communal, linked verse.

"Bashō divides haikai poets into three types," wrote Shirane. The ideal poet is "devoted to the spirit of poetry rather than to the material benefits," and those who "seek the poetic tradition of Teika and Tu Fu." Fujiwara Teika practiced an "allusive variation" of classical literature at the turn of the thirteenth century. Tu Fu, an eighth-century Chinese poet, was praised for the density of his images, the fusion of emotions and allusions to culture. The second type are those with wealth and status who see haikai as a game. The lowest are the poets who garner points. They are "the lost children of poetry," Bashō wrote to a disciple, "and yet they fill the bellies of the marker's wife and children and bring a profit to the landlord, and as a consequence, they are probably better than those who commit serious crimes."

Bashō died on November 28, 1694. He "dictated this hokku to his student Donshu" three days before his death:

> on a journey, ailing
> my dreams roam about
> on a withered moor

"As it was a balmy day, many flies had gathered around the sliding screens, and the students were trying to catch them with a lime stick," wrote Ueda. "Bashō, amused that some were more skillful than others in handling the stick, laughed and said, 'Those flies seem delighted to have a sick man around unexpectedly.' He spoke no more. He breathed his last at around four that afternoon."[27]

Bashō was amused, and the image of the flies moves with me by experience and the book. Bashō might have teased me over this scene, my haiku about fat green flies at a restaurant in Ellsworth, Wisconsin:

> fat flies
> dance on the grapefruit
> honor your partner[28]

Japanese poets were once the warriors of fusions, classical allusions, and impermanence, and many were actual road poets, a meditative, situational tradition of literature. Bashō traveled and wrote *haibun*, a distinctive form of prose and haiku, in his *Narrow Road to the Deep North*.

Haruo Shirane observed that "*Narrow Road to the Interior* is marked by a great variety of prose styles, which range from a heavily Chinese style to the soft classical style to vernacular prose to a mixture or fusion of all three. In some sections, the style is extremely dense and terse, falling into strict couplets, and in others it resembles the mellifluous, lengthy flow of *The Tale of Genji*." The Matsushima section, for instance, is "extremely Chinese in style and content."

I was truly inspired by the association of the poet and pine islands. Bashō was a master of natural reason, and he had put his "body to the wind." I had no idea at the time that the creation of a *haibun* place was a fusion of styles.

Although often praised as a work of confessional literature or regarded as part of the long tradition of travel accounts, *Narrow Road to the Interior* is best seen as a kind of fiction, loosely based on the actual journey, leaving out most of what actually happened. Key individuals are not mentioned or appear under fictitious or altered names. Bashō added incidents and characters for dramatic effect, and often rearranged or reconstructed those events that did occur. "Bashō depicted an ideal poetic world," wrote Shirane. "Like a linked verse sequence, to which it has often been compared, *Narrow Road to the Interior* has no absolute center, no single overarching perspective. Instead, a focal point emerges, climaxes and then is replaced by a new focal point."

Europeans have celebrated a travel literature of conquest. Not only of new worlds, but of new ideas and experiences. "But for medieval *waka* and *renga* poets," noted Shirane, "the object of travel was to confirm what already existed, to reinforce the roots of cultural memory."[29] That too was an *anishinaabe*, and generally, a native, existential sense of travel, and a visionary cultural memory.

Issa wrote *haibun* on his journey, *The Year of My Life*. "At long last I made up my mind to travel north," he wrote in a translation by Nobuyuki Yuasa, "to get more experience in writing *haiku*. No sooner had I slung my beggar's bag round my neck and flung my little bundle over my shoulder than I noticed, to my great surprise, that my shadow was the very image of Saigyo, the famous poet-priest of times gone by." Saigyo was a twelfth-century *waka* poet and priest.

Issa, at age fifty-seven, writes at the end of *The Year of My Life*, in December 1819, "Those who insist on salvation by faith and devote their minds to nothing else, are bound all the more firmly by their singlemindedness, and fall into the hell of attachment to their own salvation. Again, those who are passive and stand to one side waiting to be saved, consider that they are already perfect and rely rather on Buddha than on themselves to purify their hearts—these, too, have failed to find the secret of genuine salvation. The question then remains—how do we find it? But the answer, fortunately, is not difficult.

"We should do far better to put this vexing problem of salvation out of our minds altogether and place our reliance neither on faith nor on personal virtue, but surrender ourselves completely to the will of Buddha. Let him do as he will with us—be it to carry us to heaven, or to hell. Herein lies the secret."[30] Fate and chance are common sentiments of experience in haiku and native literature.

Issa, the "poet of destiny," died eight years later. The frogs continue to croak his name, skinny Issa in the secret marsh, and he is celebrated everywhere by crickets, mosquitoes, flies, many insects, and many birds in the voices of nature and survivance.

Notes

Introduction

1. Clifford Geertz, *The Interpretation of Cultures* (New York: Basic Books, 1973), 7, 10, 416.

2. Giorgio Agamben, *Means without End: Notes on Politics* (Minneapolis: University of Minnesota Press, 2000), 56, 57.

3. Geertz, *The Interpretation of Cultures*, 5.

4. Gerald Vizenor, *Cranes Arise: Haiku Scenes* (Minneapolis: Nodin Press, 1999); Gerald Vizenor, *Matsushima: Pine Islands* (Minneapolis: Nodin Press, 1984), no page numbers.

5. Gerald Vizenor, *Fugitive Poses: Native American Indian Scenes of Absence and Presence* (Lincoln: University of Nebraska Press, 1998), 15. "The connotations of transmotion are creation stories, totemic visions, reincarnation, and sovenance; transmotion, that sense of native motion and an active presence, is *sui generis* sovereignty. Native transmotion is survivance, a reciprocal use of nature, not a monotheistic, territorial sovereignty. Native stories of survivance are the creases of transmotion and sovereignty."

6. Gerald Vizenor, *Manifest Manners: Narratives on Postindian Survivance* (Lincoln: University of Nebraska Press, 1994), 64. "The shadow is that sense of intransitive motion to the referent; the silence in memories. Shadows are neither the absence of entities nor the burden of conceptual references."

7. Vizenor, *Manifest Manners*, 7, 9.

8. Vizenor, *Fugitive Poses*, 120, 121. Englishman, "You have put out the fire of my French father. I became cold and needy, and you sought

me not. Others have sought me. Yes, the Long Knife has found me. He has placed his heart on my breast. It has entered there, and there it will remain."

9. Duane Niatum, ed., *Harper's Anthology of 20th Century Native American Poetry* (San Francisco: Harper and Row, 1988), ix, x.

10. David Treuer, *Native American Fiction: A User's Manual* (Saint Paul MN: Graywolf Press, 2006), 195, 196, 197, 201.

11. Paul Shepard, *The Others: How Animals Made Us Human* (Washington DC: Island Press, 1966), 90, 91.

12. Janet Martin Soskice, *Metaphor and Religious Language* (Oxford, UK: Clarendon, 1985), 15, 58, 59, 60.

13. John Searle, "Metaphor," in *Metaphor and Thought*, ed. Andrew Ortony (New York: Cambridge University Press, 1979), 93, 105, 123.

14. Louise Erdrich, *Tracks* (New York: Harper and Row, 1988), 10, 37, 54, 60, 89.

15. N. Scott Momaday, *The Ancient Child* (New York: Doubleday, 1989), 17.

16. Charles Woodward, *Ancestral Voice: Conversations with N. Scott Momaday* (Lincoln: University of Nebraska Press, 1989), 22.

17. Leslie Silko, *Ceremony* (New York: Viking Penguin, 1977), 132, 133.

18. Louis Owens, *Other Destinies: Understanding the American Indian Novel* (Norman: University of Oklahoma Press, 1992), 184.

19. Gordon Henry Jr., *The Light People* (Norman: University of Oklahoma Press, 1994), 170, 171.

20. Louis Owens, *Bone Game* (Norman: University of Oklahoma Press, 1994), 96.

21. Gerald Vizenor, *Hiroshima Bugi: Atomu 57* (Lincoln: University of Nebraska Press, 2003), 144.

22. Vizenor, *Fugitive Poses*, 142.

1. Unnamable Chance

1. Gerald Vizenor, *Interior Landscapes: Autobiographical Myths and Metaphors* (Minneapolis: University of Minnesota Press, 1990), 21, 22.

2. Vizenor, *Interior Landscapes*, 28, 29.

3. Georges Bataille, *The Accursed Share* (New York: Zone Books, 1988), 72, 73.

4. Gerald Vizenor, "Visions, Scares, and Stories," in *Contemporary Authors* (New York: Gale Research, 1996), 22:255–77. See also *Contemporary Authors*, 2003, 205:401–33.

5. Gerald Vizenor, with A. Robert Lee, *Postindian Conversations* (Lincoln: University of Nebraska Press, 1999), 63.

6. Gerald Vizenor, *Chancers* (Norman: University of Oklahoma Press, 2000).

7. Gerald Vizenor, "Mister Ishi: Analogies of Exile, Deliverance, and Liberty," in *Ishi in Three Centuries*, ed. Karl Kroeber and Clifton Kroeber (Lincoln: University of Nebraska Press, 2003), 363–72.

8. Albert Camus, *Lyrical and Critical Essays* (New York: Random House, Vintage Books, 1968), 151, 152.

9. Owens, *Other Destinies*, 93.

10. Isaiah Berlin, *The Roots of Romanticism* (Princeton NJ: Princeton University Press, 1999), 146, 147.

11. Albert Camus, *American Journal* (London: Abacus Book, 1988), 31.

12. Primo Levi, *If This Be a Man: Remembering Auschwitz* (New York: Summit Books, 1960), 93.

13. Edmond Jabès, *The Little Book of Unsuspected Subversion* (Stanford CA: Stanford University Press, 1996), 49.

14. Samuel Beckett, *The Unnamable* (New York: Grove Press, 1958), 179.

15. Owens, *Other Destinies*, 13.

16. Diane Glancy, *Claiming Breath* (Lincoln: University of Nebraska Press, 1992), 29.

17. Edmond Jabès, *The Book of Questions* (Hanover: Wesleyan University Press, 1964), 1:31.

2. Native Liberty

1. Daniel Littlefield, "Newspapers, Magazines, and Journals," in *Encyclopedia of North American Indians*, ed. Frederick Hoxie (Boston: Houghton Mifflin Company, 1996), 428.

2. Senate Committee on Indian Affairs, *Testimony in Relation to Affairs at the White Earth Reservation, Minnesota*, subcommittee hearing, March 8, 1887.

3. Survivance Narratives

1. Charles Alexander Eastman, *From the Deep Woods to Civilization* (Chicago: Lakeside Press, 2001), 7.

2. Francis Paul Prucha, *American Indian Treaties* (Berkeley: University of California Press, 1994), 264.

3. Francis Paul Prucha, *The Indians in American Society* (Berkeley: University of California Press, 1985), 41, 42.

4. Robert Utley, *The Frontier Regulars: The United States Army and the Indian, 1866–1891* (Lincoln: University of Nebraska Press, 1973), 130, 131.

5. Jay Winik, *April 1865: The Month That Saved America* (New York: HarperCollins, 2001), 189, 419.

6. Ulysses S. Grant, *The Papers of Ulysses S. Grant*, microfilm, series 7, reels 32, 33. Reproduced at www.mscomm.com/ffiulysses/page 63.html.

7. Robert Utley, *The Indian Frontier of the American West, 1846–1890* (Albuquerque: University of New Mexico Press, 1984), 75.

8. Thomas Britten, *American Indians in World War I* (Albuquerque: University of New Mexico Press, 1997), 11, 25.

9. Britten, *American Indians in World War I*, 26.

10. Britten, *American Indians in World War I*, 61, 185, 186.

11. John M. Coward, *The Newspaper Indian: Native American Identity in the Press, 1820–90* (Urbana: University of Illinois Press, 1999), 16.

12. Coward, *The Newspaper Indian*, 17.

13. Coward, *The Newspaper Indian*, 129.

14. Utley, *The Indian Frontier*, 193.

15. Mark H. Brown, *The Flight of the Nez Perce* (New York: G. P. Putnam's Sons, 1967), 407.

16. Brown, *The Flight of the Nez Perce*, 408.

17. Bruce Hampton, *Children of Grace: The Nez Perce War of 1877* (New York: Henry Holt and Company, 1994), 307.

18. Coward, *The Newspaper Indian*, 131.

19. Hampton, *Children of Grace*, 325.

20. Chief Joseph, "An Indian's View of Indian Affairs," *North American Review*, April 1879.

21. Chief Joseph, "An Indian's View," 432; and Hampton, *Children of Grace*, 326.

22. Otis Halfmoon, "Joseph (Heinmot Tooyalakekt)," in *Encyclopedia of North American Indians*, ed. Frederick Hoxie (Boston: Houghton Mifflin, 1996), 311.

23. Utley, *Frontier Regulars*, 315.

24. Gerald Vizenor, *The People Named the Chippewa: Narrative Histories* (Minneapolis: University of Minnesota Press, 1984), 78.

25. Vizenor, *The People Named the Chippewa*, 80.

26. Vizenor, *The People Named the Chippewa*, 92.

27. Vizenor, *The People Named the Chippewa*, 94.

28. James Mooney, *The Ghost-Dance Religion and the Sioux Outbreak of 1890* (Lincoln: University of Nebraska Press, 1991), 782. First published by the Bureau of Ethnology, 1896.

29. Mooney, *The Ghost-Dance Religion*, 776.

30. Mooney, *The Ghost-Dance Religion*, 773.

31. Mooney, *The Ghost-Dance Religion*, 781.

32. *I Wear the Morning Star: An Exhibition of American Indian Ghost Dance Objects*, exhibition catalog (Minneapolis: Minneapolis Institute of Arts, 1976).

33. Michael Hittman, *Wovoka and the Ghost Dance* (Lincoln: University of Nebraska Press, 1997), 163.

34. Utley, *The Indian Frontier*, 256, 257.

35. William Coleman, *Voices of Wounded Knee* (Lincoln: University of Nebraska Press, 2000), 309.

36. Coleman, *Voices of Wounded Knee*, 312.

37. Coleman, *Voices of Wounded Knee*, 309.

38. Eastman, *From the Deep Woods to Civilization*, 234.

39. Eastman, *From the Deep Woods to Civilization*, 237, 238.

40. Luther Standing Bear, *My People the Sioux* (Lincoln: University of Nebraska Press, 1975), 223, 224. First published in 1928.

41. Standing Bear, *My People the Sioux*, 226.

42. L. G. Moses, *The Indian Man: A Biography of James Mooney* (Lincoln: University of Nebraska Press, 1984), 54.

43. S. Alice Callahan, *Wynema: A Child of the Forest* (Lincoln: University of Nebraska Press, 1997), 101. First published by H. L. Smith and Company, Chicago, 1891.

44. Callahan, *Wynema*, 80.

45. Callahan, *Wynema*, 81.

46. Callahan, *Wynema*, xvii.

47. Callahan, *Wynema*, xxvi, xxvii.

48. Zitkala Sa, "Impressions of an Indian Childhood: The Big Red Apples," *Atlantic Monthly*, January 1900, 46, 47. Reprinted by the Electronic Text Center, University of Virginia Library, http://etext.virginia.edu/toc/modeng/public/Zitimpr.html.

49. Dexter Fisher, "Zitkala Sa: The Evolution of a Writer," *American Indian Quarterly* 5, no. 3 (1979): 238. Reprinted in Janet Witalec, ed., *Native North American Literature* (Farmington Hills MI: Gale Research, 1994).

50. Ruth J. Heflin, *"I Remain Alive": The Sioux Literary Renaissance* (Syracuse NY: Syracuse University Press, 1994), 106.

51. Zitkala Sa, "Why I Am a Pagan," *Atlantic Monthly*, December 1902. Reprinted in the *Online Archive of Nineteenth-Century U.S. Women's Writings*, ed. Glynis Carr, http://etext.virginia.edu/toc/modeng/public/Zit impr.html.

4. Aesthetics of Survivance

1. Vizenor, *Fugitive Poses*, 167, 168.

2. Antoine Compagnon, *Literature, Theory, and Common Sense* (Princeton NJ: Princeton University Press, 2004), 9, 12.

3. William Warren, *History of the Ojibway Nation* (Minneapolis: Ross and Haines, 1957), 34, 47, 88. Warren, the first *anishinaabe* historian, was born May 27, 1825, at La Pointe, Madeline Island, Lake Superior. He was an interpreter, elected as a member of the Minnesota Territorial Legislature. He died on June 1, 1853. *History of the Ojibway Nation* was first published by the Minnesota Historical Society in 1885. The crane totem, *ajijaak*, is also known as the "echo makers."

4. Warren, *History of the Ojibway Nation*, 368, 373. See also Vizenor, *Interior Landscapes*, 4, 5, 6. The Long Knife is a name for the Americans. The name is a translation of *gichimookomann* (*gichi*, big or great; *mookomaan*, knife) a descriptive metaphor of the first contact with white men who carried swords.

5. George Lakoff and Mark Johnson, *Metaphors We Live By* (Chicago: University of Chicago Press, 1980), 3, 193, 229, 235.

6. N. Scott Momaday, *The Names: A Memoir* (New York: Harper and Row, 1976), 3.

7. Searle, "Metaphor," 93, 105, 123. "The question, 'How do metaphors work?' is a bit like the question, 'How does one thing remind us of another thing?' There is no single answer to either question, though similarity obviously plays a major role in answering both. Two important differences between them are that metaphors are both restricted and systematic; restricted in the sense that not every way that one thing can remind us of something else will provide a basis for metaphor, and systematic in the sense that metaphors must be communicable from speaker to hearer in virtue of a shared system of principles."

8. Soskice, *Metaphor and Religious Language*, 15, 58, 59, 60.

9. James Welch, *Winter in the Blood* (New York: Harper and Row, 1974), 1, 2.

10. Woodward, *Ancestral Voice*, 17.

11. N. Scott Momaday, *House Made of Dawn* (New York: Harper and Row, 1968), 31, 32, 33, 64.

12. Silko, *Ceremony*, 132, 133.

13. Erdrich, *Tracks*, 10, 37, 54, 60, 89.

14. David Treuer, *The Hiawatha* (New York: Picador USA, 1999), 8.

15. Treuer, *The Hiawatha*, 79.

16. Treuer, *The Hiawatha*, 5.

17. Treuer, *The Hiawatha*, 310.

18. Momaday, *House Made of Dawn*, 212.

19. Treuer, *Native American Fiction*, 3, 4.

20. Dorothy Lee, *Freedom and Culture* (Prospect Heights IL: Waveland Press, 1959, 1987), 60, 61, 65.

21. Vizenor, *Manifest Manners*, vii.

22. Ernest Stromberg, ed., *American Indian Rhetorics and Survivance: Word Medicine, Word Magic* (Pittsburgh: University of Pittsburgh Press, 2006), 1.

23. Clifford Geertz, *Available Light* (Princeton NJ; Princeton University Press, 2000), 250.

24. George Steiner, *After Babel: Aspects of Language and Translation*, 3rd ed. (Oxford, UK: Oxford University Press, 1998), xiv. The word *survivance* was not used in the first edition.

25. George Steiner, *Real Presences* (Chicago: University of Chicago Press, 1989), 209, 210. Steiner observed that it is the "aesthetic which, past any other mode accessible to us, is the felt configuration of a negation (however partial, however 'figurative' in the precise sense) of mortality. Imaging to ourselves the fictive situation or personae in the text, recomposing perceptually the objects or visage in the painting, making audition resonant to the music via an inner complementarity, at once conceptual and bodily, we remake the making."

26. Jacques Derrida, *Negotiations: Interventions and Interviews* (Stanford CA: Stanford University Press, 2002), 111, 112.

27. Jacques Derrida, *Archive Fever: A Freudian Impression* (Chicago: University of Chicago Press, 1996), 60.

28. Peggy Kamuf, ed., *A Derrida Reader: Between the Blinds* (New York: Columbia University Press, 1991), 59.

5. Mercenary Sovereignty

1. Nayan Chanda, *Bound Together: How Traders, Preachers, Adventurers, and Warriors Shaped Globalization* (New Haven CT: Yale University Press, 2007), 227. "Within a span of just seventy-odd years, eighty to a hundred million natives perished because of the disease brought by Europeans from across the seas: smallpox, influenza, diphtheria," wrote

Chanda. "One of things English pilgrims gave thanks for at Plymouth in 1621 was the fact that 90 percent of the indigenous peoples of New England had died of disease brought by previous visitors."

2. Peter Singer, *One World: The Ethics of Globalization* (New Haven CT: Yale University Press, 2002), 5, 197.

3. Agamben, *Means without End*, 111, 112.

4. Stephen Krasner, *Sovereignty: Organized Hypocrisy* (Princeton NJ: Princeton University, 1999), 9.

5. John Paul Prucha, ed., *Documents of United States Indian Policy* (Lincoln: University of Nebraska Press, 1974), 36, 37.

6. David Wilkins, *American Indian Sovereignty and the U.S. Supreme Court* (Austin: University of Texas Press, 1997), 298.

7. N. Bruce Duthu, *American Indians and the Law* (New York: Viking, 2008), 70.

8. Robert Dahl, *How Democratic Is the American Constitution?* (New Haven CT: Yale University Press, 2001), 16.

9. Michael Hardt and Antonio Negri, *Empire* (Cambridge MA: Harvard University Press, 2000), 169, 170.

10. Martin Ridge, ed., *Frederick Jackson Turner: Wisconsin's Historian of the Frontier* (Madison: State Historical Society of Wisconsin, 1896), 33.

11. Ridge, *Frederick Jackson Turner*, 7.

12. Ridge, *Frederick Jackson Turner*, 27.

13. Hardt and Negri, *Empire*, 170.

14. Hardt and Negri, *Empire*, 171.

15. Hardt and Negri, *Empire*, 172.

16. Tyler Cowen, *Creative Destruction: How Globalization Is Changing the World's Cultures* (Princeton NJ: Princeton University Press, 2002), 55, 56.

17. Singer, *One World*, 136, 137.

18. John Boli, "Sovereignty from a World Polity Perspective," in *Problematic Sovereignty*, ed. Stephen Krasner (New York: Columbia University Press, 2001), 53.

19. Philippe Legrain, *Open World: The Truth About Globalization* (London: Abacus, 2002), 7, 297.

20. Chanda, *Bound Together*, 275.

21. Daniel Cohen, *Globalization and Its Enemies* (Cambridge MA: MIT Press, 2006), 165, 166.

22. John Broder, "Californians Hear Grim News on Budget," *New York Times*, January 11, 2003.

23. Gerald Vizenor, "Gambling," in *Encyclopedia of North American Indians*, ed. Frederick Hoxie (New York: Houghton Mifflin, 1996), 212, 214.

24. "The Last Shall be First: Indian Tribes and Casinos," *The Economist*, April 14, 2007.

25. Stephen Krasner, "Sovereignty," *Foreign Policy*, February 2001, 1. Reprinted by Global Policy Forum, www.globalpolicy.org/nations/realism.htm.

26. Hardt and Negri, *Empire*, xi, xvi, xv.

27. Alexander Aleinikoff, *Semblances of Sovereignty* (Cambridge MA: Harvard University Press, 2002), 128, 150.

28. "Median Household Income Rises for Tribes," *Santa Fe New Mexican*, September 7, 2002.

29. Donald Barlett and James Steele, "Indian Casinos: Wheel of Fortune," *Time*, December 16, 2002, 46, 47.

30. Ernest Stevens Jr., "A Different View," *Time*, January 13, 2003, 9.

31. James May, "Gaming Leaders Denounce Magazine Slant," *Indian Country Today*, December 18, 2002.

32. "Bureau of Casino Affairs," *Wall Street Journal*, September 3, 2002.

33. David Chen and Charlie LeDuff, "With Growth in Gambling, Casinos Create Bitter Divisions among Indians," *New York Times*, October 28, 2001.

34. Vizenor, *Manifest Manners*, 146, 147.

35. Mark Taylor, *The Moment of Complexity* (Chicago: University of Chicago Press, 2001), 19, 47.

36. Peter van Ham, "The Rise of the Brand State," *Foreign Affairs*, September/October 2001, 2, 3.

37. Friedrich Nietzsche, *Human, All Too Human* (Cambridge, UK: Cambridge University Press, 1986), 40, 179.

38. John Forrester, *Truth Games* (Cambridge MA: Harvard University Press, 1997), 2, 24, 25.

39. James Bernauer and David Rasmussen, eds., *The Final Foucault* (Cambridge MA: MIT Press, 1988), 1, 16.

40. Bernauer and Rasmussen, *The Final Foucault*, 15.

41. James Chatters, "Politics Aside, These Bones Belong to Everybody," *Wall Street Journal*, September 9, 2002.

42. Timothy Egan, "U.S. Takes Tribe's Side on Bones," *New York Times,* September 30, 2000.

43. "Scientists Win Kennewick Man Ruling," *Tri-City Herald* (Kennewick, Pasco, and Richland, Washington), August 31, 2002.

6. Genocide Tribunals

1. William Schabas, *An Introduction to the International Criminal Court* (Cambridge, UK: Cambridge University Press, 2001), 125, 126.

2. Gerald Vizenor, "Ojibways Seek Right to 'Regulate' Rice on Wildlife Refuge," *Minneapolis Tribune,* September 13, 1968.

3. Prucha, *American Indian Treaties,* 385.

4. Albert Hirshman, *Rhetoric of Reaction: Perversity, Futility, Jeopardy* (Cambridge MA: Harvard University Press, 1991), 168, 169.

5. Schabas, *An Introduction to the International Criminal Court,* 32.

6. Samantha Power, *"A Problem from Hell": America and the Age of Genocide* (New York: Harper Perennial, 2003), 66, 157.

7. Power, *"A Problem from Hell,"* 67.

8. Power, *"A Problem from Hell,"* 168, 169.

9. Power, *"A Problem from Hell,"* xxi, 61.

10. Geoffrey Robertson, *Crimes against Humanity: The Struggle for Global Justice* (New York: The New Press, 1999), 452.

11. William A. Galston, "Practical Philosophy and the Bill of Rights: Perspectives on Some Contemporary Issues," in *A Culture of Rights,* ed. Michael J. Lacey and Knud Haakonssen, Woodrow Wilson International Center for Scholars (Cambridge, UK: Cambridge University Press, 1991), 221, 222.

12. Vizenor, *Manifest Manners,* vii, 3, 5; Vizenor, *Fugitive Poses,* 15.

13. Michael Mann, *The Dark Side of Democracy: Explaining Ethnic Cleansing* (Cambridge, UK: Cambridge University Press, 2005), 34, 529.

14. Clinton Dick, "Jessup Moot Court Team Wins Regionals," *Harvard Law School Record,* March 4, 2004, http://www.hlrecord.org/media/paper609/news/2004/03/04/News/ Jessup.Moot.Court.Team.Wins.

15. Moot Court Web, "The European Law Moot Court Competition," http://zealot.mrnet.pt/mootcourt/.

16. Rome Statute of the International Criminal Court, Preamble, Article 24, 29, http://www.un.org/law/icc/.

17. Antonio Cassese, *International Criminal Law* (Oxford, UK: Oxford University Press, 2003), 318, 319.

18. Cassese, *International Criminal Law,* 96, 97. See also David

Nersessian, "Rethinking Cultural Genocide Under International Law," Carnegie Council on Ethics and International Affairs, http://www.cceia.org/.

19. Schabas, An Introduction to the International Criminal Court, 31, 32.

20. John R. Bolton, "The United States and the International Criminal Court," United States Department of State, November 14, 2002, http://www.state.gov/t/us/rm/15158.htm.

21. Mann, The Dark Side of Democracy, 92, 93.

22. Roger L. Di Silvestro, In the Shadow of Wounded Knee (New York: Walker and Company, 2005), 56.

23. Di Silvestro, In the Shadow of Wounded Knee, 92. "General Nelson Miles, rumored to be interested in running for president, said, 'I have never heard of a more brutal, cold-blooded massacre than that at Wounded Knee.'"

24. Coleman, Voices of Wounded Knee, 148, 341.

25. Paul M. Robertson, "Wounded Knee Massacre, 1890," in Encyclopedia of North American Indians, ed. Frederick E. Hoxie (New York: Houghton Mifflin Company, 1996), 694, 696, 696. "The Ghost Dance frightened many whites in the region, and rumors were rampant," wrote Robertson. "Although there were no incidents of raiding outside the newly established reservation boundaries, many whites left their isolated homesteads and took temporary residence in towns." One hundred and six warriors were "separated from the approximately 250 women and children. Their separate camps were surrounded by 470 soldiers and 30 Indian scouts. On a hill overlooking the camp, four rapid-fire Hotchkiss cannons, capable of firing fifty two-pound explosive shells per minute, were trained on Big Foot's band." On December 29 Colonel James Forsyth, commander of the Seventh Cavalry, "ordered the disarmament of Big Foot's band. The search for weapons added to the tension. Soldiers treated the women roughly and disrespectfully." An officer "reported that one 'squaw' was thrown on her back to make accessible the rifle she had under her dress. Joe Horn Cloud recounted how soldiers took off the blankets the women had around them against the chill, raised their dresses, and laughed. The alcohol the soldiers had consumed the previous night probably contributed to the situation." Soon after the "women were searched, and the tipis ransacked for guns, the men were subjected to a body search. About forty rifles were seized in all. What happened next is not certain, but one man apparently refused to relinquish his weapon. Soldiers grabbed for it, and

in the struggle a shot went off. Shooting immediately began on both sides. Half of the warriors were killed on the spot. Others ran to rescue their families, and a few broke through the line of troops. Many women and children standing by their tipis under a white flag of truce were cut down by deadly shrapnel from Hotchkiss guns. The rest fled under withering fire from all sides. Pursuing soldiers shot most of them down in flight, some with babes on their backs. . . . General Nelson Miles was outraged by the deaths of women and children, and he removed Colonel Forsyth from command. Besides the women and children, a large number of the warriors had no firearms."

26. Coleman, *Voices of Wounded Knee*, 21; Colonel Richard I. Dodge, "Bullets and Bread," first published in the *Army and Navy Journal*, December 6, 1890.

27. Coleman, *Voices of Wounded Knee*, 130, 131.

28. Ralph K. Andrist, *The Long Death: The Last Days of the Plains Indian* (New York: Macmillan Company, 1964), 347, 351. "The line of bodies was afterward found to extend for more than two miles from the camp—and they were all women and children."

29. Coleman, *Voices of Wounded Knee*, 309, 315, 316, 318.

30. Cassese, *International Criminal Law*, 403, 404.

31. Schabas, *An Introduction to the International Criminal Court*, 120, 125. "The International Criminal Court has jurisdiction over four categories of crimes: crimes against humanity, war crimes and aggression." Ralph Lemkin created the word *genocide* in *Axis Rule in Occupied Europe: Laws of Occupation, Analysis of Government, Proposals for Redress*, published by the Carnegie Endowment for World Peace in 1944. The treaty on genocide was enacted a few years later (21, 29).

32. Mann, *The Dark Side of Democracy*, 90, 91.

33. Vizenor, "Mister Ishi," 363, 364.

34. Gerald Vizenor, *Bear Island: The War at Sugar Point* (Minneapolis: University of Minnesota Press, 2006). The United States Army declared war on the *anishinaabe*, or Chippewa, band of Pillagers at Bear Island and Sugar Point on the Leech Lake Reservation, October 5, 1989.

35. Mann, *The Dark Side of Democracy*, 91.

36. Vizenor, *Bear Island*, 9, 10.

37. Robertson, *Crimes against Humanity*, 228, 229, 334.

38. Guenter Lewy, "Were American Indians the Victims of Genocide?" History News Network, November 22, 2004, http://hnn.us/articles/7302.html. First published in *Commentary*. "As for the larger society,

even if some elements in the white population, mainly in the West, at times advocated extermination, no official of the U.S. government every seriously proposed it," reasoned Lewy. "Genocide was never American policy, nor was it the result of policy." Churchill overstated the causes of disease in native communities, an ideological revisionism. Lewy, however, by his counterargument, seems to justify a denial of genocide by simplified summaries of the cultural diversity of Native American Indians. "The Indians were not prepared to give up the nomadic life of a hunter for the sedentary life of the farmer. The new Americans, convinced of their cultural and racial superiority, were unwilling to grant the original inhabitants of the continent the vast preserve of land required by the Indians' way of life. The consequence was a conflict in which there were few heroes, but which was far from a simple tale of hapless victims and merciless aggressors. To fling the charge of genocide at an entire society serves neither the interests of the Indians nor those of history." Lewy does not mention forced removal, treaties, constitutional deracination of natives, and the consistent fraud of the government, or native resistance to the corruption of federal agents. These distinct historical positions on genocide and situational crimes against humanity would be considered as testimony in a genocide tribunal.

39. Prucha, *The Indians in American Society*, 33, 34.

40. Robert Berkhofer Jr., "The North American Frontier as Process and Context," in *The Frontier in History*, ed. Howard Lamar and Leonard Thompson (New Haven CT: Yale University Press, 1981), 48, 49.

41. Russell Thornton, *Native American Holocaust and Survival* (Norman: University of Oklahoma Press, 1987), 100, 101.

42. Office of the High Commissioner for Human Rights, "Universal Declaration of Human Rights," http://www.unhchr.ch/udhr/lang/eng.

43. Page Smith, *A New Age Now Begins: A People's History of the American Revolution* (New York: McGraw-Hill, 1976), 2:1221.

44. Wikipedia, "Indian Massacres," http://en.wikipedia.org/wiki/Native_American_massacres.

7. Ontic Images

1. Barbara Maria Stafford, *Visual Analogy: Consciousness as the Art of Connecting* (Boston: MIT Press, 1999), 8, 28, 35.

2. Louis Dupré, *Passage to Modernity* (New Haven CT: Yale University Press, 1993), 6, 249, 250. "Modernity is an *event* that has transformed the

relation between the cosmos, its transcendent source, and its human interpreter. To explain this as the outcome of historical precedents is to ignore its most significant quality—namely, its success in rendering all rival views of the real obsolete. Its innovative power made modernity, which began as a local Western phenomenon, a universal project capable of forcing its theoretical and practical principles on all but the most isolated civilizations," writes Dupré. "Some traditional societies feeling threatened by modernity have attempted to defend themselves against it by often violent reversals to the past. Such rearguard actions are not likely to prevail. Science and technology have become inevitable and practically indispensable for survival."

3. Larry McMurtry, *Crazy Horse* (New York: Viking Penguin, 1999), 14.

4. Vizenor, *Fugitive Poses*, 23.

5. Jabès, *The Little Book of Unsuspected Subversion*, 66.

6. N. Scott Momaday, "Indian Voices," in *Wordarrows: Indians and Whites in the New Fur Trade*, by Gerald Vizenor (Minneapolis: University of Minnesota Press, 1978), vi.

7. Jabès, *The Book of Questions*, 1:31.

8. Roland Barthes, *Camera Lucida* (New York: Hill and Wang, 1981), 87.

9. "*There is no archive without a place of consignation, without a technique of repetition, and without a certain exteriority,*" asserted Jacques Derrida in *Archive Fever*. Moreover, "*every archive . . . is at once institutive and conservative.*" The indian is an archive—the simulations in translation and fugitive poses in photographs, and the aesthetics of tragic victimry.

10. Mick Gidley, "Edward S. Curtis' Indian Photographs: A National Enterprise," in *Representing Others*, ed. Mick Gidley (Exeter, UK: University of Exeter Press, 1994) 103, 104.

11. David Freedberg, *The Power of Images* (Chicago: University of Chicago Press, 1989), 438, 439.

12. W. J. T. Mitchell, *Picture Theory* (Chicago: University of Chicago Press, 1994), 13, 14.

13. Susan Sontag, *On Photography* (New York: Farrar, Straus and Giroux, 1977), 9, 68, 111, 158.

14. Susan Schindehette and Danelle Morton, "Native Son," *People*, December 14, 1998, 83.

15. Schindehette and Morton, "Native Son," 84, 85.

16. Barthes, *Camera Lucida*, 12.

17. W. S. Penn, *All My Sins Are Relatives* (Lincoln: University of Nebraska Press, 1995), 53, 61.

18. Barthes, *Camera Lucida*, 6.

19. Sontag, *On Photography*, 80.

20. Penn, *All My Sins Are Relatives*, 54, 56.

21. Roland David Laing, *Self and Others* (London: Tavistock Publications, 1961), in *The Wing of Madness: The Life and Work of R. D. Laing*, ed. Daniel Burston (Cambridge MA: Harvard University Press, 1996), 179. "The intensification of the being of the agent through self-disclosure, through making patent the latent self, is the meaning of Nietzsche's 'will to power.' It is the 'weak' man who is not potentiating himself genuinely who may counterfeit his impotence by dominating and controlling others," wrote Laing.

22. Laing, *Self and Others*, 178.

23. Patricia Penn Hilden, *When Nickels Were Indians: An Urban Mixed-Blood Story* (Herndon VA: Smithsonian Institution Press, 1995), 201.

24. Marge Anderson, "Reflection on Racism," in *American Indian Report*, Falmouth Institute, Fairfax, Virginia, December 1998, 8.

25. Warren, *History of the Ojibway Nation*, 58, 60, 61.

26. Robert E. Bieder, *Science Encounters the Indian, 1820–1880* (Norman: University of Oklahoma Press, 1986), 59, 61. Johann Friedrich Blumenbach's dissertation *On the Natural History of Mankind* was published in 1775.

27. Bieder, *Science Encounters the Indian*, 69, 70, 83. Samuel Morton's *Crania Americana* was published in Philadelphia in 1839.

28. Barbara Katz Rothman, *Genetic Maps and Human Imaginations* (New York: W. W. Norton and Company, 1998), 46, 47, 57. Rothman asked, "Can there be a science of race that is not scientific racism? Is it possible to maintain the concept of race without being racist? I don't think so."

29. Russell Means, *Where White Men Fear to Tread: The Autobiography of Russell Means* (New York: St. Martin's Press, 1995), 551, 553.

30. Rothman, *Genetic Maps and Human Imaginations*, 64, 65. "The discriminating, discerning, trained eye that can recognize the 'essential' or defining characteristics in the individual that confer race categorization will now be looking not at the face, the angle of the cheek, the color of skin, but at the DNA."

31. Burston, *The Wing of Madness*, 190.

32. Rothman, *Genetic Maps and Human Imaginations*, 232, 234, 237.

8. Anishinaabe Pictomyths

1. Frances Densmore, *Chippewa Customs* (Minneapolis: Ross and Haines, 1970), 174.

2. Densmore, *Chippewa Customs*, 174, 175.

3. Selwyn Dewdney and Kenneth E. Kidd, *Indian Rock Paintings of the Great Lakes* (Toronto: University of Toronto, for the Quetico Foundation, 1962), 20.

4. Gerald Vizenor, "Ojibway, Christian Funeral Rites Conducted for State Indian, 124," *Minneapolis Tribune*, December 11, 1968.

5. Bruce White, *We Are at Home: Pictures of the Ojibwe People* (Saint Paul: Minnesota Historical Society Press, 2007), 53.

6. Barthes, *Camera Lucida*, 4, 6, 12, 13.

7. White, *We Are at Home*, 4.

8. Barthes, *Camera Lucida*, 27, 28.

9. Barthes, *Camera Lucida*, 45.

10. White, *We Are at Home*, 33.

11. White, *We Are at Home*, 34.

12. White, *We Are at Home*, 42, 43.

13. White, *We Are at Home*, 67, 68, 69.

14. Vizenor, *Bear Island*.

15. White, *We Are at Home*, 157.

16. White, *We Are at Home*, 203.

9. Edward Curtis

1. David Stout, "No Place for John Wayne at Indian Bureau," *New York Times*, September 22, 2000. Likewise, JoAnn Chase, the executive director of the National Congress of American Indians, was recently photographed in front of an original native portrait by the expressionist painter Fritz Scholder.

2. Walter Benjamin, *Illuminations: Essays and Reflections* (New York: Schocken Books, 1969), 225, 226. Benjamin pointed out that "as man withdraws from the photographic image, the exhibition value for the first time shows its superiority to the ritual value."

3. Richard Kearney, *The Wake of Imagination* (Minneapolis: University of Minnesota Press, 1988), 15. "The imminent demise of imagination is clearly a postmodern obsession," wrote Kearney. "Postmodernism undermines the modernist belief in the image as an *authentic* expression. The typically postmodern image is one which displays its own artificiality, its own pseudostatus, its own representational depthlessness."

4. Johannes Fabian, *Time and the Other: How Anthropology Makes Its Object*

(New York: Columbia University Press, 1983), 107, 154. "Certainly there has been progress in anthropology from mere counting and mapping of cultural traits toward accounts of culture which are attentive to context, symbols, and semantics," wrote Fabian. "Still, sooner or later one will come upon syntheses of knowledge whose organizing metaphors, models, and schemes are thoroughly visual and spatial."

5. Vizenor, *Fugitive Poses*, 38. "Modernity, that mirror of science, material culture, and the courier of the other as *indian*, causes the disenchantment of essence, traditional authority, and overruns natural reason. The scrutiny of traditions, however, is never the same in the case of *indians* or natives."

6. Stafford, *Visual Analogy*, xv, 2, 3. "I thought it time to develop a sophisticated theory and practice of resemblance rather than continuing endlessly to subdivide distinctions," wrote Stafford. "I also believe the moment ripe to look at the rich and varied imaging or figurative tradition, rather than linguistics, for a connective model of visual rhetoric adequate to our networked, multimedia future."

7. Barbara Maria Stafford, *Good Looking: Essays on the Virtue of Images* (Boston: MIT Press, 1996), 5. "In most American university curricula, graphicacy remains subordinate to literacy. Even so-called interdisciplinary 'visual culture' programs are governed by the ruling metaphor of reading," wrote Stafford. "Consequently, iconicity is treated as an inferior part of a more general semantics."

8. Semir Zeki, *Inner Vision: An Exploration of Art and the Brain* (New York: Oxford University Press, 1999), 9, 10, 11. "To equate artists with neurologists, even in the remote sense intended here, may surprise many among them since, naturally enough, most know nothing about the brain and a good many still hold the common but erroneous belief that one sees with the eye rather than with the cerebral cortex," wrote Zeki. "Their language, as well as the language of those who write about art, betrays this view."

Donald Hoffman made a similar point in *Visual Intelligence* (New York: W. W. Norton and Company, 1998), xi, xii. "Our visual intelligence richly interacts with, and in many cases precedes and drives, our rational and emotional intelligence. To understand visual intelligence is to understand, in large part, who we are," wrote Hoffman. "What you see is, invariably, what your visual intelligence constructs. Just as scientists intelligently construct useful theories based on experimental evidence, so your visual system intelligently constructs useful visual worlds based on images at the eyes. The main difference is that the constructions of scientists are done consciously, but those of your visual intelligence are done, for the most part, unconsciously."

9. Stafford, *Visual Analogy*, 51. 61.

10. Bieder, *Science Encounters the Indian*, 11, 12. "But if the Indian were an inferior species of man, what then was his fate? Would the effect of the environment be the same on the Indian as it had been on European man? Were Indians capable of further progress, or had they reached the limits of their potential?"

11. Roy Harvey Pearce, *Savagism and Civilization: A Study of the Indian and the American Mind* (Berkeley: University of California Press, 1988), 49, 110.

12. Coward, *The Newspaper Indian*, 16, 17, 20.

13. Coward, *The Newspaper Indian*, 34, 229.

14. *New York Times*, July 10, 1876. Quoted from Coward, *The Newspaper Indian*, 159, 190.

15. Standing Bear, *My People the Sioux*, 184, 185.

16. Mick Gidley, *Edward S. Curtis and the North American Indian, Incorporated* (Cambridge, UK: Cambridge University Press, 1998), 74, 75. "In essence, the picturesque genre approach to Native American culture, when fused with the ideology of Native Americans as a vanishing race, created images that naturalized the predicament faced by indigenous North American peoples at what was, in fact, at the turn of the century, the very nadir of their experience on the Continent," wrote Gidley.

17. Christopher M. Lyman, *The Vanishing Race and Other Illusions: Photographs of Indians by Edward S. Curtis* (New York: Pantheon Books, in association with the Smithsonian Institution Press, 1982), 79. Lyman cited Edward S. Curtis, "Vanishing Indian Types: The Tribes of the Northwest Plains," *Scribner's Magazine*, June 1906. President Theodore Roosevelt and other government agents expressed similar racialist views about natives. Curtis, it should be remembered, was beholden to Roosevelt for his letter of introduction to John Pierpont Morgan.

18. Gidley, *Edward S. Curtis and the North American Indian, Incorporated*, 21; Victor Boesen and Florence Curtis Graybill, *Edward S. Curtis: Photographer of the North American Indian* (New York: Dodd, Mead and Company, 1977), 15.

19. Lyman, *The Vanishing Race*, 65.

20. James C. Faris, *Navajo and Photography* (Albuquerque: University of New Mexico Press, 1996), 108, 114, 115, 116. "Curtis tells us he staged

the Nightway photographs not because he was there at the wrong time of year but because of the resistance to his photography—a rather minor logistical matter," writes Faris. "The type of resistance is never explained in detail, though we can probably assume it came from assimilationist bureaucrats (Navajo and non-Navajo) who resented Curtis's emphasis and manipulation to achieve some representation of 'aboriginality.'"

21. Lyman, The Vanishing Race, 35. "Among the Photo-Sessionists, however, Stieglitz tolerated the often manipulative styles of Edward Steichen and Gertrude Käsebier, and even the visual polemics of Frank Eugene," wrote Lyman. "Although he often spoke to the contrary, Stieglitz's criteria, it appears, had less to do with technique than with the attitudes of the artists and their faithfulness to the elevation of photographic art."

22. Beaumont Newall, The History of Photography, 4th ed. (New York: Museum of Modern Art, 1981), 106, 111.

23. John Tagg, The Burden of Representation (Amherst MA: University of Massachusetts Press, 1988), 56, 58, 59. "What Walter Benjamin called the 'cult' value of the picture was effectively abolished when photographs became so common as to be unremarkable; when they were items of passing interest with no residual value, to be consumed and thrown away," wrote Tagg.

24. Lyman, The Vanishing Race, 78.

25. Lyman, The Vanishing Race, 86, 106.

26. Dino A. Brugioni, Photo Fakery: The History and Techniques of Photographic Deception and Manipulation (Dulles VA: Brassey's, 1999) 17, 202. "After the turn of the twentieth century, heavily manipulated photos were produced to create supposed intrinsic and artistic values," wrote Brugioni. "The photomontage was used as an important propaganda weapon both for and against Nazi Germany. Communists and other nations often rewrote history by removing people and events from photos, despite the fact that copies of the original photos were usually available throughout the world."

10. George Morrison

1. George Morrison, as told to Margot Fortunato Galt, Turning the Feather Around: My Life in Art (St. Paul: Minnesota Historical Society, 1998), 146.

2. The Chippewa and Ojibwe are the anishinaabe, plural anishinaabeg, in the language of the people.

3. Jane Katz, ed., *This Song Remembers: Self-Portraits of Native Americans in the Arts* (Boston: Houghton Mifflin, 1980), 53–60.

4. John Nichols and Earl Nyholm, *A Concise Dictionary of Minnesota Ojibwe* (Minneapolis: University of Minnesota Press, 1995).

5. Morrison, *Turning the Feather Around*, 29.

6. Morrison, *Turning the Feather Around*, 17, 18.

7. Morrison, *Turning the Feather Around*, 39, 40.

8. Morrison, *Turning the Feather Around*, 37.

9. Morrison, *Turning the Feather Around*, 49, 50.

10. Lawrence Abott, "A Time of Visions: Interviews with Native American Artists," http://www.britesites.com/native_artist_interviews/gmorrison.htm.

11. John Berger, *Ways of Seeing* (New York: Penguin Books, 1977), 105.

12. Morrison, *Turning the Feather Around*, 71.

13. Morrison, *Turning the Feather Around*, 170.

14. Phillip Ball, *Bright Earth* (New York: Farrar, Straus and Giroux, 2001), 107, 251.

15. Morrison, *Turning the Feather Around*, 168, 169, 170.

16. Same Olbekson, "Beyond the Horizon: An Interview with Anishinabe Artist George Morrison," *Akwe:kon: A Journal of Indigenous Issues* 10, no. 1 (1993): 27.

17. Elizabeth Erickson, "An Interview with George Morrison," *Art Paper* 6, no. 30 (1987): 28.

18. Morrison, *Turning the Feather Around*, 192.

19. Charles Dickens, *A Tale of Two Cities* (New York: Dover, 1999), 1.

20. Morrison, *Turning the Feather Around*, 63.

21. Morrison, *Turning the Feather Around*, 97.

22. Ross Wetzsteon, *Republic of Dreams, Greenwich Village: The American Bohemia, 1910–1960* (New York: Simon and Schuster, 2002), 552.

23. Morrison, *Turning the Feather Around*, 128; *George Morrison: Reflections*, film, produced and directed by Lorraine Norrgard (Duluth-Superior: WDSE TV, 1998).

24. Morrison, *Turning the Feather Around*, 90.

25. Morrison, *Turning the Feather Around*, 92.

26. Morrison, *Turning the Feather Around*, 99, 104.

27. Wetzsteon, *Republic of Dreams*, 528.

28. Morrison, *Turning the Feather Around*, 105.

29. John Sherman, "George Morrison's Art Lyrical and Subjective," *Minneapolis Tribune*, February 13, 1959.

30. Morrison, *Turning the Feather Around*, 125.

31. Morrison, *Turning the Feather Around*, 142, 144.

32. Morrison, *Turning the Feather Around*, 135.

33. Morrison, *Turning the Feather Around*, 147.

34. Philip Larson, "George Morrison and Philip Larson: An Interview," in *George Morrison: Drawings*, exhibition catalog (Minneapolis: Walker Art Center, 1973).

35. Stafford, *Visual Analogy*, 3, 10.

36. Morrison, *Turning the Feather Around*, 163.

37. Morrison, *Turning the Feather Around*, 169, 192.

38. Charleen Touchette, "George Morrison: Standing on the 'Edge of the World,'" *American Indian Art*, Winter 2001.

39. Mark Anthony Rollo, "George Morrison's Superior Life," *The Circle*, December 31, 1998.

40. The White House, "Red Totem," *Twentieth Century American Sculpture at The White House: Honoring Native Americans*, November 1997, http://clinton4.nara.gov/WH/Tours/Garden_Exhibit6/morrison.html.

41. Katz, *This Song Remembers*, 60.

42. Mary Abbe, "Distinguished Artist George Morrison, Dies," *Minneapolis Star Tribune*, April 18, 2000.

11. Bradlarian Baroque

1. Elizabeth Sasser, "A Room with a View: David P. Bradley," *Southwest Art*, December 1983, 86, 87, 88.

2. Gerald Vizenor, *Survivance: Narratives of Native Presence* (Lincoln: University of Nebraska Press, 2008), 6. "The theories of survivance are elusive, obscure, and imprecise by definition, translation, comparison, and by catchword histories, but survivance is invariably true and just in native practice and company. The nature of survivance is unmistakable in native stories, natural reason, remembrance, traditions, and customs, and it is clearly observable in narrative resistance and personal attributes, such as the native humanistic tease, vital irony, spirit, cast of mind, and moral courage. The character of survivance creates a sense of native presence over absence, nihility, and victimry."

3. Interview with Gerald Vizenor, Albuquerque, New Mexico, March 27, 2008.

4. Rosemary Diaz, "Send in the Clowns," *Santa Fean Magazine*, August 2003, 144.

298

5. Suzan Shown Harjo, "David Bradley: A Good Indian Man," in *Restless Native: David Bradley*, exhibition catalog (Moorhead MN: Plains Art Museum, 1991), 14, 15.

6. John Sillevis, "Botero's Baroque," in *The Baroque World of Fernando Botero* (New Haven CT: Yale University Press, 2006), 13.

7. Walter Benjamin, "A Child's View of Colour," in *Colour*, ed. David Batchelor (Whitechapel, London: MIT Press, 2008), 63.

8. Don H. Jones, "David P. Bradley, Artist," *Santa Fean Magazine*, August 1981, 52.

9. Nicole Plett, "Message from Two Worlds," interview with David Bradley, *Art Lines*, August 1984, 6, 7.

10. "Restless Native, Coming Home: Inside the World of David Bradley," *Indian Country Today*, June 3, 2004.

11. "Restless Native, Coming Home."

12. David Bradley, "Artist's Statement on the Occasion of the Mid-Career Retrospective," in *Restless Native: David Bradley*, exhibition catalog (Moorhead MN: Plains Art Museum, 1991), 5.

13. Henri Matisse, "The Role and Modalities of Colour," in *Colour*, ed. David Batchelor (Whitechapel, London: MIT Press, 2008), 98, 99.

14. MedaliaArt, "The History of Haitian Art," www.medalia.net/HHistory.html; and the Haitian Art Gallery, www.galleryofwestindianart.com/haitianthumbnails.htm.

15. MedaliaArt, "The History of Haitian Art."

16. Susan Moldenhauer, *David Bradley: Postcard from Santa Fe*, exhibition publication (Laramie: University of Wyoming Art Museum, 2002).

17. Mary Abbe, "Artist David Bradley Had a Stint in the Peace Corps," *Minneapolis Star Tribune*, May 27, 2004.

18. Interview with Gerald Vizenor, Albuquerque, New Mexico, March 27, 2008.

12. Mister Ishi of California

1. Mary Ashe Miller, "Indian Enigma Is Study for Scientists," *San Francisco Call*, September 6, 1911; Robert Heizer and Theodora Kroeber, *Ishi the Last Yahi: A Documentary History* (Berkeley: University of California Press, 1979), 97.

2. "Ishi's Capture," *Oroville Register*, August 29, 1911; Heizer and Kroeber, *Ishi the Last Yahi*, 92.

3. Theodora Kroeber, *Alfred Kroeber: A Personal Configuration* (Berkeley: University of California Press, 1970), 81.

4. Heizer and Kroeber, *Ishi the Last Yahi*, 99.

5. Theodora Kroeber, *Ishi in Two Worlds* (Berkeley: University of California Press, 1965), 171.

6. Grant Wallace, "Ishi, the Last Aboriginal Savage in America, Finds Enchantment in a Vaudeville Show," *San Francisco Call*, October 8, 1911; Heizer and Kroeber, *Ishi the Last Yahi*, 107.

7. Kroeber, *Ishi in Two Worlds*, 148.

8. Saxon Pope, "The Medical History of Ishi," *University of California Publications in American Archaeology and Ethnology* 13, no. 5 (1920); Heizer and Kroeber, *Ishi the Last Yahi*, 225.

9. Wallace, "Ishi, the Last Aboriginal Savage in America"; Heizer and Kroeber, *Ishi the Last Yahi*, 108.

10. Alfred Kroeber, "Ishi, the Last Aborigine," *The World's Work*, July 1912. Reprinted in Alfred Kroeber, *The Mill Creek Indians of Ishi* (n.p.: University of California Printing Department, 1972); and Heizer and Kroeber, *Ishi the Last Yahi*, 221.

11. Heizer and Kroeber, *Ishi the Last Yahi*, 240; Alfred Kroeber to E. W. Gifford, March 24, 1916, in Kroeber, *Ishi in Two Worlds*, 234.

12. Heizer and Kroeber, *Ishi the Last Yahi*, 240; E. W. Gifford to Alfred Kroeber, March 30, 1916, in Kroeber, *Ishi in Two Worlds*, 235.

13. Kroeber, *Ishi in Two Worlds*, 236, 237.

14. Kroeber, *Ishi in Two Worlds*, 236.

15. Kroeber, *Ishi in Two Worlds*, 225, 230; Pope, "The Medical History of Ishi."

16. John Cruickshank, *Albert Camus and the Literature of Revolt* (London: Oxford University Press, 1959), 32, 33.

17. Tony Judt, *The Burden of Responsibility* (Chicago: University of Chicago Press, 1998), 97.

18. Mario Vargas Llosa, *Making Waves* (New York: Farrar, Straus and Giroux, 1996), 108.

19. Vargas Llosa, *Making Waves*, 108, 109.

20. Albert Camus, "Helen's Exile," in *Lyrical and Critical Essays* (New York: Random House, Vintage Books, 1968), 151.

21. Camus, "Helen's Exile," 152.

22. "Naming Ceremony," *California Magazine*, March/April 2007, 29.

23. Momaday, *The Names*, 26.

13. Haiku Traces

1. Matsuo Bashō, *The Narrow Road to the Deep North and Other Travel Sketches*, trans. Nobuyuki Yuasa (Baltimore: Penguin Books, 1966), 115, 116.

2. Makoto Ueda, *The Path of Flowering Thorn: The Life and Poetry of Yosa Buson* (Stanford CA: Stanford University Press, 1998), 1, 16.

3. R. H. Blyth, *A History of Haiku* (Japan: Hokuseido, 1963), 1:1.

4. Kenneth Yasuda, *The Japanese Haiku* (Rutland VT: Charles E. Tuttle Company, 1957), 24, 32.

5. Kobayashi Issa, *The Year of My Life* [*Oraga Haru*], trans. Nobuyuki Yuasa (Berkeley: University of California Press, 1960), 103, 104.

6. R. H. Blyth, *Haiku*, vol. 4, *Autumn-Winter* (Japan: Hokuseido, 1952), 230. Blyth wrote, "The poet or someone else has been playing the harp and at last leaves it on the tatami. Standing on the verandah, he gazes out at the rain which has fallen all day. It grows darker and darker. Suddenly, the *koto* gives out a slight sound; a mouse must have scuttled across it."

7. R. H. Blyth, *Haiku*, vol. 1, *Eastern Culture* (Japan: Hokuseido, 1949), 90.

8. Daisetz T. Suzuki, *Zen and Japanese Culture* (New York: Pantheon Books, 1959), 247.

9. Donald Keene, *Japanese Literature* (New York: Grove Press, 1955), 28, 29.

10. Francis Densmore, *Chippewa Music* (Minneapolis: Ross and Haines, 1973), 15.

11. Gerald Vizenor, *Summer in the Spring: Ojibwe Lyric Poems and Tribal Stories* (Minneapolis: Nodin Press, 1965), 23, 29; Densmore, *Chippewa Music*.

12. Densmore, *Chippewa Customs*, 78, 79.

13. François Jullien, *The Propensity of Things* (New York: Zone Books, 1999), 11, 139, 140, 267.

14. John DeFrancis, *The Chinese Language* (Honolulu: University of Hawaii Press, 1984), 78, 92, 93.

15. Jullien, *The Propensity of Things*, 16, 143.

16. Kitaro Nishida, *An Inquiry into the Good* (New Haven CT: Yale University Press, 1990).

17. Blyth, *Haiku*, 4:343.

18. Donald Keene, *World Within Walls* (New York: Holt, Rinehart and Winston, 1976), 366. Keene asserted, "Issa is an unforgettable poet, but in the end he leaves us unsatisfied because he so rarely treated serious subjects. As a young man he must have known the horrors of the natural disasters that struck his part of the country, especially the eruption of Asama in 1783, but he never refers to them."

19. Vizenor, *Cranes Arise*.

20. Vizenor, *Summer in the Spring*, 25, 29.

21. Densmore, *Chippewa Music*, 129, 130.

22. Nishida, *An Inquiry into the Good*.

23. Suzuki, *Zen and Japanese Culture*, 225.

24. Nishida, *An Inquiry into the Good*.

25. Blyth, *Haiku*, 1:272.

26. Makoto Ueda, *Bashō and His Interpreters* (Stanford CA: Stanford University Press, 1991), 4.

27. Haruo Shirane, *Traces of Dreams: Landscape, Cultural Memory, and the Poetry of Bashō* (Stanford CA: Stanford University Press, 1998), 157, 158.

28. Gerald Vizenor, *Matsushima: Pine Islands* (Minneapolis: Nodin Press, 1984).

29. Shirane, *Traces of Dreams*, 223.

30. Issa, *The Year of My Life*, 139.

Index